ISSUES IN LIBRARY MANAGEMENT
A Reader for the Professional Librarian

Knowledge Industry Publications, Inc.
White Plains, NY and London

Professional Librarian Series

Issues in Library Management: A Reader for the Professional Librarian

Library of Congress Cataloging in Publication Data
Main entry under title:

Issues in library management.

    Bibliography: p.
    1. Library administration--Collected works.
I. Knowledge Industry Publications, Inc.
Z678.I88   1984   025.1   84-7861
ISBN 0-86729-095-1
ISBN 0-86729-094-3 (pbk.)

Printed in the United States of America

Copyright © 1984 by Knowledge Industry Publications, Inc., 701 Westchester Ave., White Plains, NY 10604. Not to reproduced in any form whatever without written permission from the publisher.

10   9   8   7   6   5   4   3   2   1

Table of Contents

List of Tables and Figures ii

List of Photographs ii

Foreword iii

1. Planning Decision Tasks and Information Needs,
   by *Michael R.W. Bommer* and *Ronald W. Chorba* 1

2. A Data Base Approach to Decision Support,
   by *Michael R.W. Bommer* and *Ronald W. Chorba* 11

3. The Process of System Development and the Role of the
   Library, by *Audrey N. Grosch* 29

4. Issues in Automating Acquisitions, by *Richard W. Boss* 40

5. The Ideal Acquisitions System, by *Richard W. Boss* 52

6. The High Cost of Serials, by *David C. Taylor* 64

7. Serials Management: Issues and Recommendations, by *David C. Taylor* 82

8. Developing Preservation Programs in Libraries, by *Carolyn Clark Morrow* 97

9. Basic Publicity Techniques for Public Libraries, by *Benedict A. Leerburger* 128

10. Marketing Academic and Special Libraries, by *Benedict A. Leerburger* 155

Bibliography 177

About the Authors 184

List of Tables and Figures

Figure 1.1:	The Planning Process	2
Table 1.1:	Decision Tasks	8
Figure 2.1:	Model of Functional Components of an Academic/Research Library	14
Figure 2.2:	Classification Portion of Data Base Schema	21
Figure 2.3:	Utilization and Availability Portion of Data Base Schema	23
Figure 2.4:	Productivity Portion of Data Base Schema	27
Table 3.1:	Study Phase Steps	32
Table 3.2:	System Requirements Definition. Suggested Table of Contents	33
Table 3.3:	System Design Objectives. Suggested Table of Contents	34
Table 3.4:	System External Specification. Suggested Table of Contents	36
Figure 8.1:	Conservation Treatment	115
Figure 8.2:	Preservation Program Models	122
Figure 9.1:	The Press Release	131
Figure 9.2:	Clippings from *The Cairo Messenger* Weekly Library Column	134
Figure 9.3:	Special Event Public Service Announcement	136
Figure 9.4:	General Public Service Messages	138
Table 9.1:	Typical Newsletter Printing Costs	145
Figure 9.5:	Newsletter with an Eye-catching Masthead from the White Plains (NY) Public Library	147
Figure 9.6:	Front Cover and Sample Page from the New Orleans Public Library Annual Report	151
Figure 10.1:	University of North Carolina—Faculty Newsletter	158
Figure 10.2:	Seattle-First National Bank's Library Usage Questionnaire	172

List of Photographs

A hygrothermograph used to record temperature and humidity	102
"Save a Book" poster published by the Illinois Cooperative Conservation Program	107
Book "drops" often result in damage to volumes	108
Custom-made protective enclosures for rare/fragile materials	119
Routine book repair station	121

Foreword

"May you live in interesting times," says the Chinese proverb.

The library manager of the 1980s certainly does that. Opportunities for innovative policies and expanded services have never been greater. But the opportunities are accompanied by a host of problems and issues that make effective management increasingly difficult. Today's manager must, it seems, be an expert on everything from systems design to public relations techniques.

Of the countless issues in modern library management, five of primary interest are discussed in this volume.

First is the manager's need for timely, relevant information required for decision making. Michael Bommer and Ronald Chorba propose a database approach to this problem, offering a conceptual model of a computer-based decision support system for libraries.

The second area is library automation, which is no longer the province solely of major institutions but is spreading to libraries of even limited resources. Audrey Grosch describes the library's role in minicomputer systems development. Richard Boss discusses a specific application—acquisitions—and raises many questions important in the automation of any library function.

Two "crisis" issues confronting libraries are also examined here. David Taylor considers problems in serials management stemming from the spectacular growth and rising costs of publications. He describes the failures of the present journal system and offers some suggestions for improvement. Carolyn Clark Morrow provides guidelines for combating the dangerous deterioration of library materials. Included in her analysis are five models for organizing preservation programs in a range of library sizes and types.

At a time of tightening budgets, libraries must make a special effort to enlist the support of their communities and parent organizations. The final issue discussed in this volume is marketing, as Benedict Leerburger suggests creative ways to publicize library services in public, academic and special libraries.

The chapters in this *Reader* are drawn from previously published books in the Professional Librarian series: *Decision Making for Library Management* (1982), *Minicomputers in Libraries, 1981-82: The Era of Distributed Systems* (1981), *Automating Library Acquisitions: Issues and Outlook* (1982), *Managing the Serials Explosion: The Issues for Publishers and Librarians* (1982), *The Preservation Challenge: A Guide to Conserving Library Materials* (1983) and *Marketing the Library* (1982).

This book should be useful to library managers, other information practitioners, teachers and students who wish an introduction to the topics reviewed. Those who need more detailed information on particular subjects are advised to read the appropriate monographs in their entirety.

Adrienne Hickey
Senior Editor, Knowledge Industry Publications, Inc.
April 1984

1

Planning, Decision Tasks and Information Needs

by Michael R.W. Bommer and Ronald W. Chorba

Planning is the process of identifying organizational goals and objectives, developing programs and services to accomplish these objectives and evaluating the success of those programs. The planning process acknowledges that organizations cannot do everything and that resources must be allocated on a priority basis to those activities that lead to the most effective accomplishment of goals and objectives. McClure (1978) suggests that the activity of planning provides a rational response to uncertainty and change; focuses attention on what is to be accomplished; is important as an aid in resource allocation by establishing priorities for funding; serves as a basis for determining individual, departmental, organizational or program accountability; facilitates control of organizational operations by collecting information to evaluate various programs or services; and orients the organization to a futuristic stance.

Sellers believes that the keystone in planning is careful analysis of the library's role to formulate a statement of mission. Based upon this, projects can be developed and a review process can be established to track success and failure. He stresses the need for consistent participation of all personnel in the planning process to insure its success.

Miller proposes a user-oriented planning tool whereby user preferences for current services and for suggested change in library information center operations are collected and analyzed to offer comparisons between different potential means for improving service.

A strategy presented by Webster calls for planning and effecting change in the management of academic libraries through the employment of the Library Management Review and Analysis Program (MRAP). Such MRAP studies involve a systematic investigation of the top management functions in an academic library using self-study and group process methods for planning, identifying problems and developing alternatives within a set of management topics. A review of a cross section of the MRAP studies reveals an emphasis on the individuality of each library with resulting differences in the identified strategies and directions developed.

As depicted in Figure 1.1, academic and special library directors have the responsibility of insuring that their library's overall objectives are developed. Further, they are ultimately responsible for seeing that the library's resources are effectively distributed to

---

Reprinted from *Decision Making for Library Management* (White Plains, NY: Knowledge Industry Publications, Inc., 1982).

the programs which contribute most to the achievement of these objectives. Performance measures for evaluating the progress or success in attaining these objectives must also be specified. To insure a high degree of success in this planning process, library directors must actively seek advice and involvement of their staff and clientele.

Figure 1.1 The Planning Process

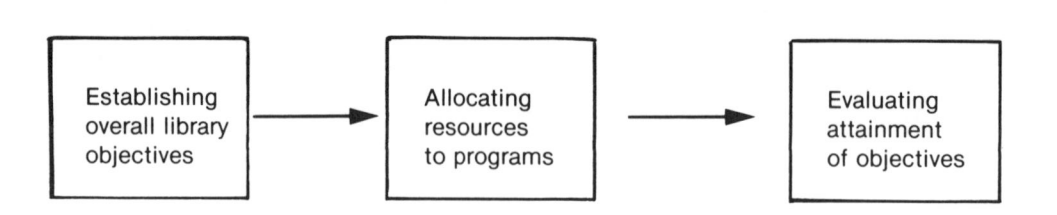

```
┌─────────────┐      ┌─────────────┐      ┌─────────────┐
│ Establishing│      │ Allocating  │      │ Evaluating  │
│overall library│──▶│  resources  │──▶│ attainment  │
│ objectives  │      │ to programs │      │of objectives│
└─────────────┘      └─────────────┘      └─────────────┘
```

This chapter will stress the need for developing clearly defined overall objectives for the library; it will deal with the allocation of resources and overall performance measures viewed in terms of how these contribute to goals achievement; and finally, it will examine decision tasks and information needed for evaluation as they relate to functional area and organizational level.

OVERALL OBJECTIVES

The effectiveness of any system depends in part upon an explicit set of overall objectives describing what the system is attempting (or should be attempting) to achieve. This set of objectives should be comprehensive and as free from internal conflicts as possible. Conflicts, if they exist, should be resolved if the accomplishment of one objective will have a negative effect on the achievement of another. Equally important is that the set of objectives becomes an integral part of the decision-making process at all managerial levels. This requires that managers at all organizational levels become involved with the system's objectives and cultivate an awareness of how each decision affects these. Without a set of precise and consistent objectives to provide guidance and direction, managers cannot make decisions and develop plans which yield the greatest contribution to the system's performance. The effectiveness of a special or academic library is no exception to this rule.

As the concept of management during the past two decades has moved away from the management of activities and toward results-based management, increased emphasis and importance have been placed on the setting of goals and objectives. One result is that institutions have become interested in incorporating the concepts of goal-oriented management into the overall institutional management process. Harvey cites the following assumptions on which this management process is based:

- "The clearer the idea one has of what one is trying to accomplish, the greater the chances of accomplishment."

- "Progress can only be measured in terms of what one is trying to progress toward."

- "Clear objectives for each program, unit and individual within an institution provide the basis for establishing concise authority and accountability relationships."

Chait has drawn attention to the recent intensity of activity on the part of colleges and universities to define goals and publish statements of purpose. Trustees, college presidents and administrators are requiring their institutions to develop a mission statement specifying goals and objectives. Establishing such a stance for an academic library may be somewhat less demanding than for the total institution. However, unless care is exercised, the statement can be so general as to lose operational significance for the library staff and administration.

McClure (1978) has noted that mission statements for libraries usually include two types of organizational philosophies. One involves assumptions regarding the role of the library within its institutional environment, together with the identification of external factors such as technology and information production which are having an impact on that relationship. The other involves value judgments and expectations regarding the nature of the clients to be served and the types and extent of services which are to be provided.

A further guide to the formulation and application of goals and objectives in academic libraries is provided by the Office of University Library Management Studies, Association of Research Libraries (see Gardner and Webster). This work presents the general and operational issues associated with designing and implementing a goals and objectives program. It includes several examples of mission statements of university libraries as well as specific goal and program objective statements for various levels of organizational hierarchy within academic libraries.

Similarly, objectives for a special library should be clearly defined and should be consistent with the objectives of the institution which it supports. The objectives should define the specific functions and responsibilities which justify its continuing support and provide internal direction for library administration. In general, the objectives for most special libraries should be more precise than those for libraries serving the diffuse teaching and research activities prevalent in an academic setting. For examples of objectives for special libraries see Strable and Special Libraries Association.

RESOURCE ALLOCATION

The need for a systematic procedure for channeling available resources in a manner consistent with institutional goals and objectives has been cited in a number of studies (see, for example, Webster and Hamburg et al., 1976). Decisions must be made as to the distribution of funds and personnel among library units, such as company and departmental libraries, and among the various functions and service areas within individual libraries. A system or systems must also be devised for monitoring and controlling these resources.

Allocations to library units, programs and services should be made consistent with the library's goals and objectives and the expected performance or benefits to be gained.

In recent years, a number of resource allocation models have been proposed to help library management make better funding decisions. Rouse (1975) has developed a mathematically based procedure for the optimal allocation of resources among the many processes of a library system. This allocation is defined as one which considers the chance of success as well as the outcome of the decision. Hamburg et al. (1976) suggest developing cost/benefit ratios for each service, then concentrating resources on those services offering the greatest return. A model for book budgeting based upon rate of use of materials, how the use contributes to the institution's goals and the associated costs is proposed by Gold. Kohut and Walker have devised a model for making resource allocations on monograph and serial purchases, while McGrath (1969a) offered an allocation model based upon factor analysis for allocating funds to different subject areas.

Goal programming models have been developed by McGeehan, and Gross and Talavage to deal with the problem of allocating scarce resources in an organization complicated by the presence of multiple, and often conflicting, managerial objectives. This is particularly applicable to academic and special libraries which are being pressed by both funders and users of their services to improve the effectiveness of their operations.

Summers describes the various methods which have been used to apply formulas and their associated disadvantages. The latter arise mainly from political factors which must be taken into account in the final decision making. Perhaps the most famous allocation formula is that of Clapp and Jordan, which unfortunately has the drawback of relying on the experience of librarians to determine the recommended resource levels for materials acquisition instead of being guided by independent institution-wide parameters. The lack of specific dependence of library allocations on independent parameters is illustrated by Baumol and Marcus who found little correlation between library resources for acquisition and student enrollment.

Formula methods of resource allocation may be useful in times of growth. However, in times of relative decline, the recipients may be inclined to favor more politically responsive allocative methods, especially if they believe they will achieve more favorable outcomes than from the former method.

Raffel (1974) has expanded on his earlier analysis of economic considerations in library decision making, which was based on studies at MIT. Because of the nature of the library's role, the more critical the decision, the more the thrust of the decision moves from the strictly economic to the political. He cites campus surveys of alternatives for library services that clearly indicate that subgroups of the university community either have different objectives in mind or view different alternative actions as being best for meeting common objectives. This means that the alternatives faced by library and university administrators involve major choices among various subgroups on campus.

Since there is often no economic way to resolve differences among alternatives which meet different objectives adhered to by different subgroups, a political solution is suggested. Raffel cites Easton's model and analysis as a basis for consideration of the political issues in such a situation. Easton defined politics as the authoritative allocation of values for a society, and cited universities as examples of private governments, as opposed to public governments where all citizens are members. The questions then arise: Can private governments be democratic? Who gets what, when and why?

Recognizing that the rational analysis of decisions and decision makers in libraries is a very complex and difficult subject, Raffel suggests that there are several areas that librarians should consider relative to their decision making:

- The definition of the relevant library system;

- The extent of the environmental constraints which limit or appear to limit the available choices;

- Which groups make demands and to what extent do such groups represent all potential users;

- What is the general climate of support for the library and what assumptions are made by users or administrators which limit the consideration of alternative policies;

- Who plays a role in decisions about the library;

- Who benefits from library services, who pays for the library and how well is each group served;

- What feedback is available to evaluate current allocations, and do non-users have an opportunity to provide feedback?

The point is made that economic analyses alone are insufficient to deal with all library decision making, and that political system analysis can help identify and clarify the broader environment in which library decisions are being made.

PERFORMANCE MEASUREMENT

Closely related to library objectives is the need for meaningful measures of performance to assess what the library is attempting to achieve and whether it is successful in achieving it. Without appropriate performance measures, it is difficult to determine how well the organization is progressing. These measures are needed to determine whether a particular decision or course of action should be pursued and whether funds are being allocated in the most effective manner.

Skeptics argue that library performance is too subjective, too complicated and too intangible to be measured. Increasingly, however, library managers are being required to demonstrate the positive role played by the library system in implementing the institution's overall goals and strategies. It should also be pointed out that decisions are being made by library managers keeping some form of criteria in mind. What is needed is to explicitly define and articulate these measures which are already being used in an implicit or informal sense.

Critical to any evaluation of a program is the availability of measures of performance by which the output of a system can be assessed according to some stated criterion. For service activities, three types of effectiveness measures have been cited by Elton and Vickery:

- Performance measures — the extent to which actual services to actual users are effective;
- Impact measures — the extent to which potential use is actualized;
- Availability measures — the extent to which potential services are actually provided.

Herner, in a basic paper covering system design and evaluation, notes that there has been a procession of evaluation methodologies available ranging from surveys to management studies, to user studies, to technically based performance measurements on specific operations. He advocates considering the total information operation as a system and considering a broader evaluation process which includes a combination of those earlier methodologies. Evaluation is a matter of quality control, and the important questions to be posed are therefore:

- What services should the system be performing?
- Is the system performing all the services it should be performing?
- Is the system performing any services it should not be performing?
- Is it performing the services as efficiently as possible?
- If not, what are the causes and what can be done to remedy the problem?

Some measures of effectiveness for such managerial decision making and planning for information processing and delivery activities appear to be emerging. Early measures dealt with level of effort or standards for library resources. Later studies focused on measuring user characteristics. Many other studies attempt to measure value by user satisfaction.

Musselman and Talavage advocate evaluation based upon three attributes of service itself:

- Quality from a user's viewpoint;
- Value to the organization;
- Effectiveness from a performance standpoint.

These attributes are further divided into such factors as accessibility, applicability, technical quality, timeliness, recall ratio and precision ratio. The two authors conclude that application of this evaluation methodology will allow information center managers to recognize when a system is not responding to the needs of those who use it and to direct improvements.

Starting from the premise that the library deals with information in the service of knowledge, Kantor (1976a) argues that one would really like to measure the contribution a given library makes to the transmission and growth of knowledge within a given time period. The direct measurement of knowledge is not possible, so related events which can be identified are measured. Kantor arrives at the concept of Contact Time per Potential User to measure the usefulness of a library transaction either within the library, or external to the library as occurs in a circulation transaction.

Hamburg et al. (1974) have analyzed the relationship of a library's goals and objectives to overall performance measures and warn that some university library objectives may be too general to yield suitable performance measurements. However, certain performance measures, such as the proportion of users satisfied, document retrieval time, document exposure counts, item-use-days and document exposure time can be used to relate back to library objectives.

Urquhart (1975) stresses the need for measures of performance based upon availability factors relating marginal increments in cost to marginal increments in service. Wills and Oldman present a concept of subjectively derived value; Weinberg formulates a concept for subjectively assessing the probable value of an information document; while Orr (1973) suggests a document delivery test as an overall measure of user satisfaction.

More recent studies have focused on a broader institutionally based criterion of information input as related to user output. For industrial or corporate libraries, Kates proposes as a measure the percentage of references used in papers published by company staff which were contributed or obtained by the information center. Rosenberg (1969) and White (1979b) suggest measures based on the benefit or contribution to project success supplied by the library in relationship to library costs as a way of evaluating industrial library performance. A series of field experiments to assist an information systems manager in assessing various programs for improving the overall system is suggested by Rubenstein and Birr. Finally, Allen (1977) identifies the "gatekeeper" function (that person who links his organization to the technological world at large) and suggests special support for enhancing this person's role as an information resource. These represent some of the few reported attempts to directly measure the productivity of information services.

DECISION TASKS AND INFORMATIONAL NEEDS

In addition to determining library objectives, resource allocation modes and overall measures of performance, library managers must make a number of decisions at both the strategic and management control levels. Each of these decisions would benefit from access to appropriate decision models and pertinent information. As a means for specifying relevant modeling aids and informational elements to be included in a decision support system, key decision tasks are identified and categorized by library functional areas and organizational level. A decision task is defined as the set of decisions which must be made with regard to a problem or opportunity which directly affects library performance.

Interviews with selected library managers showed substantial agreement in identifying the key decision tasks, although there was disagreement as to the ranking of importance or priority for each task. These differences of opinion reflect different phases of a library's evolution and differing environmental influence. For example, a library with adequate space for collection expansion will not rank the weeding decision task as high a priority as a library with space limitations. A library with severely constrained resources for collection development will rank the access to other collections decision task higher than a library with substantial resources for collection development. A listing of key decision tasks and selected performance measures associated with them is given in Table 1.1.

In addition to mapping out key decision tasks, a search was performed to identify the more significant literature pertaining to each of these tasks. This literature was reviewed and summarized for two important reasons.

1) To provide library managers with a brief overview of the types of decision models, formal as well as informal, proposed as aids in solving problems relating to each

Table 1.1 Decision Tasks

Key Functional Objective Area	Strategic Planning Decisions	Management Control Decisions	Performance or Effectiveness Measures
Collection Development	Determining collection development goals.	Allocation of funds to subject areas; Funds allocated for books, serials and reports; Types of books and serials to be acquired; Degree of duplication; Weeding policy and procedures; Current vs. retrospective acquisitions; Replacement of lost, damaged or worn documents; Selection process.	Percent held of sample bibliographies; Patron complaints; Number of reserves for books; Circulation/subject area/document; Circulation/user group; Citation distribution analysis; Selection cost/document; Minimum standards; Ratio of documents selected/documents published; Document retrieval time for local/interlibrary loan; Percent demands satisfied.
Technical Services	Level of cataloging; Timeliness and cost efficiency of document processing.	Acquisition process; Cataloging data source; Type of public bibliographic record; Maintenance of public bibliographic records; Physical preparation and maintenance of documents.	Request-receipt time; Receipt-shelf time; Cost/document processed; Entry points in catalog per document; Patron complaints; Public service staff complaints.
Reference and Bibliographic Service	Level, coverage and quality of reference assistance; Level, comprehensiveness and quality of document identification service.	Ready reference; Bibliographic search; Current awareness; Public relations.	Bibliographies prepared; Searches conducted; Search time; Percent relevant citations obtained; Patrons served; Cost per search; Cost per relevant citation; Sample recall ratio; Response time; Relevant bibliographies services/subject area; Number served by SDI; Requests per SDI. Reference questions received: Directional Informational Reference; Percent questions answered; Cost per question; Test score for sample questions; Percent time staff providing reference service; Percent telephone requests; Number patron orientation programs; Number patrons contacted; Number of class presentations; Complaints.

Table 1.1 Decision Tasks (cont'd.)

Key Functional Objective Area	Strategic Planning Decisions	Management Control Decisions	Performance or Effectiveness Measures
Collection Access	Ease of access to collection.	Hours of library service; Arrangement and location of collection; Level of collection security; Reshelving and shelfreading activities; Circulation control policy and procedures; Quantity and type of AV equipment; Reserve collection policies and procedures.	Reshelving time; Percent documents misshelved; Percent requests in remote storage; Storage cost/document; Percent documents lost; Half-life/periodical subject area; Percent documents in correct location; User access time; Document retrieval time; Percent demands satisfied; Number of patrons; Number of user hours; Percent collection in open stacks; Circulation/user group; Circulation cost/documents circulated; Circulation/document in open stacks; Circulation/document in closed stacks.
Access by Interlibrary Loan	Interlibrary loan cooperative arrangements.	Accessing documents held by other libraries; Supplying documents to other institutions.	Retrieval time; Percent documents obtained; Cost per document; Number of documents borrowed.
Physical Facilities	Quality and adequacy of user area and furnishings.	Allocation of area; Number and type of user furnishings.	Number of users; User hours; Seating/student; Staff area/staff member; Density of document storage.

decision task. Review of these decision models should be helpful to managers in developing further understanding and improved mental conceptualizations of decision problems.

2) To identify informational elements which have been proposed or have proven to be of value in each of the decision tasks. These informational elements serve to define the data to be collected and stored in the library's data base to be accessed by a decision support system.

2

A Data Base Approach to Decision Support

by Michael R.W. Bommer and Ronald W. Chorba

The customary procedure to follow in designing a decision support system (DSS) is to plan the user/data base interaction, i.e., the report formats and inquiry dialogue required by the manager. Then the designer "backs into" the design of necessary software, file structures and data capture procedures. This approach is not followed here for two reasons. First, the objective of this study is not to produce a system for a specific institution. Academic and research libraries differ widely with respect to problems, priorities and economic constraints; there exists no "typical" library for which one can tailor a system design. Second, the file structure which is to be proposed is new to the field of library management. The potential for decision support which is implicit in this file structure must be fully understood before attempting to identify specific retrieval objectives. Many forms of support are possible which, heretofore, have not been anticipated by library managers.

Designers of DSS have come to realize that most of the important decisions are unstructured. Structured decisions are recurring decisions with well-defined solution techniques and information requirements. To support unstructured decisions, the information system must be flexible, broad in scope and capable of relating data in a variety of ways. As time passes priorities will shift, planning objectives and performance standards will change and managerial styles will vary. The DSS must be capable of evolving in response to these changing needs.

The general nature of this discussion requires taking the broadest possible view of decision support. Then, recognizing that a complete implementation of all possibilities would not be feasible or necessary, various ways are suggested to identify a feasible subset consisting of those support measures dictated by needs and constraints. The data base approach allows one to do this. Within a general data base framework a specific, limited implementation is possible, as is the ability of a system to evolve with changing and growing needs.

To maintain a general decision support system capable of evolution, the underlying data base must be a model of all relevant features of the institution being managed and its environment. Components of this model include all relevant entities which exist, permanently or temporarily, and all relevant events which take place at various points in time.

Reprinted from *Decision Making for Library Management* (White Plains, NY: Knowledge Industry Publications, Inc., 1982).

For example, an entity might be a document or a set of documents, faculty member, employee, student, course, project or department. An event could be a circulation transaction, acquisition of a book, an interlibrary loan request, a student enrolling in a course or a researcher assigned to a project. The scope and detail with which events and entities are described is a design decision based on need and feasibility. Often it is sufficient to describe aggregations of entities of a certain type or of events over a period of time. Entities and events are described by their attributes—measurable values of relevant characteristics. Again, the choice of which attributes are worth recording is a design decision.

In addition to entities, events and their attributes, it is important to describe the relationship between entities and events. Relatedness is often overlooked when designing files and reports to support a specific decision. A general approach to designing a data base must include a capability to relate data in a flexible fashion. For example, the attributes of circulation transactions may be recorded in one file, while the attributes of the user community are recorded in another file. At some time a problem may arise which requires an analysis of the attributes of users having initiated circulations of a journal or of books in a specific Library of Congress (LC) category. At another time an analysis of the attributes of circulation transactions initiated by a specific subset of users may be required. Given the availability of data in the two files, programs could be written to produce either report. However, the cost of programming and the delay in waiting for a report often makes such an analysis impractical. A direct means of relating data of different types is necessary if the information system is to support *ad hoc* management requests.

A further illustration should demonstrate the variety of unanticipated ways in which data might have to be rearranged to address a specific problem. Suppose a periodic control report on interlibrary loan requests identifies an abnormally large number of requests for books in a specific LC category. A number of reports might be necessary to identify the cause of the problem. A profile showing the number of holdings in each LC category might identify inadequate coverage in the category of interest. A profile of acquisitions over the past few years by LC category might indicate that portions of the collection have become out of date. If neither of the above is true, then it is possible that poor selections of new titles are being made within that LC category. More detailed profiles of holdings, acquisitions, circulation and interlibrary loan requests within that LC category may be required. By identifying the various users in this LC category, the librarian can analyze their attributes and transaction patterns to see what specific demands are being met and not met. Key users can be identified and contacted. Depending on whether the demand pattern is judged to be transient or to represent a continuing shift in interest, a new acquisitions policy might be formulated.

No single, concise report could have provided the clues necessary to pinpoint the source of the above problem. Furthermore, the need for the various reports was generated only after the problem was recognized. Providing all of these data in periodic formal reports would quickly bury the library in computer output. Yet such data are regularly collected by libraries, especially those with automated circulation systems. Much of the cost of data capture and storage is already incurred. What is lacking is a flexible system for retrieving the appropriate data in a useful format at the time it is needed.

This chapter will attempt to establish a useful conceptual model upon which a library DSS can be based. We will then present a detailed, comprehensive specification of the relevant entities, events, attributes and relationships necessary to form a practical application of these concepts. Of course, the scope of this general data base will be far greater than any library would want to implement. Much of the data will produce redundant information. Some data are more useful than others, and some data are more costly to capture than others. Practical considerations in implementing a subset of the data base in specific environments is discussed in later chapters.

CONCEPTUAL DATA BASE MODEL

Certain conceptual components of the library system can be identified and related to form a "functional data base model." A major thrust of this discussion is to identify valid operational parameters which are descriptive of the activity of these functional components. What follows in this section is a discussion of these components and an explanation of their role in the functional data base model (refer to Figure 2.1 as terms are defined).

Productivity of Users of an Academic/Research Library

Productivity of users is measured in the organizational context as the effective contribution a user makes to the solution of a research problem or the accomplishment of an educational mission, as manifested by tangible achievements such as:

- Intellectual products such as course offerings, project activities, lectures, devices, materials, processes, patents, procedures, term papers and theses;

- Informational by-products such as published works, technical reports, patents, research and project proposals, formal presentations and demonstrations;

- Marks of recognition such as honorary designations, professional awards, promotions, monetary rewards, supervisor or peer evaluations, student evaluations and citations by colleagues.

Depending upon the context, a user may be an individual student or faculty member, employee, class, group, task force, program or a community of users with related interests. Since users often engage in a number of concurrent research or educational activities, it is helpful to initially separate each user's needs into sets or "problem spaces." The concept of a problem space is borrowed from Newell and Simon, who use it in a model of human problem-solving. As we use the term, a problem space is the way in which a researcher, teacher or student conceptualizes a problem or task in order to work on it. A problem space might be derived from a specific project, course or institutional unit specializing in a particular activity; a user associated with such an entity would adopt a portion of the entity's attributes as a problem space.

Information relevant to a problem space resides in one or more internal or external "information bases," a term used to represent any repository of text-format information within or outside of the institution. The user's personal holdings—books, periodicals or other sources of data previously acquired—form one of these information bases. Personal information bases include published versions of documents such as books, monographs, technical reports and journals (either in paper or microform), as well as duplications of

14   ISSUES IN LIBRARY MANAGEMENT

Figure 2.1   Model of Functional Components of an Academic/Research Library

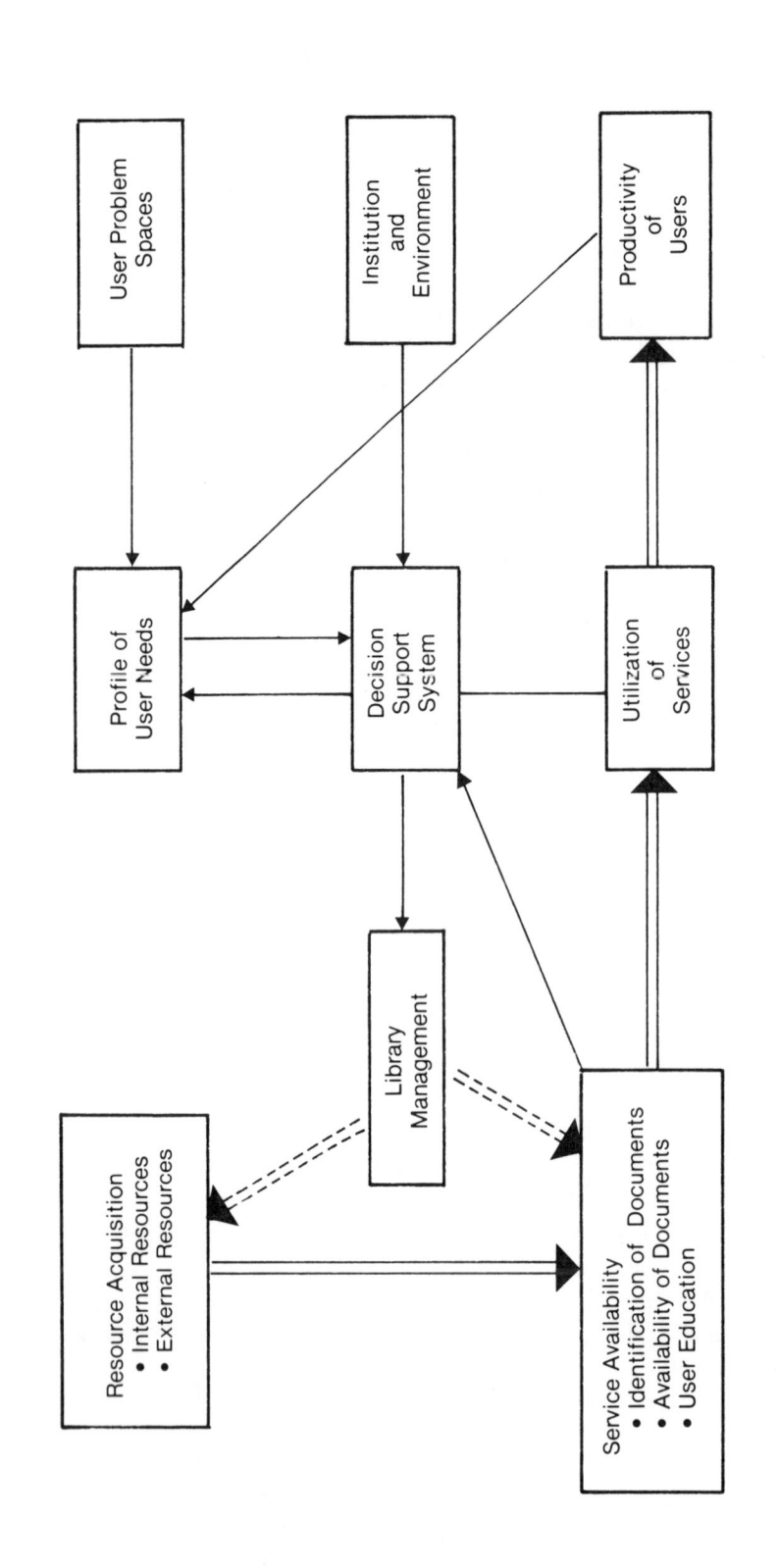

such documents which are products of previous retrieval transactions and which constitute a continuing use of information. Other information bases that might contain relevant information are at the primary library of the institution employed by the user, at other libraries that the user may contact directly or at libraries whose holdings are available indirectly through interlibrary loans.

In order to identify information relevant to a problem space within these information bases, the problem space must first be characterized in terms of a profile of user needs. This profile must then be mapped or translated according to the keys or descriptors commonly used by libraries or retrieval services to classify bibliographic material. In a method suggested by Swift et al. and Leggate et al., each user is characterized by a profile of his/her information needs mapped into "information descriptors," which are classification terms used to structure the manner in which information is acquired, stored and retrieved. These descriptors may be ranked within the profile by importance or organized into a hierarchical structure.

Over time, a user will complete research or teaching tasks, take on new tasks and make progress on continuing tasks. Therefore, the user's profile of needs changes with time and constitutes a dynamic component in the functional model. Taking the user's set of problem spaces as input to the library system and user productivity as the ultimate objective, some of the intervening attributes of the system will now be examined.

Utilization of Services

Utilization of services occurs when a user actually receives information from the system as evidenced by retrieval transactions. However, utilization is only an intervening step and not the ultimate productive act. An analogy can be drawn with management information systems theory where data are said to become information only when they are useful in a decision-making context. Likewise, unless user productivity is included, we are only studying a document transfer system, not an information transfer system. Measures of utilization of information services will require that a link be specified between utilization and productive activities.

Availability of Data

Availability is an attribute of an identified subset of the total holdings of information bases accessible by the user. To be available, a document must reside in one or more of the information bases and sufficiently match the user's information needs profile. Availability can be more precisely characterized by the following subconcepts:

1) *Completeness:* the proportion of all potentially identifiable documents which have actually been identified. This is seldom, if ever, known in relation to all possible documents, but it is a useful relative concept for comparing the completeness of specific data bases.

2) *Relevance:* the degree to which identified documents are, in fact, useful contributions to a problem space.

3) *Proximity:* the "nearness" of documents to the user, most usefully measured in units of time. Two types of time may be distinguished:

   a) *access time,* during which the user is actively engaged in retrieval effort, and
   b) *wait time,* during which a copy of the document is being transported to the user.

4) *Cost:* what it costs the user to acquire access. This can present a barrier to access since, in an economic context, the value of a document may not exceed the cost, or the user may have a limited budget to allocate for information retrieval.

5) *Psychological factors:* what causes users to be reluctant to use new technology or media. Training or learning barriers may exist, or differing user perceptions of availability may exist even though all physical factors are equal (see Gertsberger and Allen, Rosenberg (1966b), and Zipf). Library management may choose to conduct user education activities designed to encourage new utilization patterns.

Management is responsible for acquiring resources and providing services in response to user needs within the context of institutional objectives and subject to institutional constraints. Trends and shifts in the aggregate profile of the user community, as well as environmental inputs, form the nucleus of the DSS and give direction to resource allocation decisions concerning acquisitions and services.

Incorporating Functional Components into a Decision Support System

Maximization of availability is probably not the ultimate goal of most library managers. The degree to which the available resources are used and the ultimate contribution of a library to user productivity should also be monitored and reported. The relationships between availability, utilization and productivity have been the subject of some primary research, the results of which can be usefully applied in many settings. A DSS requires that ongoing feedback on utilization and productivity must be provided to the library manager for evaluating the potential impact of actions taken to improve the user community's exposure to available information and to improve user productivity. Thus, the key task of our work has been to demonstrate that practical and valid measures of these concepts may be implemented on an operational basis in an academic/research library. As demonstrated in Figure 2.1, the following necessary information flows are required by the DSS:

- resource availability
- resource utilization
- user productivity
- user problem spaces
- institutional and environmental impacts.

The last element of information flow requires some elaboration.

Library management will always be called upon to interpret institutional objectives and environmental opportunities in executing their planning and control activities. Formal, quantitative indicators of these factors are difficult to develop, and our approach only suggests that information assessments be explicitly recognized through assigning priorities which will put the aggregate institutional needs profile into a specific perspective. Some important institutional classifications of needs under which priorities may be assigned are:

- by project or general class of research activity;
- by undergraduate education/graduate education/research;
- by school, department or other institutional unit.

The degree of institutional emphasis among these categories can be assessed subjectively and expressed quantitatively by electronically adjusting or rearranging the aggregate profiles developed from individual users so as to emphasize one or another classification.

In summary, the explicit structuring of a library to meet institutional objectives requires a DSS comprised of a number of unique features to be developed and implemented. In particular, an active effort to obtain and periodically update individual and aggregate user need profiles is essential. The concepts and relationships employed in this conceptual schema have been demonstrated as useful in experimental settings. However, their articulation and structure in an operational setting, where factors such as system cost and user inconvenience are important, has not progressed to the point where implementation is straightforward. The following sections will discuss an operational approach intended to facilitate an implementation of the preceding concepts.

OPERATIONAL DATA BASE MODEL

With a conceptual framework established, the principal objective can be addressed: How can the DSS concepts be measured in a valid and economic fashion? This section will deal with the problem from a very broad perspective that will include all approaches which were thought to be feasible at the outset. The primary constraint placed on the measurement problem was that the methods must be capable of implementation on a continuing basis. This eliminated many valid approaches previously employed in research studies on a one-time basis.

Reliance on methods that involved extensive and costly capture of data not normally generated in the daily operation of an institution or its library was unacceptable. This was certainly the case with data capture requiring extensive user involvement or substantial clerical effort by library personnel. Furthermore, the differences that exist between academic/research libraries in the amount of available resources and technology which might be applied to developing a DSS must be recognized. Finally, at least some of the suggestions should be applicable in small libraries using limited computer technology.

CLASSIFICATION OF SUBJECT MATTER

Initially, we must deal with a crucial issue, the solution to which will form the foundation of the DSS. A user's activity or interest can be conceptualized as a profile, that is, as an expression of relative strength or emphasis across a set of categories or classes of subject matter. Similarly, circulation and available bibliographic resources can also be expressed as a profile of relative emphasis or strength across subject matter categories. In order to relate, compare or assess user activity, circulation and resources for management problem-solving, the set of subject matter categories must be identical in all profiles or at least capable of juxtaposition—i.e., the different sets can be mapped onto each other. There exists no such single, universal, generally accepted subject matter classification. A number of approaches are possible, none of which are ideal.

Classification via Bibliographic Data Base Profiles

Research interests of users are probably most validly expressed in the type of syntax used by bibliographic data bases. Many researchers employ these services and have profiles on file with their library. Many industrial firms and universities provide a selective dissemination service to their research and development personnel and faculty.

A dissemination system used at IBM was studied for possible applicability in a DSS setting. However, the management of the many technical libraries maintained by IBM appeared to be independent of the dissemination system. There appeared to be no formal attempt to report data from personnel profiles to library managers and no indication that this was a resource in making decisions concerning collection management. The profiles themselves were quite complex with no obvious means available to summarize or aggregate the data for an entire set of users.

The IBM experience points to the major drawbacks of bibliographic data base profiles in general. There appears to be no common thesaurus of terms applicable across a wide range of subject matter. Aggregations based on the relative occurrence of specific terms would also be misleading, since they appear within a logical, Boolean syntax within each profile. Furthermore, only a minority of the typical research community subscribes to such a service. Direct use of such profile information by library management seems doubtful unless some additional mapping of the profile onto a less robust set of terms is performed.

Publishers of abstracts in various fields usually employ a broad classification of their fields of interest, such as is done by the Association of Computing Machinery and the International Federation of Operations Research Societies. The NASA SCAN service also employs a limited thesaurus without Boolean constructs. However useful such profile sources might be, there still exists no single, universal set of categories for an entire academic/research community. Ultimately, some practical means of aggregating these diverse sources might emerge. Presently they are useful only if their terms can be mapped onto a more comprehensive set.

Perhaps the greatest difficulty with independently developed thesauri of subject matter terms is that the body of literature which is made available and circulated is only classified in these terms by the diverse means employed within various commercial services. These various thesauri are neither comprehensive in their coverage of the literature nor compatible with one another. Additionally, they are under constant revision since the state of the art in bibliographic searching is not fully developed.

None of the existing bibliographic search or abstracting service thesauri can be recommended as the common denominator for establishing profiles in a library DSS at this time. It would appear that what remains is either the Library of Congress (LC) or Dewey systems. Of these, the LC system is used in the vast majority of academic and research libraries. Employing the LC system, however, is not without its drawbacks.

Classification via the LC System

The principal advantage of the LC system is that the bibliographic material being managed is already classified within this system. Libraries have taken advantage of cataloging services such as OCLC to increase the productivity of their cataloging activities. To suggest to a library that it introduce additional cataloging tasks to classify its acquisitions according to another method of organization is simply not acceptable. Furthermore, OCLC provides a means of constructing a computer file of current acquisitions and existing holdings based on the LC system. The only practical means of creating a file based on another classification is to create a systematic mapping of terms. The reclassification could then be automated.

If mapping between systems of classification is to be undertaken, there are a number of important points to be considered. First, the DSS must not pose an excessive clerical burden on library resources; that is, the additional data capture activities required by the DSS must represent a small percentage of existing clerical activity. The acquisition of profiles of user activity and problem spaces would seem to pose the greatest additional burden. It would make sense to automate the mapping of these profiles onto the LC classification rather than take on the far greater task of mapping the collection and circulation statistics onto an independent system of classification employed for user profiles.

A second consideration is that the LC classification constitutes the natural language with which librarians work. The collection is already categorized in this mode and all activities relating to its management are organized accordingly. Management information must be expressed and organized in the natural language of the manager. To do otherwise would reduce the value of the information.

A final consideration is more technical but nonetheless important. A mapping from LC to any other system of classification would not necessarily be on a one-to-one basis and could result in simply renaming categories. For example, a book on the electrical properties of materials could be classified within many areas of physics and electrical engineering. If this book circulates, is it counted once or as many times as it appears in various categories of the user-oriented system? How will the manager interpret statistics based on multiple counts of circulations? For some problems, such a representation would be useful; for others it is not. This mapping could take place at the time the manager requests information if the data base is organized in LC terms. The reverse mapping is not possible, however, and true circulation counts by LC class would not be recoverable. It would appear, then, that the organization of the data base should be LC-oriented. Processing costs of data capture transactions and data base updates would be minimized. Mapping onto other systems of classification could then be effected at run time when reports requiring alternative categorizations are requested.

The HEGIS System

Having made the decision to employ the LC classification, some valuable existing research has proven useful. Of particular importance is the work of Evans (1978b) and Evans et al., in which a comprehensive mapping of the LC categorization onto the HEGIS

(Higher Education Generalized Information System) classification for academic programs is developed. The HEGIS system classifies academic programs and is used in New York State as a framework for reporting statistical and financial information by the Department of Higher Education (see Allman, Wing and McLaughlin). The mapping method developed by Evans indicates how library holdings and acquisitions contribute to the support of academic programs. The mapping is many-to-many; that is, one LC category may apply to several programs and one program is usually supported by many LC categories.

Many of the activities associated with a university and its members are conveniently classified by the HEGIS code. Events and entities such as faculty affiliation, departments, courses, student enrollment and research grants are easily categorized in the HEGIS code. In turn, the attributes of these events and entities can now be related to library activities and resources. However, the HEGIS code is much less specific than the LC categories we chose to employ. For this reason, some university activities may be best classified directly into the LC code or into independent classifications such as the NASA SCAN codes. Nonetheless, the mapping into the HEGIS classification is always available for reporting purposes. This is vital since the HEGIS code is made up of terms which are part of the natural language of university administrators and is generally accepted among faculty, administrators and legislators.

Data Base Interaction of Classification Systems

A code, similar to the HEGIS, could be developed for any industrial or research institution. Such a code would reflect the detailed content of continuing activities, issues and concerns of the institution and its industry. As the relative emphasis of the institution shifts over time, so should the emphasis of library management. Such a code could be assembled from several of the existing classifications of the type mentioned above.

Figure 2.2 shows the portion of the data base schema representing the classification system and its interaction with the rest of the data base. Each node represents a computer file containing occurrences of records. Each record occurrence corresponds to an actual entity and contains values of the attributes of those entities. In this case, some of the entities are logical, for example, the set of LC categories and the set of HEGIS categories.
For industrial or research institutions, the HEGIS classification would be replaced by a unique subject matter code for the institution.

The arrows in the schema represent relationships between files. For example, the arrow from DEPARTMENT to USER indicates that for every department record there exists one or more faculty records associated with (or "owned" by) the department. In place of DEPARTMENT, one may substitute or add other USER affiliations such as project or program. This is usually a one-to-many relationship. To represent a many-to-many relationship, such as between LC-SERIAL and HEGIS, we require an intervening file, LC-HEGIS. This intervening file is essentially a matrix with each record representing one cell of the matrix. The files LC-DIV and HEGIS-DIV are simply broader aggregates of the LC-SERIAL and HEGIS codes and serve to illustrate that various levels of aggregation are possible to describe both subject matter and institutional activities. Note that users are directly classified by the HEGIS (or equivalent) code independently of department affilia-

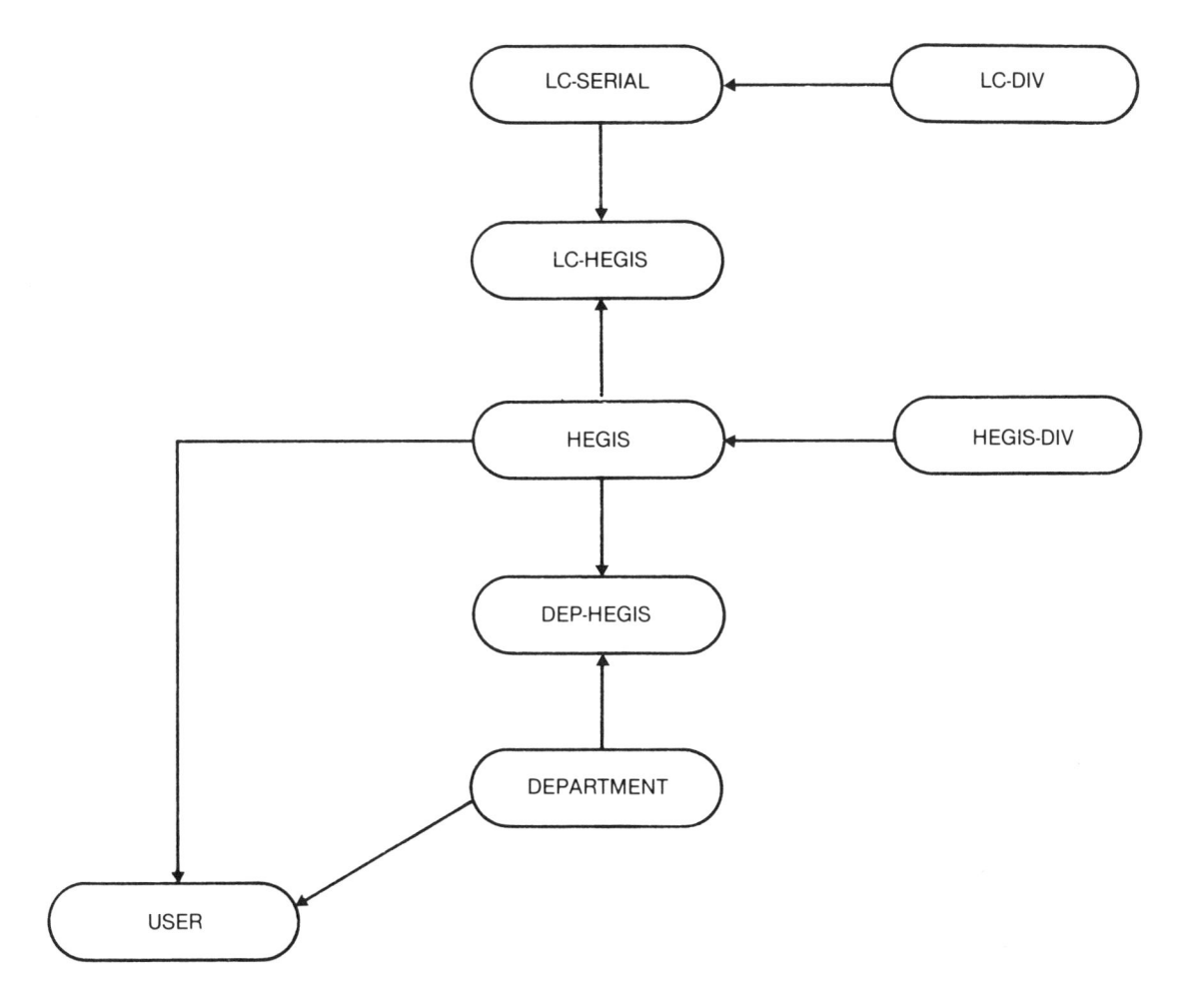

Figure 2.2 Classification Portion of Data Base Schema

tion. Such a classification may be based on education, training or previous experience not wholly reflected by the attributes of the currently assigned department.

Adoption of the LC system of classification also provided an opportunity to employ a mapping technique developed by McGrath (1969b and 1975). This technique employs the skills of a catalog librarian to classify university courses within the LC system, a methodology used in field research with considerable success. Furthermore, the concept was extended to the classification of research interests, dissertation topics and the NASA SCAN categories. These applications will be described later in the section on profiling of user problem spaces and productivity. The method can also be applied to mapping an institutional equivalent to the HEGIS code onto the LC classification.

UTILIZATION PROFILES

Although a library provides a wide variety of user services, the data base development phase of this work limited the scope of the term utilization to document delivery. Document delivery services include circulation of the local collection, interlibrary transactions, photocopying (excluding self-service facilities) and in-library use. The approach to gathering information about other services would be analogous to the methods explored in the case of document delivery, but might differ among libraries, depending on how the library defines the scope of its activities.

The LC system provides a natural classification for utilization transactions and can be easily mapped onto the HEGIS or equivalent classifications to observe the use of materials provided to support various institutional programs. Other links must also be established in the data capture procedure. For each transaction (event) which occurs, with respect to any of the services listed above, the data capture procedure must record user data (identification number), document data (LC code) and reference data (date, time and usage location). Additional data concerning users, LC category, location, etc., are assumed to be on file in the data base and may be linked to the transaction during processing. There are obvious relationships of interest to observe among employees, faculty, students, departments, etc., with respect to utilization behavior. For example, type of utilization, LC category, and trends over time may all be possible dimensions for observing patterns of use.

Minimizing Data Base Retrieval Costs for the DSS

Minimizing the cost of data capture is critical to the success of the DSS. In the case of utilization, the increasing use of automated circulation systems can be of great help. In fact, a wide array of statistical reports is usually available from these systems but librarians have not yet been able to exploit their value fully. This experience is similar to what has occurred in business data processing systems over the past 20 years. The principal business application of computers has been in routine transactions processing with management reports being a tangential by-product. Such management reports have always been subject to the constraints of timing, format and available data which are imposed by the requirements of transactions processing. Files of stored data were always organized to optimally meet the needs of transactions processing. Only in the last 10 years have there been any significant implementations of systems designed specifically for management support.

A DSS still relies primarily on data originating through transactions processing. The full cost of data capture, processing, storage and retrieval can seldom be justified solely by the benefits derived by management through decision support. Though some primary data collection can be justified, the vast bulk of data is available only as a by-product of the institution's normal transactions processing and operations. Despite this economic barrier, recent developments in storage and retrieval techniques have made these data available in ways which can be tailored to meet management needs.

Software developments in the areas of generalized data storage and generalized reporting and inquiry have made it possible to provide flexible, timely and inexpensive servicing of management requests for support information. This software was first available only on large computers but now is appearing even in microprocessor-based systems. Thus, the major economic and technical barriers to developing a library DSS lie in the data capture procedures and facilities.

As noted above, an automated circulation system can provide much of the data required for the DSS. At the time of a circulation transaction a record is created containing data about the user, the document and the date, time and location of the transaction. Ideally these data are recorded without manual key entry. Machine-readable labels should be available on the document and on the user's identification card.

If an automated circulation system is in use, much of the capture cost of utilization data is already being absorbed by the institution. Other means are available to capture data without resorting to automated circulation, but if that is the case, the costs incurred must be attributed to the cost of the DSS.

An automated circulation system may not be capable of handling all the transactions identified under utilization. In addition to the circulation stations, there must be input terminals for both interlibrary loans and photocopying as well as a portable device for scanning items to be reshelved after in-library use.

The schema for the utilization portion of the data base is shown in Figure 2.3. The four utilization files are CIRCULATE, INTERLIBRARY, PHOTOCOPY and INLIBUSE. All except INLIBUSE are linked to the USER file. To save storage space, a separate utilization record need not be maintained for each transaction, though this would be the theoretically straightforward way to record transactions. Each of the four utilization record types contains a transaction count for a given LC class or serial and a given publication date over a period of time, say, one year. Within some of these records, the count could be broken down by weeks though this is probably not essential. Thus, the data base update procedure only needs to take place periodically according to management reporting

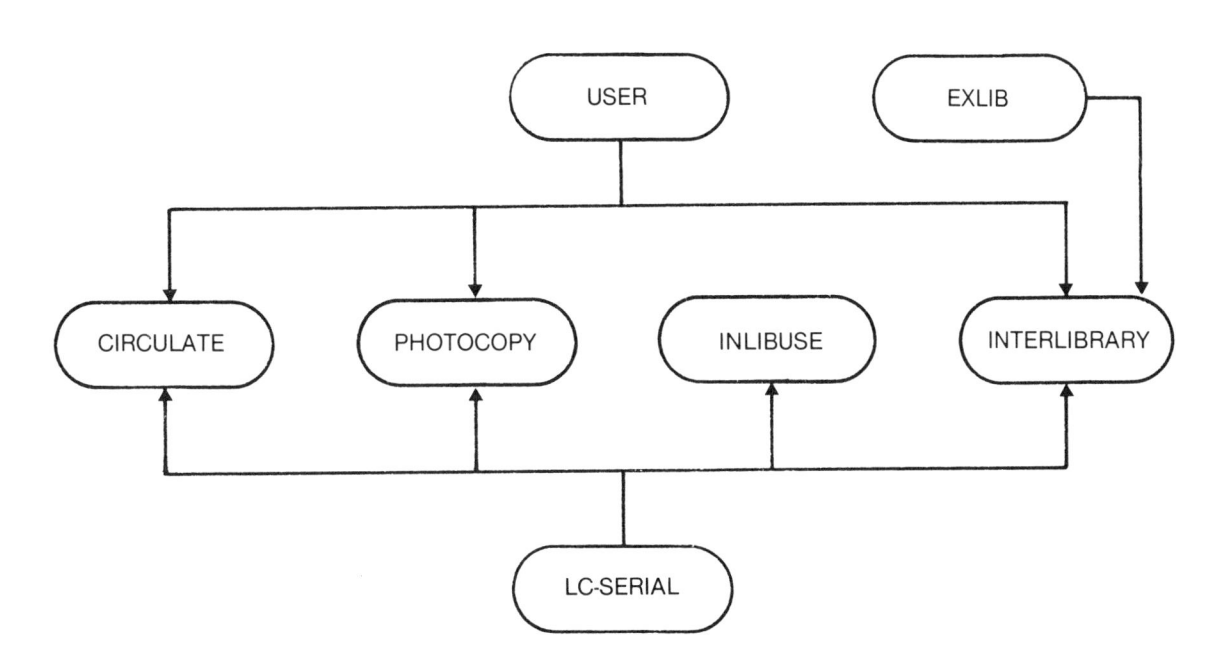

Figure 2.3 Utilization and Availability Portion of Data Base Schema

needs. Transaction records are accumulated and then processed in a batch run to update the utilization records.

At this point files have been identified to store data about users, user affiliation and utilization, and these files have been linked to both the LC and HEGIS systems of classification.

AVAILABILITY PROFILES

The existing status of available resources is an essential factor in library decision making, and some method of measuring this factor exists in any library. There may, however, be some barriers to the flexibility and timeliness with which these data may be used for decision making. At a minimum, the library should know the distribution of its monograph collection in terms of the LC classifications at a useful level of detail. This is usually known even in manual systems. Keeping track of LC class distribution, while additionally recording the age distribution by publication date within LC classes, would burden a manual system, but it is certainly feasible. Manual tracking of trends in holdings, acquisitions and weeding are also feasible but again, burdensome. However, displaying these data in a variety of formats and levels of aggregation and relating them to utilization and productivity in meaningful ways would severely overtax a manual system.

As discussed earlier, technological support for producing a computer-readable record of a monograph collection exists through cataloging services. However, the lack of such a file does not prevent the library from keeping track of availability. The number and age distribution of holdings may be based on LC classes only and updated to reflect acquisitions and weeding. Thus, both utilization and availability could be reported only by LC class and not to the document level. Most reporting requirements would not be affected by this restriction.

As in the case of utilization, the specific methods employed are largely dependent on the state of existing technology in the library. A machine-readable file of monograph holdings may already exist in the library as a result of using computer-aided cataloging and perhaps by maintaining an online catalog instead of a card file. If this is the case, then little additional cost burden is placed on the DSS. However, justifying the acquisition of a machine-readable file of monograph holdings strictly for use by the DSS would be difficult. On the other hand, a computer file of serial holdings by volume is not a significant burden on the DSS budget and should be maintained.

Another significant dimension of availability is the interlibrary loan system. An important responsibility of the library is to identify external sources for serials and monographs. Knowing where to find documents, how much they will cost and how fast they can be delivered are critical components of operational information. Data can be accumulated from interlibrary loan transactions to provide this information. Figure 2.3 shows how this is accomplished. Each INTERLIBRARY record is linked to a record describing the source library, EXLIB, for assisting loans or copy deliveries. Each of these INTERLIBRARY records contains the number of documents requested, number received and average delay time in days. Note that this schema implies that LC-SERIAL contains not only local library serial holdings but also serials previously requested through the loan system. Monograph loans are also recorded in INTERLIBRARY by LC class, publication date and source library. The concept of availability, then, extends beyond the library's holdings and this is reflected in the data base.

PRODUCTIVITY PROFILES

In all of the profile categories discussed above, the attributes to be measured and the means of measurement are very well defined. Many opportunities also exist to accomplish tangential data capture through clerical activities already taking place in the library. Further, the events and entities being recorded all reside within the library itself. However, the conceptual entities and events associated with institutional productivity lie outside the library, and additional effort is required by the library to capture data in those areas. To complicate matters, there are no widely accepted or proven ways to measure attributes of productive events or even agreement as to what the relevant productive events are.

Because of the unique problems associated with the productivity dimension of the DSS design, the authors conducted field tests of a variety of approaches in an academic setting. Of special concern was the value of information produced by the measurement alternatives as well as their cost and technical feasibility. A number of alternatives which initially appeared to have potential were selected.

Productivity as It Relates to Library Decision Making

Before discussing the alternatives which were evaluated, one must define the meaning of "productivity" in the context of library decision making. This view might be quite different from the perspective one might take in judging the merit and value of the efforts of researchers, faculty and students for other purposes. Use of the term productivity refers to the amounts and kinds of teaching or research activity which are taking place in the institution and not to the ultimate value that society might place on those activities. The library should acquire the data necessary to assist in planning for and responding to existing and potential demands for its services. Resources should be allocated according to the amounts and kinds of activities taking place and according to the way in which these activities are distributed across departments, programs, projects, fields of study and, ultimately, across the LC classification of bibliographic material.

Any attempt to modulate the activity distribution with built-in value judgments for the purpose of allocating resources is considered to be outside the terms of reference of the library DSS. Certainly, it is true that historical activity data will not reflect the impact of new programs, projects, priorities and institutional directions. Such factors, as well as historical trends, should be taken into account when forecasting future activity profiles. Aside from such forecasting activities, any attempt to modulate the activity data should be at the explicit discretion of the planners and not implicitly built into the DSS.

Classification of Courses

In a university setting, all educational and research activity is, directly or indirectly, focused on faculty activities. In the case of research libraries, the focus is on the researchers themselves, either directly or through project leaders or technological gatekeepers. Thus, the data capture system can be conveniently focused on this relatively small group of library clients. The research and learning activities of students can always be linked to and characterized by courses, projects, theses and dissertations supervised by faculty. The quantity and type of teaching activity taking place may be kept in a file associated with the courses offered at the institution and their enrollment. Courses may be linked to departments offering the courses and faculty assigned to teach them.

These data are readily available, often on university computer files, through the registration process each semester. Thus, implicit characterization of the subject matter in each course is available from the attributes of the related departments and faculty. However, an explicit characterization of the courses requires a special effort and should also be undertaken. On the other hand, the research projects conducted by faculty or assigned to employees of research and development institutions can only be explicitly characterized by the attributes of the projects themselves. The explicit classification of courses and research projects is considered below.

Three possible sources of course classification were identified within the context of the LC system of categorization. The first method was suggested by McGrath (1969b and 1975) and involves employing a catalog librarian to classify the course title and description in the same fashion as bibliographic material. With this method there is a high initial cost when the course file is first created. Revisions to course offerings every one or two years will probably result in less than 10% of the records requiring update. A second source of data about course classification comes from the textbooks required for the courses. Records from the campus bookstore may be used for this purpose. The skills of a catalog librarian would not be required for this approach since the books will already have an LC code. However, there would be considerable clerical effort associated with obtaining the codes and producing a complete file update each semester. Further, many courses have no text, and many that do will not be accurately described by the text classification itself. The next chapter explores the relative cost-effectiveness of these approaches.

A final source of classification data is the reserve list for courses. Since library material placed on reserve is already coded, this source is the easiest of all to employ for data capture. Though only a limited number of all the courses have reserve placements, the data that are available could provide a significant profile for those courses making a direct and large demand for library support. The data base schema for teaching activities is shown in Figure 2.4. All of the coding possibilities described above are included, though it is unlikely that any actual implementation would include them all.

Classification of Research Activities

With respect to research activities, there are a number of tangible indicators which could serve as sources of data capture. Lists of researcher publications and technical reports are accumulated and reported by the institution. Libraries often attempt to accumulate copies of such documents for their files. Other possible sources are research grants applied for and received, project descriptions, bibliographic searches, theses and dissertations supervised, faculty and emloyee annual reports and direct survey instruments. All of these sources require primary data capture and, therefore, their cost-benefit in the DSS must be carefully evaluated.

A Data Base Approach to Decision Support 27

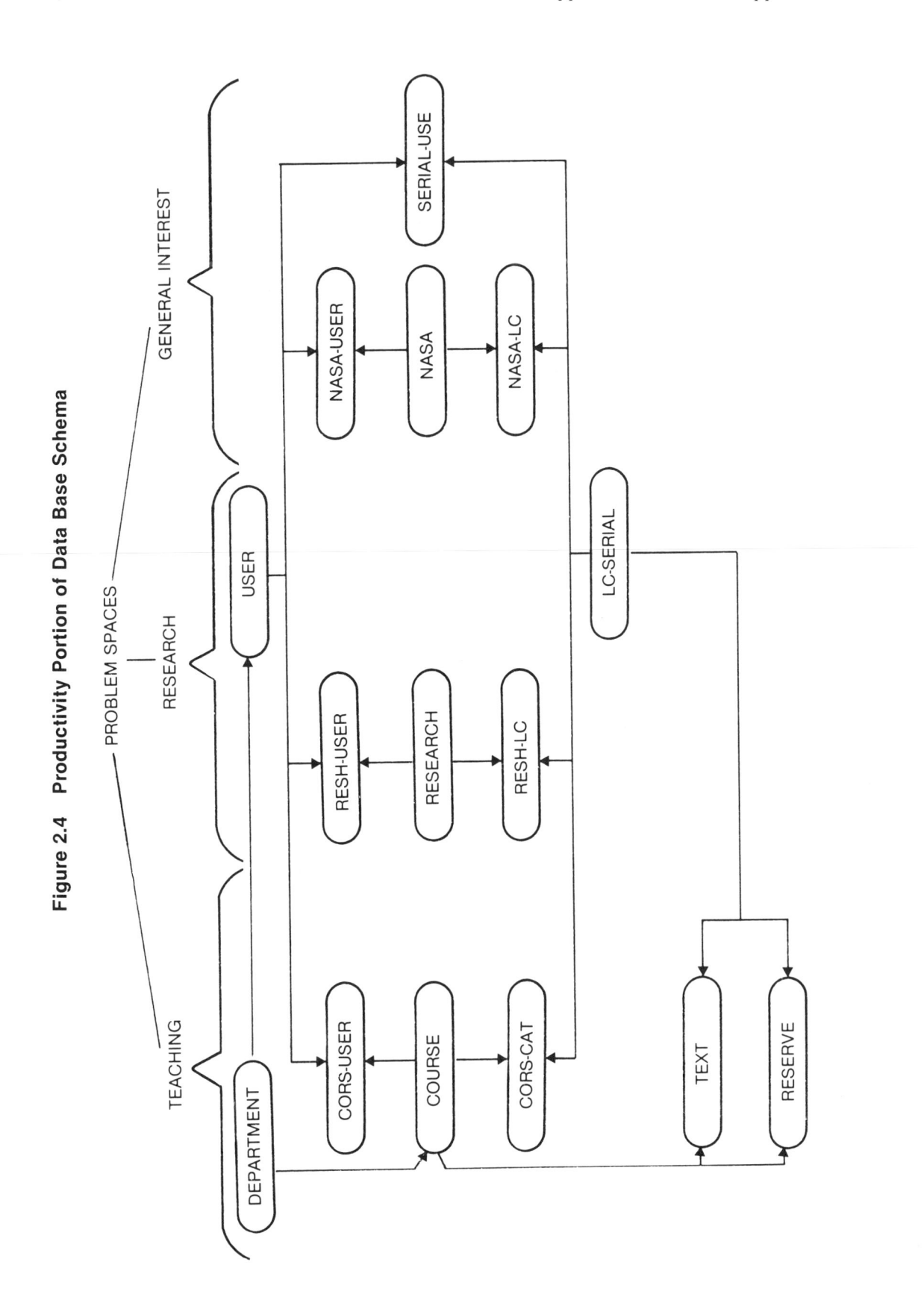

Figure 2.4 Productivity Portion of Data Base Schema

Direct surveys requiring researcher input are the most costly data capture devices. Attaining a high response rate also requires considerable attention by library staff. Results then have to be coded and key-entered. Much of the data required to track research activities could be obtained from researcher annual reports provided that these are available for inspection and transcription by library staff. Another source of research data would be the institution's office charged with coordinating project and research activities and/or publication records. Data gathered from these sources may be more timely than annual reports.

Whatever the source of activity data, the most expensive aspect of research data capture is the coding of activities according to the LC classification or some other system which may be automatically mapped onto the LC system. In the case of annual reports, this coding would have to be performed by library staff. Data from publications, project or research activity and supervision of student or employee research could be self-coded by users at some point in time when formal documents describing such work are prepared. A classification system in the natural terminology of the field of study is strongly recommended. Thus, by marking a checklist of applicable categories, the coding can be accomplished with minimum effort by the most knowledgeable party. A mapping of such categories directly onto the LC system could subsequently be done by computer. Furthermore, the checklist for coding the activity could be a mark-sensitive form, thereby eliminating the need for key-entry. Bibliographic searches and other research services performed by the library could also be subject to the same coding.

To simulate the type of data which might be obtained through the research sources described above, the academic field trial included acquisition of data concerning publications, research grants and student supervised projects.

Further Sources of Data on User Interest

There are also a number of potential sources of data concerning user interest which are not directly associated with productive teaching and research activities. Some of these include the dissertation topic and degree field of the user, personal serial subscriptions and selective dissemination services such as the NASA SCAN. Each of these sources was explored in the field trial as well. Requests for monographs and serials to be added to the collection are also a potential source of data concerning current user interests and have the advantage of being voluntarily submitted and pre-coded. However, it is frequently difficult to associate these requests with a specific user, since they are often submitted to the library through a departmental representative.

The schema for research activities and general interest are shown in Figure 2.4. The file SERIAL-USE results from a survey of users who asked for serials frequently used in addition to those under personal subscription. The NASA SCAN was taken to be representative of any such selective dissemination service.

The next chapter will focus on the potential contribution of each of the above approaches for assessing user productivity and general interest. Development of availability and utilization profiles seemed to be straightforward, and therefore no primary research was necessary. Based on the results of the field trials, the data base schema developed above was refined and reduced in scope.

3

The Process of System Development and the Role of the Library

by Audrey N. Grosch

INTRODUCTION

System development is an ongoing process. It is a structured process that does not end with the installation of a computer-aided system, but continues through further development or to conversion to another system.

The library or information center is usually the client or purchaser in this process. If the role is to be played successfully, the librarian or information center manager must understand that in-house computer facilities, operating in either a stand-alone or distributed environment, demand responsive technical support for both software and hardware. Hardware must be reliable and tested in field use with standard components or a minimum of custom-engineered features. The language of application-level software must preserve maximum independence of software from hardware and allow the minicomputer vendor or language developer to supply standard support. Finally, the operating system and other system level software must be program products supported by the minicomputer manufacturer or by an established software developer.

TRENDS IN LIBRARY SYSTEM DEVELOPMENT

The trends in library system development essentially parallel the trends of noncomputational data processing. In the past, libraries used batch mode systems for acquisitions, serials management and circulation control. Now, either they have added online data entry and editing to these systems, or else they have converted to the new generation of interactive online systems that are developed internally or supplied by commercial systems houses and software vendors. The commercially supported system is more common because it is too expensive for a library to maintain a data processing unit.

Library bibliographic software, however, has not matured enough so that new development is not needed. Careful decisions need to be made among the approaches of

---

Reprinted from *Minicomputers in Libraries, 1981-82: The Era of Distributed Systems* (White Plains, NY: Knowledge Industry Publications, Inc., 1982).

different networks, and competitive offerings that will serve certain applications should be developed to provide each library with the best alternative for its particular situation.

The data processing environment still lacks certain definitions, systems and products. For example, there is still no standard definition for the parameters of the online catalog for libraries, particularly a definition with a simple and acceptable library-user orientation. Some solutions to this problem include the touch screen terminal inquiry approach from CL Systems, Inc.; the command language search of Research Libraries Group, Inc./Research Libraries Information Network (RLG/RLIN); and the experimental online catalog at Dartmouth College. Further refinement is needed in such areas as the basic operational systems for serials management; the development of patron-accessible online catalogs; and methods of searching information centers that retrieve, abstract, index and disseminate documents in a micro/minicomputer environment. Larger libraries also need products to assist them in collection development and management.

Because of the problems involved in selecting and establishing a computer system, it is important for librarians to understand the process of system development. The basic principles of system development are defined in the next section. Every librarian can expect that vendors who provide data processing service will adhere to these principles whether or not any proprietary tools, such as SDM-70 (System Development Methodology) are used to manage or facilitate the process. This generic process applies 1) whether a single host mainframe computer or a distributed system is being employed, 2) whether a generalized application software product is chosen or a completely new application software product is developed and 3) whether the data processing agency is a software house or is part of a corporation, university, not-for-profit organization or government agency at the municipal, state or federal level.

SYSTEM DEVELOPMENT PROCESS PHASES

The development of any computer system requires the careful completion of the following phases:

- Study

- Design

- Programming

- Conversion and implementation

- Review

Each phase should result in a clear document that becomes the raw material for the next phase, including an estimate of the effort required to complete the following phase and an estimate, to be revised periodically, of the effort required to complete the entire study. In the following discussion of these phases we will use the term "data processing unit" to refer to an in-house department, a commercial software or system house, a consultant data processing firm or service bureau supplier.

Study Phase

The initial study phase begins when a user or library identifies a possible application for data processing, and the data processing unit assigns the project to a system analyst. (Table 3.1 shows the study phase steps.) For the user and the data processing department the two parts of the study phase should produce two separate documents, the system requirements definition and the system design objectives. These documents provide input data for the design phase.

The library, with guidance from the data processing unit, outside consultants and library systems analysts, is responsible for developing the system requirements definition and system design objectives. Usually the library must bear 50% to 90% of the effort required for the system requirements definition. If the library assumes greater responsibility in this phase of development, the results are usually improved in the later phases. The system design objectives will require the user and the data processing unit to share 20% to 50% of the responsibility, but since system design objectives deal with the performance of the host computer, the responsibility that different libraries assume will depend on the library's familiarity with data processing and computers. However, the library should be equally involved with the data processing supplier for the completion of both parts of the study.

The system requirements definition will analyze the present system, whether manual or computer-based. (Table 3.2 presents a suggested Table of Contents.) The analysis can be a narrative with flow charts describing communication paths, document disposition, etc. It should contain estimates of file sizes, i.e., the number of bibliographic records, volumes, etc., and estimates of average and peak input or output transaction processing loads. The analysis also describes the future data for the systems and the listed or displayed outputs produced by the system and the function that they fulfill. The next section of the analysis outlines the requirements of the proposed system: its objectives, major functions, performance expectations, data base content and envisioned output products.

The definition should describe the benefits of developing the proposed system, and also present the data processing unit's appraisal of the resources that are needed to implement the system. The system design objectives of the study phase should also be specified. Finally, any supporting data collected during this analysis should be included in an appendix after the summary statement.

The document that results from the system design objectives study will assess the standards and performance expected of the system, as well as alternative suggestions for creating or procuring the environment needed for the proposed software and hardware. (Table 3.3 presents a suggested Table of Contents for system design objectives.) It is at this point that libraries must face the question of central vs. distributed computing. They will need to consider interrelationships with other systems, both computer or manual, to determine the

Table 3.1 Study Phase Steps

1. **Identify scope for analysis**
   - Gather library organization chart and subunit written descriptions
   - Gather previous functional studies of operations, feasibility studies, etc.
   - Gather sample forms
   - Gather existing system documentation and procedure manuals
   - Gather statistical data on file volumes, transaction rates, flow and disposition of forms, error rates, etc.

2. **Conduct interviews — fact finding**
   A. Formal interviews:
   - Develop an interview format that will encourage a discussion of the current library procedures
   - Schedule interviews and provide interviewees with an outline of question areas in advance
   - Conduct and document interviews

   B. Informal interviews:
   - Conduct after formal interviews to check inconsistencies or to gain more details

3. **Analyze the collected data**
   - Establish what source data is required for the application
   - Establish the necessary summary data
   - Establish what products or reports are to be produced by the application
   - Establish the file characteristics, i.e., data elements, logical record types, sequencing, searchable elements, number of records, file use and updating requirements
   - Establish the auditing requirements for data entry
   - If application is presently performed via computer, review documentation and determine what deficiencies should be improved in a new system, and document these
   - Prepare schematic diagrams and written procedural descriptions of current work flow
   - Recast the current work flow in terms of events and transactions, each event triggered by a transaction which brings new information into the workflow or system
   - If the system is to involve multiple locations communicating via computer, analyze the communications needs of each location

4. **Summarize information requirements and usage**
   - Detail the planning, decision making, control, action, or status aspects of the application system

5. **Define system application objectives**
   - Describe how the system will address problem areas
   - Describe the benefits of the system over the old approach
   - Describe what the system will not do
   - Describe performance criteria, i.e., improved operating efficiency, cost reallocation, improved work quality

6. **Prepare work plan for next phase of study — system design objectives**

7. **Prepare system requirements document using data obtained in steps 1-6 above**

8. **Begin system design objectives phase**
   - Identify constraints on the selection of system alternatives
   - Identify viable alternatives
   - From the requirements, rank the application objectives versus cost
   - Define system components, i.e., hardware, system software/application packages

Table 3.1 (Cont.)

9. **Describe alternatives**
   - Develop new application software
   - Use existing or new host computer systems or expand existing systems
   - Use online/offline/batch processing
   - Acquire vendor-developed application software or hardware/software combination and either modify or use as is
   - Contract with vendor for needed modifications
   - Modify existing manual or operational practices

10. **Identify input categories, i.e., transaction data entry, capture, data elements**

11. **Identify output categories, i.e., displays, reports, forms to be produced by the system**

12. **Identify logical file organization requirements**

13. **Compare current cost/benefits to projected cost/benefits of alternatives**

14. **Document system design objectives for steps 8-13, including discussion of alternatives and a most favorable recommended alternative**

Table 3.2 System Requirements Definition. Suggested Table Of Contents

1. **Analysis of present system**
   - A. Present system description
     - Narrative
     - Operational flow diagrams
     - Intersite communications narrative
     - Operational data
   - B. Problem or needs analysis
   - C. Special considerations

2. **Definition of requirements**
   - A. Proposed system application objectives
   - B. System functions, required and desirable
   - C. Performance constraints
   - D. Data base constraints
   - E. Informational requirements

3. **Anticipated benefits**
   - A. Tangible
   - B. Intangible

4. **Project recommendations**
   - A. Data processing appraisal
   - B. Scope for next phase

5. **Appendices and/or supporting data**
   - A. Summary of study
   - B. Summary of collected data

Table 3.3 System Design Objectives. Suggested Table Of Contents

1. **Description of proposed system and alternatives**
   A. System overview description
   B. Schematic of data flow
   C. System function descriptions
   D. System limitations
   E. Systems design considerations
      - Data entry or inputs
      - Data base or files
      - Outputs or displays
      - Principal design requirements
      - Teleprocessing requirements
   F. System controls/auditing/error handling

2. **Anticipated benefits**
   A. Tangible
   B. Intangible

3. **Analysis and plan for subsequent design phases**
   A. Project schedules
   B. Cost analysis
   C. Comparison of benefits of alternatives
   D. Comparison of manpower requirements of alternatives

4. **Recommendations**
   A. Discussion of alternatives
   B. Recommendation of best alternative

5. **Appendices and supporting data**
   A. Glossary of terms
   B. Summary of collected data

---

dimensions of the new system. A suggested scope and level of effort estimate is made for the design phase and its first function—the system external specification.

The two documents that result from the study phase must be approved by both the library and the data processing unit. At this point the library must decide whether to continue the system development. If the decision is not to proceed, the effort has, at least, brought together information that may assist in refining manual systems or in reexamining the problem at a later time. If the decision is to proceed, the library can change its decision later, but the decision not to proceed becomes more costly with each succeeding phase.

Design Phase

The design phase translates the user's requirements into specifications for the system. The two stages of the design phase, external specification and internal specification, must be performed sequentially. The external specification is usually drafted by the system analyst in a data processing unit. However, it will be a stronger design if a representative of the library and the systems analyst share the responsibility. If the library has a systems librarian who is an experienced and technically qualified analyst, it should give that individual the responsibility for developing the external specification. Otherwise, the library should arrange for assistance on a consulting basis.

The external specification is essentially a structural walk-through of the system from the library's viewpoint. (Table 3.4 presents a suggested Table of Contents for this phase.) Computer terminology should be minimal and clearly defined in text and glossary. Library terminology should also be defined in text and glossary so that both data processing personnel and library staff understand the document. A clear and readable document is essential since the library management and staff will use it to judge the system. In addition, the system's internal design will depend on the external specification document, as modified and finally accepted by the library. The design should be frozen at this point, since any changes will have an impact on the delivery of the internal design and, subsequently, on the completed software.

Once the external design document is completed the initial version of several user-level documents can be prepared, such as a terminal operator's manual, a dictionary of the data that will be part of the system and a description of the major products of the system, including a system overview.

The library must recognize that this external specification will be the ultimate method of determining whether the software, both in test and ultimately in use, actually enables the system to fulfill the design objectives. Moreover, the library can insure that the data entering the system is stored in the data base with necessary checks; that internal data, which is stored in coded form, is properly displayed in the common language; that the command language works smoothly with good operator prompts; and that necessary "help" data screens are well constructed and understandable.

The data processing technical group, which supplies or creates the software for the library's applications, is responsible for the second stage of the design phase, the internal specification stage. Their technical management should insure that the internal design specification will produce a system or application that agrees with the external specification. The costs and schedule for the programming phase and the actual software will depend on the processing, data flow and data base design that are specified in the internal design. Consequently, if the internal specification is not consistent with the external specification the software will not produce the necessary results for the library, even if the programming has been well tested and relatively error free.

Programming Phase

This phase, the responsibility of the data processing unit, has two stages; writing programs and testing them. During this phase, programs are written in a source programming language, and these programs are tested to insure that they perform reliably and logically. Part of the external specification should have included a test plan for processing records and performing data transactions after error and logic tests are completed and the programs are integrated into the application system. The library should gather the data for this test during

Table 3.4   System External Specification. Suggested Table Of Contents

1. **Management summary**
    A. System overview
    B. System schematic diagram
    C. Design constraints
    D. Future contingencies
    E. Special management reporting features
        - Operations measures
        - Cumulative/comparative historical reporting
        - Other potential management reporting

2. **System design specifications**
    A. Overview of system modules
        - Functional organization
        - Data entry method
        - Data communications
        - Data management facilities
        - Output preparation
    B. Data entry/input requirements
        - Source documents
        - Data entry procedures/error correction
        - Record and transaction content
        - Input processing/auditing
    C. File update requirements
        - Code tables: contents and processing
        - Data base/master files: contents and processing
        - Other files: contents and processing
    D. Output description: processing requirements
    E. Algorithms and calculations
    F. System supplied messages and prompts
    G. Data control procedures and processing requirements
    H. Interface requirements with other systems

3. **System security and auditability**
    A. Security provisions
    B. Audit trails

4. **Conversion and implementation requirements**
    A. Conversion and implementation schedule and plan
    B. Creating initial files
    C. Phase-over procedures
    D. Startup requirements

5. **System acceptance plan**
    A. Acceptance criteria
    B. Test plan

6. **Preliminary operations data**
    A. Required system components
    B. Preliminary requirements for testing and conversion

7. **Supporting data and appendices**
8. **System changes agreement and impact statement**
9. **Estimates of cost and time for internal design and remaining phases to project completion**

the design phase. These data should include a good sampling of records. For example, a catalog data base application dealing with Library of Congress (LC) MARC records in various languages should test samples of varying complexity and length for each language. They might include 100 selected records with varying fields. This mix should insure that the data validation provisions are functioning, that search indexes are properly built, that the handling of extended-character sets functions correctly, and that display- or printed-product formats smoothly accommodate data with varying characteristics.

Programs that make up an application system are comprised of smaller groups of program statements, called routines and subroutines. Combined subroutines form routines, and a program may be comprised of a varying number of routines, e.g., the program that checks errors will normally contain a routine to test the value and length of each type of data element or of specific data elements.

This program may be incorporated into an application system in such a way that it is used by all data entry processes for the system. For example, it may check data for the entry of a purchase order for a book, as well as the entry of a cataloging record or the modification of the purchase order record into a cataloging record. When programs are coupled for testing (an integration test), the user begins to see the results of the programming. The library must now be prepared to work closely with the data processing unit, taking responsibility for evaluating the results and reviewing the documented reports of each test to insure conformity with the external specification and system requirements. When the library is sure that the application system functions correctly, then the conversion and implementation phase can begin.

Conversion and Implementation Phase

While the data processing unit is in the programming phase, the library should prepare the conversion plan. This plan can be written either as part of the external specification stage or as a separate document completed during the internal specification stage and programming phase. This plan establishes the timing and sequence of events for conversion to the new system, including the training of personnel, reorganization of personnel functions and a period for parallel operation and retrospective conversion. The library and data processing unit should develop this plan jointly since the library must be sure that the system will perform according to the external specifications and that the necessary documentation is present both at the user and system level.

The time may vary, from a week to a year, before the library staff is fully trained and able to use the application system to replace the former method completely. The management of the data processing unit must take the main responsibility to insure that the library staff is trained in system operation. Good management support in the library is important during the installation period, especially if it becomes obvious that organizational or administrative restructuring is needed to achieve full benefit from the computer-based application. Librarians who have witnessed the introduction of computer-assisted acquisitions and cataloging systems have seen that the new system requires the organization to serve different functions from those served prior to computerized operation. For example, there are no longer LC card ordering units or their record files when systems such as OCLC or

MINI-MARC are used for cataloging data entry, selecting pre-machine readable records and building files. The unit that performs pre-order and pre-cataloging searches also disappears.

During the implementation period the system will be subject to live testing according to criteria agreed upon by the library and the data processing unit in the external specification document. Here it may be necessary to modify the system to improve its performance. Also, hardware components that may create problems can be changed or altered. During the test stage the system should meet the specifications contained in the system requirements definition, system design objectives statement, and system external specification. Therefore, the fine tuning performed during implementation should address those aspects of the system that may be difficult to test thoroughly under simulation. For example, actual terminal loads in operation may differ from test loads. This difference may require changes in the data base structure or in the transaction-processing software. The amount and complexity of change that is necessary during this phase will depend on the degree of independence in the system for the data and application programs.

System Review Phase

This review, sometimes called a post-implementation review, should be carried out 12 to 18 months after the application is installed, the institutional reorganization completed, and the operation stable. The purpose of this review is to determine if the system still meets the library's needs, whether system changes or modifications have been made that improve the functioning and if major enhancements or extensions are necessary.

The library should make periodic reviews to monitor continued viability throughout the life of the system. The data processing unit should also take part in this review, particularly in examining the program code modifications and associated documentation, to insure that proper standards are being maintained. It should also insure that the software can continue to be adapted to future needs and that a minimum of new errors are introduced into the software through changes.

This review is the beginning of a process that uncovers new system requirements or design objectives and regenerates the system development cycle outlined in this chapter. For example, if a system has a rapidly growing data base, has doubled peak transaction loads and requires additional physical locations, a review could determine:

- if the present system can accommodate the present growth rate;

- if the present hardware can accommodate increased file sizes, processing loads, and telecommunications demands;

- if the hardware needs upgrading;

- if the system software needs to be changed;

- if the data base or indexes need to be redesigned or restructured to accommodate larger file extents across disk volumes;

- if improvements in file reorganization/regeneration/recovery are needed;

- if file updating programs can handle increased updating transaction loads;

- if the time that is required to swap programs into and out of main memory from a disk volume acting as a system disk can be reduced by increasing main memory size or using a dedicated faster disk as a system disk.

CONCLUSION

This structured approach to system development insures that both the library and the data processing unit give proper consideration to all aspects of the system. The documents from each phase provide a guide for measuring progress and maintaining management direction and control and are ultimately the ingredients of the entire system's documentation. This approach helps a library to avoid the problem of an undocumented system, a badly designed and tested system, or a system that does not address the library's needs. The system development approach assists the developer and makes certain that the library's contribution to and investment in the system is at an appropriate level.

4
Issues in Automating Acquisitions
by Richard W. Boss

The primary motives that will prompt libraries to investigate automated acquisitions systems in the 1980s appear to be the hope of realizing cost reduction or cost containment, speeding the receipt of materials, improving fund control, expanding single function systems into integrated systems and being in the forefront of librarianship.

Nevertheless, the major initiative in automating acquisitions appears to be coming from the vendors of automated library systems, both commercial and noncommercial. The bibliographic utilities and turnkey circulation system vendors have substantially completed the development of software for their initial products and are seeking to broaden their range of services. Book wholesalers with in-house computer systems see significant financial benefits from having libraries submit orders online.

Circumstances have changed dramatically since the 1960s when most libraries first became aware of the potential of acquisitions automation. Twenty years ago the library's greatest concern was ordering. Acquisitions funds were somewhat more plentiful than today and libraries were often pressed to spend all of their money before the end of the fiscal year.

Twenty years ago the cost of full-size or mainframe computers was so high that few libraries considering automation could afford to obtain their own computers; most had to rely on sharing a large full-size computer with other departments in their organization. In this climate there were two options for automating acquisitions: develop the system in-house or transfer the software developed by another library. Developing software in-house was extremely expensive, and purchasing software from another library was extremely difficult because the programming languages in use at that time were very hardware specific and therefore difficult to transfer or "transport" from computer to computer.

At the beginning of the 1980s, the concerns of the acquisitions librarian are no longer primarily associated with ordering, but with collection development and sound management

---

Reprinted from *Automating Library Acquisitions: Issues and Outlook* (White Plains, NY: Knowledge Industry Publications, Inc., 1982).

of funds. The problem for most libraries is how to make the best collection development decisions in light of scarce resources and the mission and goals of the parent organization. It has frequently been said that the most significant part of acquisitions work—that which involves the planned selection of materials, both new and old, best calculated to strengthen the institution's resources—takes place before the books are actually ordered. Modern acquisitions systems are increasingly expected to do more than provide purchase order writing, accurate outstanding order information, timely reports and good funds control. They must also become tools for selectors by providing detailed collection information.

The early acquisitions systems were tied to expensive full-size computers. The dramatic hardware developments of the 1970s have now made it possible for almost any library, even one with a limited budget, to consider an online system. Full-size computers are more powerful and less expensive than ever before. Minicomputers and microcomputers offer more limited, but considerable, processing power at even lower cost. Twenty years ago a minimum investment in automated system hardware was over $1 million; today it is less than $15,000.

The options for automating acquisitions now include not only in-house development, but also the purchase of a system or services from a vendor. The number of vendor options had grown to at least twenty automated acquisitions systems or subsystems by early 1982. For the first time the offerings of the major bibliographic utilities (OCLC, RLIN and UTLAS) duplicate those of the vendors of turnkey stand-alone systems (CLSI, DataPhase, Geac, etc.). A turnkey system is one that includes, in a single procurement, all hardware, software, installation, training, hardware/software maintenance and software enhancement. In addition, wholesalers with established bookselling relationships with libraries are offering systems, and some companies previously not associated with libraries are entering the field.

The number of choices appears overwhelming at first, especially to someone who does not regard him/herself as an expert in library automation. The natural tendency is to rely on "experts" to make a recommendation. Yet many of the issues that must be addressed are not of a technological nature. A librarian may unintentionally abdicate important judgments to someone with a more limited, less informed perspective.

Among the issues which must be addressed are:

A. *Integration or connection with other automated functions*—Given the large number of sources for the automation of acquisitions, how can the library coordinate the automation of this function with the automation of other library functions?

B. *Features*—What is the relative importance of each of the following to the library:
   1) Data base access
   2) Name/address file
   3) Purchase order writing
   4) Online ordering
   5) In-process file
   6) Claiming

7) Receiving/paying
8) Funds accounting
9) Management information
10) Vendor monitoring

C. *Cost over time*—What is the projected cost of the automated system over a period of time (generally calculated for five years), including both capital and operating expenses?

D. *Ease of adoption and cancellation*—How easy will it be to adopt the system and how easily could the library discontinue the system if it did not work well or if a more attractive option became available?

E. *Vendor reliability*—Does the vendor of the system have the financial resources to continue to support it, and have its previous customers been satisfied with its performance?

HISTORY OF AUTOMATED ACQUISITIONS

Librarians have been thinking and writing about library automation for at least four decades. Ralph Parker was working on the implementation of library automation during the 1930s at the University of Texas. The automation of acquisitions and circulation was contemplated, but it was nearly 20 years after the first experimental automated circulation system before both activities were, in fact, automated. The Montclair (NJ) Public Library adopted a punched-card circulation system in 1941 after several years of investigation. The library staff at the University of Illinois, Circle Campus, was aware of the potential of automation from the very founding of the library in 1947, although it again took a number of years to implement a plan. In his first annual report the librarian stated:

> Thought has also been given to the possibility of making use of the undergraduate division's extensive installation of IBM punched card equipment in the book order procedures and it is not at all unlikely that some application of this sort will eventually be undertaken.[1]

Early Library Automation

Acquisitions operations were a popular target for the application of automation during the first growth period of library automation: the late 1950s through 1970. Hundreds of libraries automated their procedures for the ordering, receipt and payment of library materials. The early systems tended to be order/receipt control systems or funds accounting systems. Only a few combined the two functions. Virtually all of the development was done in-house on equipment owned by the libraries' parent organizations.

As long ago as 1957, the University of Missouri Library was printing its purchase orders using punched-card equipment. Within a few years several other large academic and public libraries were punching Hollerith cards and feeding order information into computers to print purchase orders. The Brown, Harvard and Yale University libraries were among the first to automate order/receipt control.

Automation was also applied to claiming. By the mid-1960s, the University of Michigan had a system that printed claim notices on overdue orders at monthly intervals. The system provided for specification of the period after which any particular order was to be regarded as overdue—e.g., the period might be longer for orders sent overseas than for domestic orders. The system also printed lists of exceptional orders—such as those for which three claim notices had been issued—for detailed investigation. The Michigan system was among the most popular for transfer to other libraries that wished to avoid the expense of developing their own programs for acquisitions automation. The University of Utah Library was one which sought to adopt the Michigan system. However, the programs of the day were highly machine-dependent, and even though both universities had Univac 1108 computers the programs had to be extensively rewritten before they could be transferred.

Funds accounting systems were popular because many of the libraries' parent institutions were providing financial information in formats that were not useful to the libraries. Monthly reports of encumbrances and expenditures were not available until two to four weeks after the close of the month, and they summarized information by purchase order number without identifying the individual items ordered or the unit of the library for which they were acquired. Libraries, therefore, sought to develop more timely and detailed reports.

Growth of Acquisitions Automation

More sophisticated acquisitions automation began in the mid-1960s—a period of rapid growth for many institutions. At the time, the author was the acquisitions librarian at a major academic research library where the acquisitions budget grew by 350% over a six-year period. Such growth was common to a number of libraries and emphasized the need to increase staff productivity. Some of the automated acquisitions systems developed at this time sought to address ordering and funds accounting. While still produced in-house, the systems were able to control the various aspects of ordering: producing purchase orders; issuing open order reports; printing in-process reports; and summarizing expenditures by purchase order, vendor, unit of the library or requestor. The greatest drawback was that the systems operated in batch mode. The data were periodically fed into the computer and were output solely in hard-copy form at fixed intervals.

The mid-1960s was also the period of blanket order development. A number of libraries, primarily in academic institutions, began to place orders with jobbers to automatically supply all research level material produced by major publishers. The libraries were thus relieved of much of the paperwork of ordering. But the two solutions for improving library productivity were often in conflict. The automated systems were developed by librarians, while blanket ordering procedures were developed by book wholesalers. Some libraries that were producing individual purchase orders by computer were once again forced to revert to manual methods because they could not find an effective way to use the computer to handle the blanket orders which represented an increasingly larger percentage of total acquisitions.

While some comprehensive systems were developed, a majority of the systems started before the late 1970s did not automate all acquisitions functions because of the serious limitations—technical, financial and political—on the libraries that developed them. A market, therefore, existed for comprehensive vendor-produced systems for which the developmental costs could be spread among a number of library clients.

Development of Vendor-supplied Systems

The first vendor-supplied system was a batch software package called BATAB, a product of North America's largest book wholesaler, Baker & Taylor (B&T). The system was first made available in 1969 and was purchased by more than four dozen libraries, which mounted it on their local full-size computers. The system, although still used by several libraries, is no longer supported. During the eight years that B&T actively marketed BATAB it was the most comprehensive commercially developed system available, offering selection lists, purchase orders, multiple-part order sets, open order reports, in-process reports, detailed funds accounting, invoice clearing, the capacity to detect problem invoices, claim and cancellation notices, vendor lists, statistics, and various exception and historical reports.

In 1972 a new company, CLSI, introduced an online minicomputer-based acquisitions system. The system featured creation and printing of purchase orders, on-order/in-process control, accounting, etc. At least nine systems were sold before the company changed its focus to circulation control (when it discovered that acquisitions automation was extremely difficult to standardize because each library wanted different purchase order formats and accounting procedures).

The next vendor-supplied system was IROS (Instant Response Order System), an online ordering system developed by Brodart, a major book jobber, in 1978. The system allowed libraries to access Brodart's files to determine what titles were available and to place orders online. Users only needed a computer terminal and a modem to access the system, but its range of function was limited, excluding such operations as open order control, in-process files, funds accounting, etc.

The Washington Library Network (WLN), a regional bibliographic utility, was the first utility to offer an acquisitions system. Introduced in 1978, the system provides a full range of ordering and accounting functions.

By the late 1970s, as the number of vendor-supported systems grew, many of the in-house systems in use in libraries were more than a decade old. Almost all of them were batch systems, developed for full-size computers available to the libraries. Batch systems are those in which data are stock-piled and only periodically fed into the computer, which is almost always a full-size computer outside the library. Punched cards or magnetic tape are the most common forms of input; output is usually a printout. Batch systems normally have response times measured in days and are almost always limited to single functions. In contrast, online systems, such as those developed by Brodart and WLN, measure response times in seconds and can handle many related functions concurrently. There was, therefore, a gradual movement from batch to online systems in the late 1970s, with a majority of the libraries adopting vendor produced systems.

Approximately one out of five libraries with annual acquisitions budgets of more than $200,000 were using an automated acquisitions system by late 1981.[2] The most common systems in use were the online ordering systems of the major book wholesalers: Baker and Taylor's LIBRIS and Brodart's OLAS (the successor to IROS). Nearly 100 libraries were using these systems, the majority of them large public libraries. The second most common approach to automating acquisitions was the use of in-house systems, most of them batch systems installed in the late 1960s and early 1970s. Most of the 60 in-house systems that could be identified were in academic libraries. The smallest, but fastest growing segment was of bibliographic utility systems. Approximately 15 libraries were using the Washington Library Network's system, the oldest comprehensive online acquisitions system developed for use in a multi-library environment. Another 20 libraries were using the OCLC (Online Computer Library Center) acquisitions system released in late 1981 and more than 30 other libraries had placed orders for it. Eleven Research Library Information Network (RLIN) users had committed themselves to use that utility's acquisitions system, still under development in 1981.

THE MOTIVATION

Before a library begins the process of developing or selecting an automated acquisitions system, library administration should examine its motivation in undertaking the activity. This is not to suggest that there are good or bad reasons for automating, but there must be a clearly stated rationale to the process, so that the many decisions which must be made can be made quickly and consistently. Common motivations include:

1) Reducing ordering backlogs
2) Reducing acquisitions costs
3) Containing acquisitions costs
4) Speeding order writing and/or receipt of materials
5) Improving funds control
6) Expanding a single function automated system into an integrated system
7) Improving management information
8) Achieving compatability with resource sharing partners
9) Committing the library to the use of technology

The motivation may be to seek a solution to an existing problem, to anticipate a prospective problem, or merely a wish to do something perceived to be more efficient. It is imperative that the administration of the library be very honest with itself in determining its motivation, even if it should decide not to share its reasoning with others. An objective study of the options may lead to a decision not to automate. Library automation consultants are often told that library administration wishes to automate to achieve a specified objective. When the consultant determines that the objective cannot be achieved through automation, the library administration concludes that automation will, nevertheless, be undertaken—sometimes for the originally stated reasons and sometimes for other reasons. If the motivation is a desire to automate because of a belief that automation is the modern way of administering a library, the library administrators should acknowledge this, at least among themselves.

The motivation of the library director is very important in the automation project. In more than 150 telephone interviews conducted by the author and his associates in 1981, the library director was identified by virtually all interviewees as the principal decision maker in an automation commitment. The decision to automate is apparently deemed to be one of the most important developments in a library, and directors choose to reserve the major role for themselves. The decision-making process appeared to be a source of irritation for many of the non-administrators interviewed.

The author, therefore, talked with 80 library directors to determine why they might automate acquisitions. Each director was asked whether acquisitions might be automated within the next five years, and if so why? More than 75% responded that they expected to automate the function. Almost all of the nearly 25% who did not expect to automate acquisitions cited lack of funds as the principal reason for not doing so. Only four directors said that they saw no reason to automate because the manual systems were adequate. The comments of the directors are incorporated into the balance of this chapter.

Reducing Ordering Backlogs

Automation almost always speeds the rate at which work is performed by relieving the staff of repetitive chores, improving the accuracy and integrity of files, eliminating the multiple entry of data, and facilitating the reformatting of data to accommodate changing needs.

The reduction of ordering backlogs was once a major motivation for automating, but it was cited by only two of 80 directors interviewed. Half of the directors interviewed said that problems of backlogs had been solved by declines in their libraries' purchasing power—they are buying less than in the past and there is little prospect for a change for the better.

Some libraries have been forced to reduce staff or freeze positions, and have had ordering backlogs develop for that reason. Often, the personnel retrenchments have been matched or exceeded by retrenchments in other areas. Therefore, there is no money to commit to automate the function.

Reducing Costs

One of the most frequently cited reasons for considering automation of acquisitions is the hope of reducing the cost of ordering and paying for library materials. The majority of the directors interviewed mentioned this as their principal interest.

The cost-effectiveness of automation in libraries has not been clearly established, however. Libraries have very large bibliographic files, often consisting of hundreds of thousands of records. Only a small percentage of a file will be consulted in a given day—Becker and Hayes estimate as little as 0.1%.[3] This is in sharp contrast to the activity in most business organizations, where smaller files may be consulted a hundred times as frequently each day. Therefore, libraries cannot spread the cost of creating and maintaining a large data base over very many units of activity, as can typical businesses.

It has been argued that automated cataloging using OCLC or one of the other bibliographic utilities has saved libraries a great deal of money. In the author's view it is not automation alone that has produced the great cost savings reported; rather, it is the effect of access to a rich, shared bibliographic data base that in many libraries has reduced the percentage of costly original cataloging (typically from $17 to $40 per title) to less than 10% of total cataloging. The ability to create records and edit copy without retyping would be extremely expensive if that were the only effect of using a bibliographic utility.

It is extremely difficult to acquire just enough computer capability to speed up work done manually without also acquiring capabilities that far exceed the minimal needs. Since many of these "extra" features are highly desirable, libraries tend to use them. The cost of performing a single task may be reduced, but total operating costs may rise because more work is being done. An example of this is the additional work that flows from the availability of collection use statistics produced by an automated circulation system. It results in more weeding of little used materials, more purchases of replacement and added copies, and changes in collection development patterns. One might argue that these are all things that libraries should do all of the time, but in fact automation often stimulates libraries to undertake these previously neglected tasks.

Directors of large public libraries who are responsible for purchasing large numbers of copies for several branches are the most optimistic about cost reduction. The costs of acquisitions of this type can be extremely high because of extensive bookkeeping requirements. Strikingly, of those who had automated circulation in the past five years, none thought cost reduction could be achieved by the automation of any library function because none had realized cost savings by implementing an automated circulation system. However, virtually all of these directors reported dramatic improvements in service from such installations.

While there is little evidence that any library has reduced the cost of acquisitions by automating, the future prospects for cost-effective automated library systems are quite good. Hardware costs are decreasing and the unit cost of each transaction will be lower when several functions can share computer hardware and the data base.

If cost reduction is a primary objective, current non-automated system costs should be determined, and this will probably require a cost study. A good study is time consuming and expensive. There is no point to undertaking all this work if cost reduction isn't the motive for automating. If it is, the cost study should be undertaken and the library administration should abide by the results. If it isn't, the cost study should be foregone and the library should concentrate on determining whether the other improvements sought will be realized.

Containing Costs

Many of those who are skeptical about cost reduction nevertheless believe that costs can be contained. While a little over half the library directors interviewed thought automation would reduce costs, nearly all thought it would contain costs. It is recognized that while capital investment in automation may take several years to recover, once the system is installed it can usually absorb additional work at little increased cost. Usually, the unit cost of additional work drops. This has been confirmed in many libraries with automated systems.

More and more directors are citing cost containment, rather than cost reduction, as the reason for considering automation. Several said they had previously held the view that cost reductions could be achieved, but their own experience and that of others persuaded them that cost containment was a more realistic objective. If one does opt to automate with cost containment in mind, one should be able to determine current costs and project the rate of increase in those costs. This requires adequate historical cost information—something most libraries lack. Here again, a library should undertake a cost study. The major categories of costs should then be projected, based on inflation and on prospective increases in activity.

A less expensive cost study could be undertaken by comparing the added cost of increasing (by some percentage) the level of acquisitions using existing procedures, with the cost of increasing (by the same percentage) the activity level using the automated system. That will not answer the question of whether the implementation cost of the automated system is recovered; it will only compare the capacity and cost of each to accommodate increased activity.

Speeding Order Writing and Receipt of Material

Library directors generally agree that automation will increase the speed of writing orders and receiving materials. This is particularly important to the directors of public libraries who are concerned that new books reach the shelves before reviews appear in news media or authors appear on television interview programs.

Several of the interviewees said that automating order writing got the orders to the vendors more quickly, but did little to improve the total time required to get materials. Reducing the order preparation process by a few days matters little if the vendor takes several weeks to supply the titles. Libraries experienced with wholesaler systems that transmit orders online to the vendor supplying the system and transmit printed orders to other vendors, found the following: getting the order to the vendor in machine-readable form (for direct entry into the vendor's order-fulfillment system) resulted in dramatic improvements in delivery time; however, the rapid production and mailing of printed orders for other vendors appeared to have no effect.

A few directors of special libraries (most of them libraries which order fewer than 2000 titles a year) who have had experience with automated systems said that while they liked the overall control the system provided, the total process had become more complex. One reported that automated systems which call for detailed input of data can actually increase the time required to prepare orders. Another said that a good manual system can produce purchase orders more quickly, and without creating backlogs. It is in the subsequent filing and retrieving of information and financial control that most benefits accrue from the automation of the function.

Improving Funds Control

Acquisitions consumes a large part of every library's budget and the pressures to account for expenditures are greater than ever. Most libraries have more than one fund from which purchases are made and a majority allocate the available funds among collections, departments or disciplines.

All of the directors interviewed consider improved funds control a major reason for automating acquisitions. Among the directors of large libraries it is the most important reason for considering automation.

It is imperative that the automated system be flexible enough to permit the setting up of accounts in the manner prescribed by the financial authorities in the library's parent institution. It should not be necessary to rewrite the reports from the automated acquisitions system into the formats required by the institution's accounting department. This requirement appears to have been the major reason for many libraries choosing to develop in-house acquisitions systems.

Expanding a Single Function System into an Integrated One

Over 3000 libraries have now had some experience with automation—shared cataloging, online circulation control or the searching of remote bibliographic data bases. They are, therefore, prepared to consider the automation of other library functions to create integrated systems, and modern computer hardware is capable of supporting the integration of several functions.

For most libraries cataloging and circulation control are the most important candidates for automation. Several automation options had been available for each of these functions for at least three years before viable automated acquisitions systems options began to appear. For many libraries the automation of acquisitions is, therefore, an augmentation of an existing system or systems.

The library directors interviewed want to be able to create a bibliographic record when an item is selected and to use the same record in the cataloging, circulation control and patron access catalog functions. Even when the automation of acquisitions is not cost effective in itself, it can be justified as an essential component of the overall automation program.

Improving Management Information

Automated systems can produce a substantial amount of management information, including detailed information about the relative cost of materials in various disciplines, vendor performance, etc. The library directors interviewed ranked improved management information as a high priority, but few were accustomed to using extensive management information in their work.

Unfortunately most automated systems produce more management information than an administrator can readily use. Few systems are designed to provide only "exceptional" information—for example, reporting the vendors who exceed a particular delivery time rather than producing detailed reports of how long it takes each vendor to deliver the average order.

One of the most important pieces of information in improving collection development is knowing how much the existing collection is used. The persons charged with selection should have access to information on patterns of use as one element in shaping their collection development programs. They should also be alerted when a large number of reserves or holds are placed against a title so that additional copies may be ordered.

Ideally, titles which are on order should be included in the circulation control system or patron access catalog so that reserves or holds can be checked against them and additional copies of high-demand titles ordered even before the initial order is met.

Achieving Compatibility with Resource-sharing Partners

More and more libraries are coordinating their acquisitions with other libraries. By sharing an automated system they can determine what is in each cooperating library's collection and what each has on order, thus avoiding unnecessary duplication.

A few of the library directors interviewed were already sharing automated circulation systems. Some were entering titles on order into their circulation systems before they were received so that the information could be shared.

Committing the Library to the Use of Technology

Nearly every technological advance in the past 100 years has excited the imagination of one librarian or another, and many advances have eventually been adopted by libraries. One example is the typewriter. It was in 1877, during the Conference of Librarians in New York, that the typewriter was mentioned as a possible tool for cataloging. In 1885 the typewriter was discussed at the Conference of Librarians at Lake George. Some of the librarians present had been trying different makes and models, and were convinced that the typewriter was a superior way of making catalog cards. However, there was still some question about the permanency of the ink. Those who went ahead had no proof that the ink was suitable, but they took a chance and introduced what was to become one of the most important technologies ever adopted by libraries.

The first articles in the literature explaining potential library applications of Hollerith punched cards, which were first used in the census of 1890, began to appear in the 1930s. As previously noted, the first experimental library automation was undertaken at the University of Texas in the mid-1930s; five years later the circulation system of the Montclair Public Library was changed to a punched-card machine installation. During this same period University of Florida Library staff members wrote about their experiences with a mechanized circulation system. While none of this early automation was cost- or service-effective, it laid the groundwork for the successful automated circulation efforts of later years.

By early 1982 online circulation control had matured as an application, with comprehensive systems containing nearly identical features available from several vendors. Comprehensive online acquisitions systems supported by vendors were still in their infancy. Some of those who chose to automate acquisitions sought to solve specific problems with their manual systems; others moved ahead because they were committed to a philosophy of employing new technology to improve library operations. This faith in technology has often been warranted, as it was in the case of the typewriter. It has also often led to failure—as it did with many of the dial access learning systems that were installed in the late 1960s.

There is a risk involved in automating acquisitions before all of the options are fully developed and can be observed in operation in libraries. It is extremely difficult to predict which of the vendors will offer the most comprehensive and cost-effective systems. There are, nevertheless, a number of librarians prepared to take the risk.

FOOTNOTES

1. University of Illinois, Chicago Circle, *Annual Report of the Library 1947-48* (Chicago, IL: The Library, 1948).

2. Based on a random sampling undertaken by the author's firm in 1981.

3. Joseph Becker and Robert M. Hayes, *Handbook of Data Processing for Libraries* (New York: John Wiley & Sons, 1970), p. 109.

5

The Ideal Acquisitions System
by Richard W. Boss

The ideal acquisitions system would allow an operator to search the library's own bibliographic data base online from any terminal in the library, or even from a remote external location, using any one of several access points such as author, title, keywords of the title, publisher, date of publication, etc. The operator would be able to determine the status—for example, on order, received—of any item by consulting the library's data base.

The system would allow an authorized operator to order additional copies of a title for which an order was previously placed. Not everyone with access to a terminal should be able to perform this and a number of other functions. Thus, passwords or some other form of security would be required to prevent unauthorized actions.

The system would contain a vendor (publisher/wholesaler) address file. There would be online access to a vendor data base which the operator might search, in a predetermined order of preference, to determine which vendors were able to ship the wanted material immediately, and at what price.

The system would be linked to the data base of a bibliographic utility so that bibliographic records would be stripped off to create purchase orders.

The system would be able to access vendors' inventory files which would include status notes for all titles—e.g., the item is out of print, not yet published, scheduled for later publication or scheduled for reprinting. The authorized operator, after determining the appropriate vendor on the basis of availability and/or price, would be able to place the order online to the vendor, preferably directly into the vendor's internal order fulfillment system.

The ideal system would alert the operator if an order about to be transmitted was going to deplete the funds in the account selected. At the time of ordering, the library's

---

Reprinted from *Automating Library Acquisitions: Issues and Outlook* (White Plains, NY: Knowledge Industry Publications, Inc., 1982).

financial files would be simultaneously updated to reflect an accurate encumbrance against the appropriate account.

When the order is received by the vendor, the material should be pulled from the inventory and mailed within 24 hours. The jobber's inventory record would be reduced immediately so that the next library inquiring about the title would be given correct inventory status information.

The library using an online acquisitions system would have the flexibility to provide very detailed financial information in a variety of ways. All of the areas and sub-areas against which materials are charged would be accommodated. The ideal system would also be capable of selecting titles from the master data base from which it would produce selection lists in multiple copies. These could be used for selection purposes in large branch systems.

The ideal acquisitions system would maintain a comprehensive online file giving the library complete information about every item on order but not received, as well as everything in process. Other available information would include the date of shipment by the vendor, the date of receipt by the library, the date paid, etc. The system would alert the library when expected materials did not arrive after a predetermined amount of time, so that cancellation or reordering could be undertaken.

The vendor would supply machine-readable invoices with the material. The acquisitions system would verify when all items on the invoice had been received and then write the necessary checks, pre-addressed and ready for mailing. If a library was not authorized to issue checks, the system would generate vouchers for payment. Invoices that had not been cleared would be identified by the system for further investigation. Concurrently with payment, all financial records would be updated (encumbrances cancelled, expenditures posted against the correct accounts, etc.). Also, the in-process file would be updated to reflect the date of receipt and the date of payment, including the check number and other pertinent information. The library would have the capability of converting the machine-readable information in the acquisitions system to a record for circulation control and/or to a catalog record. An online interface with the library's other automated systems would be provided, including linkages with the library's circulation and patron access catalog systems.

The system would be able to accommodate a variety of materials, including monographs, serials, continuations, government documents, deposit accounts, approval plans, blanket orders, gift and exchange agreements, and other categories of materials acquired by the library. The system should provide a complete audit trail by title and by fund for a library-specified length of time online, and then print audit trails on microfiche for permanent retention. Management information of various kinds including vendor performance statistics should be available. It would be possible for the library to determine when service performance was deteriorating or discounts were decreasing. Preferably the system would report exceptions to expected patterns that had been recorded in the system, rather than generating large numbers of reports that require time-consuming review.

54   ISSUES IN LIBRARY MANAGEMENT

There was no single system available in early 1982 that incorporated all of these features. Almost all of the features were in the preliminary design of one or more vendors' systems. It appears unlikely that any system would have all of the features before 1985.

The choice of a system, therefore, involves careful examination of the issues, and selection of the option that best meets the library's current and future needs.

CRITERIA FOR SYSTEMS COMPARISONS

The following checklist of features may be used to compare systems.

A. Files Searching
1. What files are available for searching?
   a. The library's own holdings?
   b. On order/in-process file(s)? Local and/or union?
   c. Bibliographic utility data bases?
   d. Other bibliographic data bases?
   e. Vendor file(s)?
      (1) Availability or stock information?
      (2) Current list price?
   f. Accounting file(s)?
   g. Vendor name/address file(s)?
2. How flexible is the searching system?
   a. How many access points are available?
   b. Can partial keys be used? (That is, can an operator key in an incomplete name or word and retrieve all possible matches?)

B. Ordering
1. Can the system produce selection lists if desired?
2. Can the system handle multiple copy ordering for different locations easily?
3. Does the system allow the operator to select the vendor?
4. Is online ordering (instantaneous transmission) directly to vendor possible?
5. Can the system print purchase order forms ready for mailing?
6. Can the system print multiple-part order record sets for internal use if desired?
7. Are the appropriate funds encumbered at the time of order using an estimated discount for the selected jobber?
8. Is the operator notified if the funds are exhausted?
9. Can libraries sharing the systems select different options?

C. Monitoring
1. Is the in-process file instantaneously updated so that the current status of an order can be determined at any time?
   a. On order
   b. Shipped
   c. Received

2. Is vendor fulfillment status available?
   a. Back ordered
   b. Cancelled
3. Are claim and/or cancellation notices prepared according to the library's specifications?
4. What statistics are provided by the system?
5. What kind of vendor monitoring is available?
6. What exception/error reports are produced?

D. **Receiving/Paying/Accounting**
   1. Is the in-process file instantaneously updated so that the receipt and/or payment of an item is recorded?
   2. Are the various funds updated automatically and correctly (i.e., previous disencumbered and accurate expenditures posted)?
   3. Are vendor's invoices balanced and problem invoices identified for manual resolution?
   4. Can checks be written automatically after clearing of invoices?
   5. Can payment vouchers be issued if the library is not authorized to issue checks?
   6. Are audit trails available so that the operator can determine the history of any given order or the history of any given fund?

E. **Interfacing**
   1. Can the acquisitions system connect with other systems in the library?
      a. Circulation
      b. Serials control
      c. Patron access catalog
   2. Can the system interface with the library's bibliographic utility?
   3. Can the operator order catalog records at time of order/receipt of material if desired?
   4. What machine-readable records can be obtained from or loaded into other systems?

F. **Screen Display**
   1. What screen displays are provided by the system?
   2. Are the screen displays difficult to interpret?
   3. Are they compatible with the forms currently used by the staff?
   4. Will extensive staff training be required?

G. **Cost Breakdown**
   1. Does the system vendor itemize costs in enough detail for the library to make realistic comparisons?
   2. Are all of the items necessary to make the system operational included in the cost breakdown?
   3. Are the costs capital expenses or operational expenses?
   4. What commitment is there regarding the costs in future years?

IN-HOUSE SOFTWARE DEVELOPMENT

As the foregoing checklist implies, an ideal system essentially means ideal software. Hardware supplies support only, and there is relatively little difference in equipment available from one vendor to another. Virtually the only way for a library to achieve its ideal system today is to undertake in-house development and design its own online acquisitions software. When doing so, a library maintains a high degree of control over system design, permitting it to specify the inclusion of all desired functions. The cost, however, will be extremely high and unpredictable. It can represent as much as 80% of the total cost of a computer system. When this cost is carried solely by one library, rather than by many libraries participating in a bibliographic utility, purchasing the same turnkey system or using the same book wholesaler's system, the cost can be several hundred thousand dollars.

Most of the libraries that attempted to develop their own systems did so in the late 1960s and early 1970s. Virtually all of these systems are batch systems for producing purchase orders and controlling funds. Large systems include those at the Universities of British Columbia, California at Berkeley, Columbia, Cornell, Harvard, Syracuse and UCLA. Smaller batch systems were developed at a number of public libraries.

Online acquisitions systems were generally launched in the late 1970s. Among them are the systems of the Howard University Library, University of Minnesota Biomedical Library, Pennsylvania State University Library and Denver University Library. All of the online systems are envisioned as future integrated library systems. Boys Town Center (Boys Town, NE) is developing a small integrated system with automated acquisitions. The Fraser Valley (British Columbia) Regional Library has contracted with a software house to develop its shared automated system.

The library opting for in-house development must decide between a system configured around a full-size computer (probably not located in the library except in the case of a very large library) or around a minicomputer or microcomputer (which probably would be owned by the library). The development of a system designed to be run on an existing full-size computer in the parent organization might appear to be the most reasonable choice until the library begins to explore the cost of software development.

OTHER SOFTWARE OPTIONS

One way of reducing the developmental costs of software is to purchase it from another library or library consortium. The modifications required to meet a specific library's needs will range from minor to extensive and the costs will vary accordingly. The purchase price of the software may range from $2000 to $100,000, but the total software cost may be much higher. A package that requires considerable modification to fit the library's needs and/or is written in a language that is not highly "transportable" to other equipment will add substantially to the purchase cost. This type of approach should only be undertaken by a library that has in-house data processing expertise.

Examples of acquisitions software packages that have been developed for a consortium or a single library and are now available for sale to others include the Washington Library Network's acquisitions subsystem and the Northwestern University Library's NOTIS III (Northwestern On-Line Total Integrated System). The former has recently become available through a vendor as a turnkey system. The latter may be available in the future as an off-the-shelf package with a program for ongoing software enhancements.

Although there are more than 5000 standardized software packages available, virtually none have been developed specifically for libraries. If a library turns to a "software house"—a firm that specializes in the development and sale of software—it can get custom development of software. Custom software packages developed in this way are sometimes later generalized by the firm and become "off-the-shelf" products.

There are hundreds of software houses in North America. Almost every major city has several. The standard practice is for the firm to develop the necessary software for a particular customer on the basis of specifications the library has provided. The price is usually higher than the estimated cost of in-house development by the library, but the price and delivery date are firm if the contract so stipulates. The software house often uses its experience to solicit other clients in the same field. If only minor adaptation of the initial software is required for subsequent clients, the price can be lowered for the buyers and the profitability to the vendor increased. One Texas firm did several circulation system software contracts this way. The first customer can recover some of its high cost by stipulating in its contract that it will receive a royalty on subsequent uses of the software package developed for it.

The maintenance of custom-developed software is also expensive. Again, there is no broad base of libraries over which to spread the cost of making improvements or enhancements. The cost is usually at least $40 per hour for additional programming. Enhancements may affect the original programs so that they too have to be modified.

AVAILABLE SOFTWARE PACKAGES

The balance of this chapter is devoted to summaries of three major software packages: DOBIS/LEUVEN, Maggie's Place and NOTIS. The reason for discussing these software options in a chapter on ideal systems is that the primary justification for choosing a software package is not to cut costs, but to further develop the software in-house to tailor it to the unique needs of the library. In early 1982 there were no ongoing software maintenance/enhancement programs available for either DOBIS/LEUVEN or NOTIS, but there were plans to provide ongoing support for the NOTIS software.

The Washington Library Network software, which is also separately available, is not discussed here because only three libraries had purchased WLN software as a separate package by early 1982, whereas more than 60 were using it as part of the bibliographic utility service.

DOBIS/LEUVEN

Development of the DOBIS/LEUVEN system (Dortmunder Bibliothekssystem/Leuvens Integraal Bibliotheek System) began in 1971. In that year, the University of Dortmund contracted with IBM of West Germany to develop an integrated online library management system. IBM performed additional work on the system for the University of Leuven, which created an international MARC standard for the system. The combined system supports cataloging, searching, acquisitions and circulation. In general, DOBIS is oriented to technical services and Leuven to public services.

The programs are written in PL/1 and assembler languages, and operate on IBM/370 compatible hardware. The acquisitions module resembles the WLN acquisitions module in that there is no duplication of data in the system. All subsystems share a common bibliographic file. Local information is tied to the shared bibliographic file, but retained separately.

The acquisitions functions that are part of the DOBIS system allow for immediate online additions and updates in all acquisitions files. Records are indexed by vendor, library fund, order and document number as well as by eight bibliographic indexes such as author, title and subject. Added copies can be recorded very quickly. The system also accommodates interlibrary loan activity. Financial and statistical information about vendors and funds can be updated and displayed online. Automatic claiming is performed and can be regulated by the vendor performance statistics maintained online. Order information is created and formatted to the specifications recorded in the vendor profile.

The primary memory requirements depend upon the number of active terminals, the tasks being executed concurrently and the response time desired. The minimum storage required for DOBIS is 512KB (kilobytes).

Since DOBIS/LEUVEN is not just an acquisitions system, or a circulation system, or a cataloging system, but can perform all of these functions, the workload tends to be much higher than the workload placed on a single-function system. The smallest CPU on which DOBIS/LEUVEN will operate is 1MB (megabyte) unless a library opts to perform some functions in batch mode. DOBIS/LEUVEN does not require a dedicated CPU, but can be run concurrently with other, different systems. Therefore, this one megabyte would contain the operating system and the terminal communicating system, and, depending upon usage, it could also be used to perform other functions, such as word processing or computer assisted instruction (CAI).

Minimum system configuration consists of an IBM System/370 Model 138 or comparable machine with appropriate disk storage (based on the size of the data base) and at least one IBM 3270 Display Station, a nine-track tape unit and a high speed printer for printing notices and listings.

The DOBIS/LEUVEN system is not a turnkey system. Rather, it is made up of software packages marketed by IBM to all types of libraries. While DOBIS and LEUVEN may be purchased separately, the acquisitions function may not be purchased separately from the other technical service functions.

IBM will sell the computer with the software, but it will not provide the extensive training and ongoing software enhancements that libraries are accustomed to receiving from turnkey vendors. It is expected that many customers will acquire the software for use on existing equipment, the capacity of which may have to be increased. The system cannot be used without data processing expertise to adapt the purchased software.

As of late 1981 the online DOBIS/LEUVEN software was marketed by IBM at a cost of $1500 per month for 24 months. This price includes the license fee, documentation and source code. Future maintenance and enhancement of the software is not available from IBM.

As with other IBM products, DOBIS/LEUVEN is marketed through IBM marketing representatives located in IBM offices around the country. The availability of the software was announced in the United States in February, 1980. A number of U.S. installations are in progress, but in early 1982 only one was operational—at the Austin (TX) Public Library. The system has also been installed in libraries in Canada, Europe and Africa.

Before IBM was able to obtain the marketing rights to the DOBIS product, the University of Dortmund decided that it would distribute its programs directly to one major library in each interested country. It would be up to each library to modify the product to fit its country's needs. At this point the National Library of Canada (NLC) obtained the DOBIS software directly from the University of Dortmund. The NLC chose to make extensive changes to the software to fit its requirements. To date it has implemented only the cataloging and the catalog search portion of the system from Dortmund. The version of DOBIS installed at Centennial College Bibliocentre (Toronto, Canada) was obtained from NLC. Centennial has made its own modifications to the programs. In addition, before IBM was able to obtain the marketing rights to the LEUVEN product, Centennial purchased a copy directly from the University of Leuven and modified it to correspond to its version of DOBIS. The DOBIS and DOBIS/LEUVEN software in use in Canada are substantially different from the software available from IBM in the United States.

The primary memory required for the NLC version of DOBIS is substantial. Centennial College is nearing saturation on its 2MB machine for its 19-member consortium. This is approximately eight times the primary memory of a typical installed turnkey local cataloging and circulation system. The capacity of the National Library of Canada's mainframe is currently 4MB and is to be upgraded to 6MB–8MB in the future.

Maggie's Place

The Pikes Peak Library District in Colorado Springs, CO, has developed an integrated library system called Maggie's Place. All of Maggie's Place components are designed to operate on a Digital Equipment Corp. (DEC) PDP/11 series computer with the RSTS/E operating system. The price of the hardware, which must be purchased separately from a dealer, ranges from $45,000 to well over $100,000, depending upon the number of terminals and the amount of secondary storage required.

Software for the functions of acquisitions, circulation, community resources, periodicals and administrative tasks are sold by Pikes Peak and can be installed on a DEC PDP for a license fee plus installation and training. Acquisitions software alone costs approximately $8000. There is no ongoing software maintenance or enhancement available at this low price.

Through the acquisitions system, items to be ordered are searched against the library online circulation file, if maintained, as well as the acquisitions file. The acquisitions file contains all items on order, as well as items in process, and includes standing orders that are placed with publishers or which must be renewed annually.

Read-only access can be provided from any terminal in an integrated system and the file can be searched by author, title, vendor or bar code. The system will respond with the information in the data base, including the number of copies on order and in processing.

Through the various functions, staff can search the file by several approaches, load new orders, calculate encumbrances, produce reports arranged by department, area and line item, delete items from the file, generate purchase orders sorted by vendor and title, clear invoices for payment, modify items in the file and record the receipt of items. All materials can be processed through the system except periodicals check-in and claiming. Standing orders are flagged and can be accessed separately. A separate subprogram handles claims.

The system can provide a separate encumbrance report for standing orders and serials by department or division. Orders are now mailed to the publisher or vendor, but it is projected that it will be possible to place orders online. The standards on which online ordering would ideally be based are unlikely to be developed before mid-1983.

The acquisitions system is designed to eliminate all filing related to the process, to generate orders on demand, to provide accounting information and to provide access to the file by all staff.

NOTIS

NOTIS III is a comprehensive library materials management system developed by the Northwestern University Library. The first version of the software was completed in 1970 and two major revisions had been accomplished by late 1981. NOTIS includes acquisitions, processing, serials and circulation control modules. All functions are fully integrated.

In technical services, system use begins as early as receipt of an order request, with a search of the NOTIS data base. Northwestern's practice is to capture authoritative bibliographic data, when available, at the earliest possible moment. To this end, the library has a search department responsible for both preorder and precataloging verification. This department attempts to fulfill preorder and precataloging requirements prior to the placing of an order for newly requested titles.

The starting point in any search is the library's online data base. If no record is found in the NOTIS file, the operator initiates a search of the MARC data base, unless the item is unquestionably out of MARC scope. The NOTIS system maintains the complete MARC and COMARC files offline, searching them each night and retrieving the most current records the following day, and older records according to a regular schedule. An interface to the Research Libraries Information Network (RLIN) is being developed for libraries that require access to a bibliographic utility's data base.

After the transfer of data from MARC tapes into the online system, or input from other sources such as Library of Congress (LC) or National Union Catalog (NUC) copy, or the entry of provisional data, the basic bibliographic record—with appropriate modifications—is used for the production of all hardcopy output, from purchase orders through catalog cards and punched circulation cards.

The technical services subsystem operates in two modes: bibliographic and order. Each requires a different password and, although all data may be displayed in either mode, modification in the order mode is only permitted by operators with an appropriate sign-on code.

The top line of the computer screen serves as the "request line" on which the terminal operator enters the appropriate command. The system automatically displays the most common commands, but these may be overridden at any time by the operator.

In both modes the indexes provide the major access points when the bibliographic record number is unknown. All name entries, whether main or added entries, and all title entries, including generic records, are created. The main entry and main title fields cause immediate online update of the indexes. Other indexed fields in the bibliographic record, such as name and title added entries, result in batched offline updating at periodic intervals. Corporate name entries appear in both normal and rotated forms for ease of access to the lowest level in the corporate hierarchy.

Three types of screen displays are possible in the bibliographic mode: full bibliographic data, copy holdings and volume holdings. On the bibliographic data screen, the fixed fields are formatted at the top and the variable data fields, headed with MARC mnemonic tags, display in MARC numeric order below. To create a new record in the proper format, the operator keys in a command indicating which of the MARC formats is to be used.

It is possible to generate a purchase order after the provisional bibliographic data and location/copy designation have been entered, regardless of whether or not a MARC transfer has occurred. In the order mode an operator inputs the appropriate vendor information, including any special instructions, and calls for printing of a purchase order. The bibliographic record number in conjunction with an order sequence number furnishes the purchase order number.

In the order mode, the holdings screen provides the link to all orders, with an alphabetical status code indicating if the order is open, cancelled, complete or a replacement. The operator selects the desired order number and receives a screen display that includes the brief bibliographic data, the vendor information, the copy control number and the order/payment/receipt data fields. The first of these fields, the order scope statement, indicates the order status, fund, encumbered amount and an action date for claiming purposes. Any payment statements will appear next and include the amount paid, invoice number and date, invoice control number and any necessary piece of identification. A receipt statement is used to record pieces received. For serials, a new automatic claim date is calculated based on the latest receipt statement modification date and predetermined claim interval information. Both the machine-set latest modification date and claiming action date appear on the screen.

Each night the computer generates a list of expired action dates that prompts claiming. In response to this list, an operator reviews each record and produces a claim memo by entering a statement containing an appropriate code and date. Claims can also be generated any time a gap is discerned without waiting for an action date list to prompt the claim. A wide variety of messages can be generated automatically. Approximately 50 memo-producing codes are in current use, generating claims for missing and overdue periodical issues and unsupplied monographs, requests for permission to return duplicate or imperfect items and requests for unsupplied invoices. Printed claims are produced overnight for dispatch in the following day's mail. A note statement entered in a data field in the order record is used to record vendor response as to the order status (out of stock, back ordered, etc.).

As of early 1982 the author observed keen interest in NOTIS. This interest is understandable, because NOTIS offers a more comprehensive list of features than normally available in other software packages. To summarize, the basic features are:

- preorder searching against a local data base;
- order record creation/update;
- purchase order writing;
- customized vendor correspondence (claims, cancellations, etc.);
- receipt posting;
- overdue item alerting;
- payment posting;
- commitment/expenditure reports.

The Northwestern University Library decided in 1981 that it would market NOTIS to other libraries. One system had already been sold to the National Library of Venezuela. Agreement was reached in 1981 with the University of Florida Library to provide the system after making several enhancements, including improved circulation control, subject access, call number access, cross references in indexes and authority management. Online funds control may also be included at some time in the future.

NOTIS software can be run on any computer which will support a standard IBM/370 operating system.

CONCLUSION

The ideal system is not currently available from any vendor. The cost of in-house development is prohibitive, often several hundred thousand dollars. Libraries that have electronic data processing expertise available can purchase a software package and adapt it to their unique needs. The library would then have to undertake ongoing software maintenance and enhancement. The cost for this may be high and unpredictable. Libraries that can afford to wait or that can accept less than the ideal system might be well-advised to do so.

6
The High Cost of Serials
by David C. Taylor

The rising cost of serials may have been the single factor with the greatest effect on academic libraries in the last 10 years. It has forced libraries to reexamine their basic acquisition activities and goals, and their relationships to other libraries. It has certainly introduced more hate than love into their love-hate relationship with publishers.

Why have the costs of serials to libraries risen so dramatically in the past decade? The answer is twofold: the increase in subscription prices and the increase in the number of journals (and other periodicals) being published, creating pressure on libraries to buy more and more. This chapter will consider both aspects of the problem.

Are publishers making enormous profits at the expense of libraries, or do the jacked-up subscription rates truly represent the costs of publishing? Do we really need all—or even a large percentage—of the serials now available? To answer these questions we will examine some of the financial problems that beset both libraries and publishers; the different kinds of serials and their publishers; and serials readership.

SUBSCRIPTION RATES

According to the 1981 price index for serials in the U.S. the average annual subscription price of 3425 journals was $39.13 in 1981, an increase of 13.3% over 1980. The increase the previous year was 13.7%. For five years, from 1976 to 1981, the price rose 73.8%![1]

Subscriptions have eaten up so much of the library budget that no library has been able to absorb the costs easily, no matter how well off financially it is. In fact, some of the larger libraries have been affected most, because of their larger commitment to serials.

R.H. Blackburn, Chief Librarian of the University of Toronto succinctly stated the problem. In his 1975-76 annual report, he wrote:

> The steady upward trend in the price of books and journals in the international market in which we must buy has amounted to at least a doubling in the past six years. In the last year, for instance, the average price of our subscriptions rose 16.4% to $35.93, and we were paying for 20,713 of them. Since our budget for purchases has remained fairly fixed in dollar amounts,

---

Reprinted from *Managing the Serials Explosion: The Issues for Publishers and Librarians* (White Plains, NY: Knowledge Industry Publications, Inc., 1982).

our purchasing power has dropped by more than half, though the total volume of scientific and scholarly publishing continues to go up. Moreover, our standing commitments which involve recurring costs year after year (subscription renewals, continuations, standing orders for currently published books, binding, shipping and insurance) take a share which has risen from 42% in 1968-69 to 72% in 1975-76 (and 83% in 1976-77) so that there is little money left for anything else... The purchasing power of the "discretionary" part of the book budget has sunk in eight years to only 14% of what it was in 1968-69.[2]

Library Subscription Budgets

In the past decade many libraries have discovered a mechanism at work in their libraries that few noticed before. When the price of library materials goes up faster than the library budget, an increasing proportion of money will be spent on serials and a decreasing proportion on monographs. When this tendency repeats itself year after year, the shift in funds can be ruinous to established acquisitions programs.

According to the statistics reported to the Association of Research Libraries (ARL), the University of Toronto cut its subscriptions from 47,866 in 1975-76 to 42,244 in 1979-80.[3] Nevertheless, the subscription budget doubled from $750,057 in 1975-76 to $1,546,564 in 1979-80. The proportion of acquisitions funds spent on subscriptions jumped from 24.1% to 46.7%.

ARL's statistics reveal that other libraries are experiencing similar problems. Texas A&M's spending on subscriptions went from $270,000 (19.7%) in 1975-76 to $904,190 (54.5%) in 1979-80. Syracuse University spent 27% of its acquisitions funds on subscriptions in 1975-76, and 60% in 1979-80. Temple University went from 25% on subscriptions in 1975-76 to 62.8% in 1979-80. Massachusetts Institute of Technology's (MIT) spending jumped from $481,918 in 1975-76 to $834,307 in 1979-80 and only maintained subscriptions in the 60% range by adding $438,000 in total funds between those years. None of these libraries decreased its subscriptions but none added substantially to them.

Case Western Reserve University cut its subscriptions by 651 and added $200,000 to its budget (+27%) but its subscription costs rose 76%, despite the cancellations. The subscriptions share of the Case Western library acquisitions budget rose from 58.7% to 81.6%! The amount of money available for the purchase of books fell from $309,002 to $174,957.

According to the 1980-81 ARL statistics, spending by university libraries for serials increased 13.8% per year from 1976 to 1981. Spending for books and other nonserials only increased 4.2% per year over that period.[4]

Trying To Keep Up with Inflation

Libraries faced with these budget shortfalls have desperately sought larger increases in order to keep up with the inflation in costs of library materials. In his annual report for 1979-80, Dr. Blackburn reports the bad news that despite an effort by the university to maintain the library's book purchasing power, the 11% increase for 1980-81 would not meet the inflation of book and journal prices. As he analyzes the problem:

> The situation is extremely critical because about 84% of the book fund is committed before the year even begins, to subscriptions, standing orders, continuations, binding, and shipping charges. This leaves only 16% to buy books for the reference collections and special collections of all kinds . . . for the local libraries in 15 faculties and teaching departments, for all research items which are outside the scope of our standing orders . . . and for covering unexpected rises of price. . . . This 16%, and everything that depends on it, could be virtually wiped out by one year's inflation.[5]

Most of the academic libraries in North America have experienced a similar loss in buying power and the squeezing of the acquisition budget by subscription and standing order commitments. Few university administrations can afford to increase library budgets enough to provide cost-of-living increases to personnel, keep up with inflationary increases in equipment and supplies, and provide funds to keep up with more-than-inflationary book and periodical prices.

Those who can may be self-defeating, says Richard DeGennaro in the most important single article written on this subject. "Up to now, our standard response to the problem of escalating journal prices has been to plead and beg for higher budgets from our funding authorities, for subsidies from the government, and for grants from foundations. All these and more are desperately needed, but this kind of help is certain to come too little and too late. And when such help comes, it will only encourage publishers to raise the institutional subscription rates even higher, and to publish more unnecessary, largely unread journals."[6]

In this call to action, DeGennaro accuses publishers of treating libraries as a captive audience, and increasing journal prices as much as the traffic will bear. He also claims publishers create new, specialized journals at low cost to themselves but at high cost to libraries who must buy them at inflated institutional subscription rates. He implies further that publishers used to consider themselves part of the scholarly enterprise, but that the inflation of the 1970s has created a different climate, making journal publishing an opportunity for profit and that the unquestioning slow-to-cancel libraries are targets of that opportunity. Even learned societies used inflated subscription rates to subsidize membership services.[7]

DeGennaro is easy to quote because he writes clearly and provocatively. He accuses faculty members of using journals as vehicles for self-promotion, not scholarship.[8] He accuses librarians of being illogically wed to the desire to have complete runs, and urges them to wake up and cancel the serials that sit unread.[9] If he is right, there is little possibility of dialogue between librarians and publishers. I think that much of what he says is true, but in general, he is wrong. I believe publishers and librarians have to stop being angry at each other if they are to solve their mutual problems.

THE COST SQUEEZE FOR PUBLISHERS

Librarians should understand that scholarly publishers have enormous problems. They have explored all possible means of improving income for their journals. They have gone to great lengths to reduce expenses for their journals. Still, the costs go up—15%, 20%, 30% a year.

Advertising Revenues

Publishers have gone after advertising revenue, an income producer that American journals have tapped successfully for many years. In 1898 the American Chemical Society (ACS) received $620.77 from subscriptions, $649.96 from advertising and $6490 from dues. In 1900 it received $917.29 from subscriptions, $1129.50 from ads and $7500 from dues. In 1930 the figures had grown to $167,000 in advertising and $294,000 in dues and subscriptions.[10] In recent years, the advertising dollar has risen greatly, but total income needs have risen still more—and advertising revenue has provided a smaller percentage of that income. In 1972 the ACS took in $3 million in member and nonmember subscriptions, and only $900,000 through advertising.[11] By 1981, income from printed publications and dues reached $47 million; from advertising, $6 million. To put these raw numbers in perspective, note that advertising was 9% of subscriptions and dues in 1890, 13% in 1900, 56% in 1930, 26% in 1972, and back to 13% in 1981.[12]

This trend in advertising income for the ACS is consistent with that for other scholarly publishers. A study conducted by Fry and White showed that advertising revenue, while a significant source of income for many types of publishers, declined in importance on the average for all categories of publishers (commercial, society, university press and other not-for-profit publishers) and for all subject disciplines (pure science, applied science and technology, humanities and social sciences) between 1969 and 1973. While advertising revenues went up for all categories except science journals between 1969 and 1973, it did not go up as much as total revenues (and costs) for any of the categories. Despite attempts by many publishers to increase advertising revenue, the income from this source has not been as great as hoped because advertisers are not terribly interested.[13] They know that researchers go from indexes to the specific articles wanted and do not linger over the ads.[14] In fact, advertising income for scientific and technical journals is almost negligible. Magazines do much better, but journals do poorly.[15]

Page Charges

Other sources of income to supplement subscriptions have also been tapped by publishers. Society publishers of journals in pure science have been able to achieve a great deal of income from "page charges," a form of subsidy by authors. S.A. Goudsmit of the American Physical Society (APS) estimated in 1968 that 70% of the publication costs of the *Physical Review* and *Physical Review Letters* were met by page charges, only 30% by subscriptions.[16] This has changed considerably in recent years.

According to Marjorie Scal of Cambridge University Press, page charges in the early 1960s were generally paid under the same grants that supported the original research. The National Science Foundation (NSF) announced in 1961 that federal research grants would include page charges for scientific journals, since publication of research results was a legitimate and necessary part of the research. However, in the late 1960s and early 1970s the trend began to reverse, as federal government subsidies of scientific research began to decline. Foreign authors and authors working on their own, not on grants, were unable to pay the charges. As journals experienced more and more difficulty in collecting page charges, they increased charges for authors' reprints or subscription prices significantly.[17]

The authors of *Scholarly Communication* describe the history and significance of the page charge.

> Page charges were initiated by the *Physical Review* about 1932 at $2 per published page and have risen to more than $70 a page. The rationale for the page charge, which was set to cover editorial and composition costs, was the belief that research is not complete until it is published. Subscription costs were kept low because they had to cover only the costs of production, primarily paper and press work, and distribution costs. Page charges were always assessed against the author's institution, not the author. The system worked well as long as research was well funded. When budgets tightened, payments for page charges declined precipitously. Many journals in the sciences then introduced the two-track system—relatively rapid publication (within six months) for those who paid, and delayed publication (up to two years), for those who did not.[18]

Because of the changes in the federal government's funding of research, the page charge has almost completely died out now as a significant source of income for most journal publishers.

Subsidies

Subsidies never appear to have been a major source of funds for scholarly journals but that doesn't mean publishers haven't tried. Most foundations have shunned grant requests from journal publishers, although the same foundations may issue grants to authors while they are writing books. Many scholarly journals do enjoy the indirect subsidies of universities. Those journals based at universities usually do not pay rent, the secretarial expense may be paid by the institution, and the professor who gives his or her time to editing duties may be relieved of some instruction hours or other committee assignments.

When a society budgets a certain amount from its dues income for subscriptions for members, that cannot properly be called subsidy. In fact, that budget almost never amounts to the same price per member subscription as nonmembers pay, so it could be considered a subsidy of the society by the journal!

Back Issues and Reprints

Most scholarly publishers realize some money from the sale of back issues. The study by Machlup, Leeson and Associates in 1974 showed that 2.2% of the income of 137 journals studied was from back issue sales.[19] The figure reported for the ACS journals for 1972 was $200,000, or 3.2%, but by 1981 back issue sales had dropped to $100,000, or .22% (.0022)![20]

The sale of reprints is a better source of income than back issues for the ACS: $550,000, or 8.7% of its income, in 1972 and $1 million, or 2.2% in 1981.[21] The journals studied by Macklup, Leeson and Associates reccived 4.8% of their income from reprints.[22] Probably most reprints are sold to authors in lieu of or in addition to page charges.

Reprints are a sore point between publishers and libraries. Publishers have been convinced for years that libraries illegally photocopy articles from journals and that this systematic copying robs them of subscription and reprint income. Many of them fully expected that the new copyright law of 1976 would stop this "unfair practice" by libraries. So far the copyright law has not made a substantial difference. The Association of American Publishers (AAP) and the Information Industry Association (IIA) formed the Copyright Clearance Center to handle requests for photocopying and to receive and distribute royalties. Receipts have been disappointing. To publishers this indicates that there is widespread infringement of the law. To librarians it indicates what they have been saying all along: that the massive photocopying in libraries is done by the public, not librarians, and is not and never has been illegal. The two points of view differ widely and do not show much movement toward a mutual understanding. Suffice it to say now that there does not appear to be any immediate improvement in income for publishers from copyright fees.

Cost Hikes for Publishers

As the foregoing discussion shows, all the sources of income are closed or limited to publishers except subscription fees. Meanwhile the costs of producing a journal have increased rapidly. The price of paper more than doubled between 1970 and 1980. Nelson W. Polsby, managing editor of the *American Political Science Review,* reported that the cost per issue had gone up from $.89 a copy in June 1970 to $1.52 in June 1975, and the 1970 issue had 388 pages to 312 for the 1975 issue.[23] That's 10 pages for 2.3 cents in 1970, and 10 pages for 4.9 cents in 1975, an increase of 112.4% in five years. During those same five years the consumer price index went up only 38.6%.[24]

The price of paper is just one example of the tremendous increase in the cost of doing business as a publisher. Number 3 uncoated book paper, a standard high grade paper used widely in publishing, has increased in cost at a steady rate of 9.3% since 1972. Rolls of paper that cost $307 a tone and sheet paper that cost $356 a tone in 1972 cost $480 and $555, respectively, in 1977 and $747 and $867, respectively, in 1982, according to Stewart Furlong, president of the book paper division of the WWF Paper Corporation of Bala Cynwyd, PA.*

Printing costs have risen at least as fast, postage even faster. Salaries and wages, rent, telephone rates, and all other costs have matched the cost-of-living increases or exceeded them. Publishers must show a profit to survive. If costs cannot be kept down, income will have to match them or the publisher must go out of business.

Where is the increased revenue to come from? Payments from readers. How can publishers expand this income? There appears to be little market for additional subscribers. Even though many publishers have been able to increase their sales abroad, total sales for scholarly journals appear to be down.

Two recent reports corroborate a general decline in circulation of scholarly journals. In a paper given before the Second International Conference of Scientific Editors, in October 1980, Chomet and Nejman reported on a study of circulation and income figures for physics

---

*Personal communication with author, June 1982.

journals. They concluded that most of them had experienced an initial rapid rise in subscriptions for four or five years, followed by a tapering off and decline. Most physics journals, they projected, would sell only 900 copies by the year 2000, only enough to fulfill "archival" purposes.[25] (I assume that this means only library subscribers by the year 2000.)

In a report at the same conference, Bowen stated that 12 of the 20 ACS journals had lost subscribers during the previous five years. "Further erosion of circulations will result unless successful sales campaigns can be waged to hold or expand the markets for the publications," he predicted.[26]

With the addition of *Sci Quest*, there are now 21 ACS journals. In 1981, 17 of the 21 journals lost subscribers, although most only lost a handful, and none are in danger. As it turns out, the ACS did not mount any major circulation campaigns in 1981. The low return rate from broad spectrum direct mail promotions makes it uneconomical to do so. Instead, spot campaigns appropriate for each journal are continued, to keep renewals high and to bring in enough new subscribers to replace cancellations. The American market is pretty well saturated for older ACS journals, Bowen feels, although he believes that a potential market exists overseas, particularly in underdeveloped countries. "But we don't know how to reach *those subscribers*," he says.[27]

With the number of subscribers declining, the single greatest hope for publishers probably is to increase the subscription rate for their most solid customers—the libraries. The well-known fact that libraries are reluctant to cancel subscriptions to important journals no matter how high the price has led to the "institutional subscription rate." Individuals tend to drop their subscriptions at a certain point—$40 or $50 these days. Libraries stick it out at $500, $1000, $1500.

THE CONFLICT

This growth of the institutional subscription rate is a great bone of contention between publishers and librarians. Librarians feel that the institutional subscription rate is outrageous. Only a few years ago serial publishers offered libraries discounts, and most book publishers still do. Librarians catalog, index, bind, preserve and distribute journals. Without libraries, the documentation functions of journals would no longer work. Why, say the libraries, should they pay more?

Publishers are as convinced of their own special role, and the need for money to publish must override many other considerations. A publisher may take the attitude that no self-respecting physics library can get along without the American Institute of Physics (AIP) journals; therefore few libraries will cancel their subscriptions no matter how high the prices get. They can always ask the state legislature for more money because of the rise in acquisitions costs. Or libraries can cancel subscriptions to less significant journals in order to pay for the more important ones.

This attitude appears cynical to librarians and puts them on the horns of a dilemma. Herbert White sums up charges and countercharges over the institutional subscription rates:

> Librarians . . . can argue that they are in fact subsidizing unrealistically low individual subscriber prices. Publishers undoubtedly tend to counter by saying that price differentiation is necessary to protect what little remains of a personal subscription base. Without this, library prices would have to be set still higher. They also tend to argue that there is at least some suspicion that cancellation in individual subscriptions is accelerated by the availability to the library user of expanded interlibrary loan through networks, consortia and photocopying. . . . The charge that libraries are increasingly being asked to bear a larger share of the subscription price than in the past appears to be true. Librarians argue that they are being singled out because they are largely a captive market with little ability to make competitive decisions. Publishers respond that libraries are singled out to shoulder increased prices because, despite their poverty, they are still the most affluent group of subscribers available.[28]

But times have changed since 1976, when these attitudes were reported. Libraries are no longer affluent. Government funds are drying up, as libraries' costs are increasing. At the same time, as discussed above, publishers' costs are also increasing steadily.

GROWTH IN NUMBER OF JOURNALS

Given this rather desperate situation of libraries and publishers of journals, it comes as rather a shock to receive flyers announcing new journals. If the economics of publishing are so bad, librarians want to know, why are so many new ones being started? How can a new journal be important enough to buy? The librarian asks how the world got along without these journals for so many centuries, but now finds them to be essential to a well-stocked library. Yet, the faculty want them. This surprising encounter with a new scholarly journal is the way we experience the "explosion of serials" that the historians of science tell us is only a steady growth of three hundred years that continues in our time.

Fry and White concluded that new scholarly journals were being created at a rate of 3.9% a year: that is, 403 of 2459 journals studied were born during the time frame of the study (1969-73). On the other hand, they concluded that 2% ceased during that period, leaving a net growth in journals of 2%. They also found an increase in the number of pages published by most journals.[29]

A slower rate of growth is indicated by comparing the two most recent editions of *Ulrich's International Periodicals Directory,* although one must remember that *Ulrich's* lists many other periodicals besides scholarly journals. The 20th edition (1981) lists approximately 63,000 titles—1000 more than the 19th edition (1980).[30] More than 550 cessations are also listed. This would indicate a birth rate of 2.5% per year, and a net growth of 1.6% for the year 1980.

The King study concluded that 6335 scientific and technical journals were published in the United States in 1960, 8460 in 1974.[31] That amounts to a net increase of 2.2% a year. The number of journals per scientist consuming and contributing research remained quite steady, however.

The National Enquiry into Scholarly Communications, conducted in 1976-1978, found that journals in four disciplines in the humanities (classics, English and American literature, history and philosophy) grew more than twice as fast as the scientific journals covered by the King study. The growth rate for these fields was 114% in 15 years, or 7.6% a year.[32] This is especially interesting since Fry and White's study and the National Enquiry both found that journals in the humanities were in the most financial difficulty.

What can account for this growth even in hard times? The clue is the King study's figure for journal-per-scientist, which stayed even during the period of growth. The research literature grows as researchers grow, and hence, as research grows. White, in his summary of the Fry-White findings, says:

> Concern about this assumed rate of growth among librarians and others has been so great that suggestions have been made that libraries refuse to purchase newly published journals in order to force publishers to limit their output. It appears clear, however, that most new journals arise from needs of scholars and researchers to communicate the results of their research and the needs of others to learn about that research rather than from some preconceived notion by publishers that new journals in particular fields must be issued. . . . The net annual rate of growth . . . [of] 2% [is] a figure considered neither alarming nor abnormal when compared to growth in research, particularly academic research, during the same time period.[33]

The National Enquiry concluded that the ease of entry into publication is a good thing, but that failing journals should not be kept going artificially by subsidy and that further net growth of scholarly journals should be discouraged by "a continuing scrutiny of the usefulness and quality of existing journals as well as those that are proposed."[34] That scrutiny implies a cancellation of journals that do not measure up.

However, there is no indication that librarians, scholars and university administrators are organizing journal population control efforts. There are many cancellations, but they appear to be for the reasons Dr. Blackburn mentions: library budgets losing their purchasing power.

The new journals exacerbate problems already quite difficult. They add to budget stress; to overcrowding of library shelves; to strain on scholars to read, on secondary services to index and review, on the national and international library community to catalog and provide access to all useful literature, and on existing journals as competition for papers and subscribers. Is it enough to say that scholarship is growing and therefore scholarly media must grow? Shouldn't we ask, "Who publishes them and why, in such adverse times?" Shouldn't we ask, "Who writes for them? Who subscribes to them? Who reads them?"

WHO PUBLISHES THEM?

The Fry-White study found that commercial publishers started more new journals than other publishers (35.2% new journals in four years, or almost 9% a year). Society-published journals increased only 7.4% (1.8% a year), new university press journals grew only 5.8% (1.4% annually), but other not-for-profit publishers started 19% new titles (4.5% a year). The new journals appeared twice as fast in social science (20.6%) and pure science (20.1%) as they did in the humanities (12.8%) or the applied sciences and technology (10.5%).[35] (Apparently humanities as a whole is not growing as fast as the National Enquiry found classics, English and American literature, history and philosophy to be!)

In 1982 this author conducted a brief study of cataloging for new serials in recent issues of *New Serial Titles*. One thousand randomly selected entries from the May through November 1981 issues were studied. Cross references and entries describing foreign-language publications were disregarded. Of the 350 English-language entries, only 47 were descriptions of new journals. They were divided by subject as follows: 9 humanities; 13 social sciences (including business and law); 18 science (including medicine); and 7 technical. Publishers of these 47 journals were: 21 commercial; 13 societies; 8 university presses and departments; 3 self-published (publishers created apparently for the purpose of publishing these journals); and 2 government bodies.

As the commercial publishers are the most willing to gamble on a new journal, it is probable that they are most likely to kill one that no longer pays its own way. The overall balance of publishers then may be fairly steady.

WHO WRITES FOR THEM?

There is no problem for a conscientious and energetic editor to find publishable papers. As the National Enquiry report puts it, "Careers [are] at stake." Authors need outlets for their scholarly research. "Pressures to publish for professional advancement are strongly felt and generally accepted."[36]

This is not a recent phenomenon. Harold Wooster said in 1967:

> The young scientist learns, as part of the formal code of behavior of the scientist, that publication of the results of his research in a standard, authorized, refereed scientific journal is not merely right and proper, but a high duty and a behavior expected by his peers and employers. He learns informally that promotion comes about through visibility and that, at least up to a certain critical point in his career, visibility comes about through publication. He learns that there are "good" journals and others not so good, but that every manuscript can eventually find a home somewhere and that, for all the platitudes about refraining from unnecessary publication, this must apply to someone else—it is better to publish something in anything, even if only a government report, than not to publish at all.[37]

"Publish-or-perish" has a negative connotation, but it does not necessarily mean that bad scholarship is published. Scholars who might not otherwise compete for printed space in journals are driven to do research and to publish it. That can be very good for scholarship and society. However, it puts more pressure on the editors and journal referees to evaluate contributions and to publish only the original and creative papers.

Unfortunately, they sometimes are unable to do the job of weeding out articles which should not be published. One demonstration of this is the growth of what is called the "Least Publishable Unit" (LPU). Instead of writing one article about a research project, scientists—especially in biology and medicine—have recently tended to divide the data up into three or four articles, each only slightly different from the others, and to publish them in different journals. This leads to a fragmentation of data and makes the job of the researcher who is checking all pertinent references much harder. The only solution to this problem, says William J. Broad, is to expect editors and readers to do a more thorough job in evaluating papers.[38] It is probably not realistic to suppose editors will be able to reduce this practice significantly as long as grants and promotions are handed out to those who exhibit fat *curriculum vitae* with many publishing credits.

This sort of practice makes many librarians feel angry and worry a little less about cancelling subscriptions. More and more, they are studying journal usage and are cancelling the rarely read. Libraries may be very reluctant to subscribe to a new journal now. Editors of a new journal may attempt to find readers interested in a specialized field, but they will have a difficult time surviving without library subscriptions.

WHO READS THEM?

Who reads these new journals, and all the other scholarly journals being published so prolifically throughout the world? The National Enquiry found that "the average scholar scans seven journals, follows four or five regularly, and reads three to five articles a week." According to this report, these scholars spend 10 to 12 hours a week reading books and journals. More (40%) had increased the number of articles read in the past few years than had declined (20%). They tended to read their own subscription copies of journals, rather than a library copy, and scholars at larger institutions subscribed to more journals even though they had access to more journals in their libraries.[39]

A classic study of the reading habits of psychologists conducted in 1963 found also that American scholars did most of their reading in journals obtained by personal subscription. Most reading by foreign scholars was of library copies. Since all were reading the same 13 journals, 12 of which were published in the U.S., it suggests either that American scholars aren't as library-conscious as other scholars, or that all scholars tend to depend on the library for foreign subscriptions.[40] One also assumes that almost all psychological journals read by non-psychologists are library copies. (Of course, one cannot be certain that the findings would be the same if such a study were made today.)

The King study summarized its findings on the use of scientific articles in 1977: 5470 subscriptions per journal, 382,300 articles published, 244,000,000 uses, 638 uses per article, 2,092,600,000 article copies distributed, and .12 uses per article copy distributed.[41] This last figure is discouragingly low, considering the effort and expense mustered to produce scholarly literature in journal form.

Earlier reports by Elson and Dew (1955), Sorokin (1968), The American Psychological Association (APA) (1963) and Moore (1972) indicate that this situation is not a recent phenomenon. Elson and Dew concluded that an article in a specialized journal would be likely to interest only 10% of the specialists on that subject and an article in a general journal would interest only 2% of readers. Sorokin estimated that 15% of what is published is read by *nobody*. The APA discovered that half of the research reports in core journals are read or scanned within two months of publication, by fewer than 1% of subscribing psychologists; no report will be read by more than 7%, and even the most popular journal has a large group of articles looked at by fewer than 1%. Moore studied use of the *Journal of Organic Chemistry* and concluded that the average subscriber glanced at 17% of the papers in the typical issue and read half or more of only 4%.[42]

One reason for the low readership per article appears to be the expansion of scholarship itself, requiring more and more specialization by the scholars. Journals sent as part of a society membership must cover such a range of interests that fewer and fewer articles in each issue are likely to appeal to any particular scholar. This helps account for the viability of new specialized journals. The quality of papers may not be as high as those of the well-established general journals in the field, especially at first, but the special interest in a sub-sub-branch will appeal strongly to those researchers devoting their attentions to that specialty.

This phenomenon also accounts for a new development in scholarly publication: the bulletin (a newsletter-type news medium) that publishes original papers, especially short communications of work in progress. For example, Elsevier has successfully marketed one newsletter-type periodical for biochemists and has started others for neurobiologists and pharmacologists.[43]

Even librarians, who might be expected to be as conservative as anyone in accepting new publications, show considerable interest in new periodicals. Respondents to a survey sent out with the December 1980 issue of *Title Varies** listed 38 different serials as important reading for them. Each was asked to list his or her top five. Many publications (including *Title Varies*) were relatively new, and the fifth most read title, *Serials Librarian,* is a specialized, commercially published journal begun in 1976. In sixth place was another more general periodical, the *Journal of Academic Librarianship,* begun in 1975.

The many new publications contribute to the scattering of relevant papers in a discipline. S.C. Bradford discovered that in any large literature search for a given time period, a few key journals will provide a large number of the articles, but a very large number of journals will have one or two articles each.[44] Because of this scattering, a scholar attempting to keep up with a field can find perhaps half of the articles being published by reading four or five journals regularly. By subscribing to an SDI (Selective Dissemination of Information) service he can cover 80% or 90%, but it will be very difficult or impossible for him to manage 100% coverage.

The academic librarian also has a difficult time trying to cover subject fields. Worse, he must anticipate what faculty reading interests will be not only in the next five years, but in the next 100 years. According to the study of use of the Pittsburgh University Library by Allen Kent and his associates, librarians' guesses about the use of journals in the library are poor. Use follows the Bradford distribution. Of the six departmental libraries studied, "the percent of the titles in the collection used during the sampling period varies from under 10% to a high of 37%, depending on the library sampled. In general, a very small percentage of the collection accounted for the entire journal usage in the sampling period, and could be projected for the year as the titles used predominantly."[45] While almost all journals will

---

*A newsletter published by the author six times a year from 1973 to 1980. Its audience was primarily composed of serials librarians.

eventually be used, some will be used so infrequently that they probably could be cancelled with virtually no complaint from faculty and students.

NON-SCHOLARLY JOURNALS

This chapter has concentrated on scholarly journals because that is primarily where the "explosion" of serials comes from. That also tends to focus on the problems experienced by academic libraries. But all libraries experience much of the frustration of working with serials, and some of the non-scholarly journals can create the worst problems for libraries. Before leaving this chapter we will talk a bit about the very different problems, goals and economic considerations of these publishers.

The publisher of a scholarly journal requires very little capital to get started. His potential audience is easy to find. He has minimal expenses for artwork and design, and since his publication will have limited appeal to advertisers, he does not have to impress them with lavish displays or expensive color printing.

The reverse of this is usually (although not always) true for the publisher of a general interest, nationally distributed magazine. Millions of dollars are required to assemble an expert staff of editors, writers, artists, publicists and advertising account executives. Designs, page layouts and sample tables of contents must be made up months in advance in order to gain commitments from large advertisers. Expensive test marketing must be done in advance. A heavy investment in direct mail promotions and in impressive ads in other magazines must be made. Despite enormous expenditures, the chances of success are not good. For every *People* that made it, there are many *Shows* and *Vivas* that didn't.

The entrepreneurial publishers of this kind of magazine have a different purpose in publishing from that of the scholarly publisher. Communication of ideas (and making a profit) is the aim of one; documentation of scholarship the aim of the other. A big consumer magazine usually has an identifiable (and salable) "concept," which will help editors assemble articles, stories and other features that make it unique and indispensable to a large group of readers, and therefore attractive to major advertisers.[46]

Circulation for a major magazine will be handled by a highly automated "fulfillment service" company. These companies will be highly efficient in handling new subscriptions and address changes, but will require four to six weeks to make changes in subscription records. While responsive to claims for missing issues, they will not often be able to send another copy of the issue in question, since few copies are left over and they are discarded soon to avoid high warehousing costs and inventory taxes. Even though the fulfillment managers are suspicious and cynical about the high percentage of claims from the very small percentage of their subscriptions that go to libraries, they will try to be scrupulously fair and will extend the subscription by one issue for each issue claimed as missing.

Controlled Circulation Magazines

At the opposite end of the spectrum is the publisher of the "controlled circulation" magazine designed for a particular, small, carefully defined professional group—e.g., manufacturers of mining equipment, egg farmers, institutional cafeteria managers. These magazines will live on the advertising, since there are no subscribers. Those people on the "subscription" list qualify for free distribution by virtue of their occupation, and presumably by their ability to make purchasing decisions. The carefully audited mailing list represents a high quality group of potential buyers to the advertisers, who are willing to pay much more than the usual ad rates for a small circulation magazine.

Editors will gather together three or four articles for each monthly issue, emphasizing practical methods and how-we-do-it-good articles from leading practitioners. The editor and his staff of two or three writers will also scan a few pertinent scholarly journals and competitors for new developments in the field.

As production costs are low and income from the 30 or 40 pages of ads in each issue is relatively high, a fairly steady profit is possible, even though no one is likely to make a killing. Since most of these publications are owned by closely held family corporations, no one can be too sure just what the profit figures are. Libraries do not usually qualify for controlled circulation periodicals, but exceptions can be made—especially on the basis that students at a university are being trained to enter the field the periodical serves.

Special Interest Magazines

One interesting phenomenon in the United States in the past two decades has been the growth of "special interest" consumer magazines. They are popular, generally beautifully illustrated, and aimed at a very specific audience: readers interested in a sport (*Tennis, Golf Digest* and *Bodybuilding*), hobby (*Modern Railroading, Car and Driver, Backpacker*), locality (*Southern Living, New York, Texas Monthly*) social group (*Parents, Retirement Living*), science (*Psychology Today, Astronomy, Weatherwise*) or art form (*Ballet News, Art in America*). These magazines have tended to be very successful and their formulas have influenced popular magazine publishing a great deal.

MUTUAL NEED OF LIBRARIES AND PUBLISHERS

These are only a few of the variety of serial publications that libraries need to have in their collections. The difference in the aims of the publishers and the libraries creates problems for both. While most publishers respect and use libraries, they do not devote much consideration to needs of libraries before making decisions concerning their publications.

Libraries serve a diverse set of users who tend *not* to be specialists in the academic field served by a journal. (Specialists probably subscribe already and do not read the library copy.) The library thus provides an audience for the scholarly journal that is not in the mind of the author or the editor of the journal.

The same is true of other serial publications—the general magazine, the controlled circulation magazine, the special interest magazine and countless others ranging from the shoppers' guides to intellectual journals. Because its published indexes make articles easy to find, the library helps students read articles written for housewives, blasé young professionals, poultry farmers. The library lets local history buffs read 30-year-old garage sale ads. It provides important political and literary analyses to a large non-elite audience.

The publisher sends his serial out to the reader he has in mind right now. The librarian makes it permanently available to readers 100 years from now whose interest neither one of them can imagine. The publisher creates communication between the great minds of national and international society. If anyone else is ever to understand this conversation, to learn from it in future years, to become the great mind of another generation, we will need the library's ability to provide permanence to that fleeting communication. The copy on library shelves is permanently available to read. The index to it is also available only in the library. The existence of a library copy somewhere makes possible a reference or citation to an article written and published sometime. All these are possibilities expected by publishers, assumed by authors and relied upon by readers, but provided only by libraries.

The point here is not that libraries are valuable to society or more valuable than publishers. Without publishers there is no library. They form a partnership. The point is that libraries transform the objectives and accomplishments of publishers into something else which is valuable to publishers, but may not be anticipated by them. Since the immediate objectives of librarians and publishers differ, they clash, and they trade resentment and suspicion of each other.

CONCLUSION

"Economics" is known as the "Dismal Science." The economics of journal publication are dismal indeed. Costs to publishers keep rising and income possibilities are almost exhausted. Libraries are publishers' best hope for retrieving the additional revenue required, but library budgets have been stretched as far as possible. Additional increases to library subscription budgets in the amounts required are extremely unlikely. Therefore, hopes of finding new mechanisms for getting income from libraries in another form, such as copyright fees, appear to be doomed to disappointment. On the average, subscriptions to each scholarly journal tend to dwindle. This too puts more pressure on publishers to increase subscription rates to recoup their costs. These rates can only hasten the time when more libraries and individuals will be forced to cancel. A self-feeding cyclical mechanism is taking over, and no satisfactory end is in sight.

The enormous overall costs of the journal system are difficult to defend when widely disseminated journal articles average so few readings. All authorities agree that we cannot go on this way much longer. Some new system or combination of systems will soon be taking the place of the printing of journals and their placement in libraries for readers to find when and if they ever need them.

At present, cost may be the greatest strain serials put on libraries, but prices are not the only criticisms librarians have of publishers. Serials tend to create chaos by their unstandard, unpredictable behavior in frequency of publication, delayed publication, title changes, size changes, merges, splits, absorptions, suspensions and cessations.

FOOTNOTES

1. Norman B. Brown and Jane Phillips, "Price Indexes for 1981, U.S. Periodicals and Serial Service," *Library Journal* 106 (July 1981): 1387-93.

2. University of Toronto annual report of the Chief Librarian 1975-76.

3. Association of Research Libraries, *ARL Statistics 1975-76 and 1979-80.* (It is likely that the discrepancy between the number of subscriptions cited in *ARL Statistics* and Mr. Blackburn's annual report is due to definitional problems.)

4. Association of Research Libraries, *ARL Statistics 1980-81.*

5. University of Toronto Libraries annual report 1979-80, p. 1.

6. R. DeGennaro, "Escalating Journal Prices: Time to Fight Back," *American Libraries* (February 1977): 72.

7. Ibid., pp. 69-74.

8. Ibid.

9. Ibid., pp. 69, 74.

10. American Chemical Society, *Proceedings* (1899): 15; (1901): 18; (1931): 21.

11. John K. Crum, "Sale of Reprints, Advertising, Single Issues, and Back Volumes," *Economics of Scientific Publications,* pp. 32-33.

12. American Chemical Society, "Annual Report 1981," *Chemical and Engineering News* 60 (April 12, 1982): 55.

13. Bernard M. Fry and Herbert S. White, *Economics and Interaction of the Publisher-Library Relationship in the Production and Use of Scholarly and Research Journals,* U.S. National Science Foundation Office of Science Information Service, 1975 (NTIS PB 249 108), pp. 251-292.

14. Marjorie Scal, "Page Charges; Who Should Pay for Primary Journal Publication?" *Economics of Scientific Publications,* p. 22.

15. *The Technical, Scientific and Medical Publishing Market, 1981-82* (White Plains, NY: Knowledge Industry Publications, Inc., 1982), p. 24.

16. P.M. Boffey, *Science* (1968): 884.

17. Scal, "Page Charges," pp. 22-25.

18. *Scholarly Communication: The Report of the National Enquiry* (Baltimore: Johns Hopkins University Press, 1979), p. 62.

19. Fritz Machlup, Kenneth W. Leeson and Associates, *Information Through the Printed Word,* vol. 2, *Journals* (New York: Praeger Publishers, 1978), Table 3.4.13, p. 137.

20. Crum, "Sale of Reprints," p. 32, and telephone interview with D.H. Michael Bowen, June 3, 1982.

21. Crum, "Sale of Reprints," p. 32.

22. Machlup, *Printed Word,* p. 137.

23. "Journal Costs Alarming Scholars," *Chronicle of Higher Education* 11 (November 17, 1975): 8.

24. Data based on information from *Information Please Almanac,* 1981, pp. 56, 63.

25. S. Chomet and E. Nejman, "Economics of the Physics Journal," *Journal of Research Communications Studies* 3 (1981): 194.

26. D.H. Michael Bowen, "The Economics of Scientific Journal Publishing," *Journal of Research Communication Studies,* 3 (1981): 172.

27. Bowen, telephone interview, June 3, 1982.

28. Herbert S. White, "Publishers, Libraries, and Costs of Journal Subscriptions in Times of Funding Retrenchment," *Library Quarterly* 46 (October 1976): 366. (Summary of the study carried out by the Indiana University Graduate Library School, funded by the National Science Foundation —often referred to as the Fry-White study.)

29. Fry and White, *Economics and Interaction,* pp. 172-181.

30. *Ulrich's International Periodicals Directory,* 20th ed. (New York: R.R. Bowker Co., 1981).

31. King Research, Inc. *Statistical Indicators of Scientific and Technical Communication (1960-1980),* (Rockville, MD: King Research, 1976) 2: 125.

32. *Scholarly Communication,* p. 41.

33. White, "Publishers, Libraries and Costs," p. 361.

34. *Scholarly Communication,* p. 42.

35. Fry and White, *Economics and Interaction,* pp. 173-176.

36. *Scholarly Communication,* pp. 2, 4.

37. Harold Wooster, "Books and Libraries in the Scientific Age," *Library Journal* 92 (July 1967): 2511-2515.

38. William J. Broad, "The Publishing Game: Getting More for Less," *Science* 211 (March 13, 1981): 1137-1139.

39. *Scholarly Communication,* pp. 43, 44.

40. Nancy K. Roderer, *Statistical Indicators of Scientific and Technical Communication Worldwide* (NTIS PB 283 439) (King Research, Inc., 1977), pp. 88-90.

41. David W. King, *The Journal in Scientific Communication: The Roles of Authors, Publishers, Librarians and Readers in a Vital System* (NTIS PB 296263) (King Research, Inc., 1979), pp. 258, 297.

42. F.W. Lancaster, *Toward Paperless Information Systems* (New York: Academic Press, 1978), p. 72.

43. Jack Meadows et al., "What is the Future for New Research Journals in the 1980's? A Discussion," *Journal of Research Communication Studies* 2 (November 1980): 141. (The ideas referred to here were expressed by Robert Campbell of Blackwell Scientific.)

44. S.C. Bradford, *Documentation* (London: Crosby Lockwood, 1948).

45. Allen Kent et al., *Use of Library Materials, The University of Pittsburgh Study* (New York: Marcel Dekker, Inc., 1979), pp. 68, 72.

46. See *Folio: The Magazine for Magazine Management,* May/June 1974 for several articles on starting a magazine.

7

Serials Management: Issues and Recommendations

by David C. Taylor

The serials explosion has given rise to a number of issues, some philosophical, others practical, which publishers and libraries must resolve. This chapter will discuss the major issues and offer some recommendations that might lead to an improvement in the current system. Such improvement is vital, because the system in operation today is failing readers, authors, editors, publishers and libraries.

The serial differs from the book by creating a definable community which receives and reads and to some extent writes for it. One or two issues create the expectation for a third and a fourth. Because of that community, authors have a ready-made audience for their writings. But the proliferation of knowledge and of scholarly writing has apparently reached the point of information overload. Readers can't keep up with all the articles written on subjects of interest to them. These articles are scattered throughout hundreds of journals. The reader can't find out about them or retrieve copies of them, let alone read and digest them. Meanwhile the journals that are most central to the research interests of the individual scholar only publish a small number of articles per year of great interest to him. The rest of the articles may be scanned quickly or ignored. The journal system is failing readers.

Since readers are not able to find all the relevant articles, those articles are not being read by the audience that could use them. This means that the people whom the author is writing for are not receiving the message. The journal system is failing authors.

The literature is so scattered that editors cannot possibly keep up with all of it either. How then can they know whether an article being considered has been published already in another form by another journal, either by the same or another author? Without effective control of the quality of the scholarly writing being published, the value of scholarly publications is reduced. More citations need to be checked by readers but fewer original papers of value are discovered. The journal system is failing editors.

Costs of publications are rising at a faster rate than most publishers can absorb or recover them. Many honest, important journals of consequence with smallish subscription

---

Reprinted from *Managing the Serials Explosion: The Issues for Publishers and Librarians* (White Plains, NY: Knowledge Industry Publications, Inc., 1982).

lists are faced with debt or bankruptcy. Other publishers succeed because they give up scholarship in favor of more saleable content. At the same time, all publishers are losing control of what they have published because photocopiers are cheap and ubiquitous. The journal system is failing publishers.

The publishers who are successfully riding out the storm of inflation rely heavily on high institutional subscription rates charged to libraries. Libraries are being squeezed at a time when budgets have lost elasticity. Private colleges are hurt by the lowered ability of benefactors to give them funds. Public colleges are hurt by taxpayer revolts and lowered revenues in economically troubled times. Libraries are forced to cut subscriptions, stop purchasing books or both. At the same time libraries have difficulty serving readers who need a wider and wider range of journals. They are more dependent on interlibrary loans, but the administrative burden of interlibrary loans is itself becoming intolerable. The journal system is failing libraries.

Indexers, too, have difficulties with the wide scattering of publication, but proliferation and scattering make indexes indispensable to the scholarly community. Indexers and publishers of secondary publications have solved many of their problems with the computer. First used to drive a typesetting photocompositor by an indexer (*Index Medicus*), the computer has almost completely taken over book and journal typesetting. The information produced for print was simultaneously put in machine-readable form and in this form was easily used by indexers to make cumulations and create different points of access to the file of information. The computer typesetter led to the computerized information data base as primary and secondary publishers found new ways to market the machine-readable information they created. The journal system has served indexers very well, and indexers are serving the journal system well through the use of the computer.

This is now our situation: a system in disarray but with a new technology promising miraculous solutions in the near future. However, this marvelous technology will not solve every problem instantly. Let us consider some of the issues and suggest a few solutions.

THE KNOWLEDGE EXPLOSION

Is knowledge really expanding or is the explosion of publication merely the result of self-serving careerism of university faculty? From the historical perspective the growth of knowledge has been steady, and what we are experiencing is consistent with the number of scholars and scientists who are engaged in research. Some writing is derivative and weak; some writing is fraudulent or plagiarized; and some is creative and descriptive about subjects so specialized that no one else in the world is interested. However, there is no reason to believe it has ever been different. Poor writing and research proliferate, but they do not impede the progress of knowledge.

Nearly every scholarly study proposes subjects for further study. Each advance uncovers several areas that we don't know enough about. What we learn is like a sphere. As it expands, the surface worked by scholars grows. Think of it as a mine. The face of the exposed bedrock of the unknown grows as we mine it. Some surfaces are more resistant than others. Some brilliant researchers work far ahead of others creating new branches into the unknown, while some more plodding, more ordinary workers clean up the less interesting problems left behind.

If the expansion of knowledge is real, is it responsible for us to make it more difficult to publish? Should we allow the less viable journals to die as DeGennaro proposes? Yes, the free marketplace for publication places some check on the proliferation of undeserving or second-rate research. If any research could be published freely, we would have a more difficult time yet in culling the good from the bad.

The computer, the microform, the abstract journal and perhaps other alternative forms of publication are likely to create a solution of sorts for us. In the foreseeable future we are likely to have a mix of publications, much as we have now. Fewer journals will survive in paper, but the strongest will. Those which can attract the income to pay for print will continue to publish that way because of the subscription advantages to publishers and because of reader preference for paper. Those journals with large numbers of personal subscribers will continue to sell to libraries; those with sales to libraries only will not find enough income to continue. Various forms of publication, such as abstract journals with on-demand publication support, microform journals, video disc journals and electronic journals will emerge. Some will be refereed and will have large and small audiences with personal and institutional subscriptions. Some will be collections of reports, speeches and studies, like the ERIC reports and NTIS.

Authors will be presented with a three-tiered system of publication in such a system. The greatest prestige will come from publication in the printed journals. Next best will be the refereed publications with less expensive publication mode and smaller readership. Least prestigious, but still better than not publishing, will be the catch-all collections. Some gems will be found in these, but much will have little interest to any but the most thorough of future researchers. Fortunately, the capacity of the computer to index all this material will mean none of it will be lost to future readers.

COSTS

The second major issue is the cost of serials. We know that publishers' costs are rising. But is it legitimate for publishers to charge libraries two, five or ten times as much as individual subscribers are charged? Could a publisher justify 20, 50 or 100 times the individual rate for a subscription to a consortium? Should librarians acquiesce in this money-making strategy from any publisher or should distinctions be made between profit and not-for-profit publishers?

A publisher's attitude toward libraries probably depends upon the size of the publisher's subscription list and his perception of the future potential of his list. The publisher with millions of subscribers is indifferent to libraries, treating them like any other subscribers and charging them no more for their subscriptions, even though 75% of the fulfillment problems come from libraries.

The publisher of a fairly new periodical with a growing list of thousands of subscribers is likely to court the business of libraries. A library subscriber is a recommendation—like a positive review. Library readers will discover the magazine and many of them will want their own copies. These publishers will also be inclined to charge libraries no more than individual subscribers and are more likely to offer good discounts (20%) to subscription agents.

A publisher of a scholarly journal who is dependent on libraries for a substantial portion of his income will tend to charge much more for institutional than for individual subscriptions.

Serials librarians may be bewildered by these variations. Librarians may as well adjust to higher subscription prices and to the institutional rate. There appears to be no legal limit to the price a publisher can charge libraries, and perhaps none should be sought. The marketplace is probably the best regulator.

One proposal raised by publishers is to levy "usage charges" on libraries. Every time a reader checked out a book or asked for a periodical, the library would be bound to pay a reading fee to the publisher. Such a scheme would be likely to help a few publishers of the most popular materials at the expense of the rest. The libraries would spend much more on record keeping and would be less able to purchase books and serials.

Any scheme to increase publishers' income from libraries is bound to fail, say most librarians, because libraries have only a limited amount of money available to spend. The more costs of publications rise the fewer of them libraries will be able to buy. This brings on the familiar tailspin effect of fewer subscriptions, higher prices, fewer subscriptions, etc.

Some individual publishers may do well in this situation. But it is clear that publishers as a whole must cut costs, find new sources of income, or go out of business. New sources of income seem unlikely now. Many serial publishers, it seems, must cease publication in the next decade, reversing a trend that has been continuing since 1655. More and more of those who survive will do so because they are able to utilize the new electronic technology to save costs.

PHOTOCOPYING AND COPYRIGHT

The copyright law of 1976 has been a disappointment to publishers. It seems likely that any revisions to it will be minor ones, however. For instance, libraries may be given more detailed guidance on their obligations under the copyright law for putting copied materials on reserve for assigned reading. Even without further legislation, it appears likely that any viable national library consortium will negotiate with publishers a fee payment for photocopies or uses. Whatever changes are made will probably not significantly increase publishers' income. That source of income that seemed so promising to publishers four years ago now must be written off.

One surprising development with the copyright law was the ruling by the three-judge panel of the United States Court of Appeals for the Ninth Circuit in San Francisco on

October 19, 1981. It ruled that the use of video tape recorders violated the copyright law because owners of recorders are gaining "economic control" over the copyrighted works that were broadcast. The suit was brought by two Hollywood movie studios, Walt Disney Productions and Universal City Studios. In 1979 Federal Judge Warren J. Ferguson ruled against the plaintiffs, but the Court of Appeals ruling sent the case back to him and ordered him to fashion some kind of relief for the damage done to the plaintiffs by video recorders. The Sony Corporation, manufacturer of the Betamax, will probably appeal to the Supreme Court.[1]

If this decision is not reversed, it will certainly hurt the sale of video recorders for the home market. Some kind of royalty charge could be included in the purchase price of recorders which would be paid to producers of broadcast shows, although it is hard to imagine how the royalties would be divided among all eligible producers and produce any income at all. The total pool would be required just to administer the program—a situation closely parallel to that of the Copyright Clearance Center. The producers are trying to maintain the market for video cassettes for themselves, and don't expect to receive income from the sale of video recorders. They would prefer that no home video recorders exist. On the other hand, they would like to see millions of video players in homes as a market for their cassettes.

It is chancy to predict the possible effects of this development on serials, but they could be far-ranging. For instance, if the court decision prevails, it could give video disc players a boost, since the major advantage of the tape recorder is that broadcast material can be recorded, while video disc players cannot record. If the courts prohibit free videotaping, the cheaper price and better quality of video discs may give them the advantage. A better market for video discs could make them a better future medium for serial-type publications. On the other hand, if the Appeals Court decision stands, it may take away some of the possible configurations for transmitting and using entertainment in the future, and with it could be swept away the means for publishing scholarly information in some electronic formats.*

ACCESS TO INFORMATION

The computer is creating an access problem for librarians as it creates new and better access to published literature. As its role enlarges, those seeking information become more dependent on the computer to provide it. Since the computer makes the user totally dependent on technology, it creates a means of controlling who has access to the information. The computer has also introduced a new fee-for-service precedent into American libraries that not only limits free access for some specialized services, but could spill over to become the standard relationship between library and user. To some people this is one of the most disturbing of recent developments. Others urge that it is merely a necessary adaptation of the old tax-based library book service to the needs of a modern information-based society.

Libraries have purchased millions of copies of books and serials and made them available to the citizens and guests of America. Each book and serial is a capital investment already paid for by the library for which no reimbursement is necessary. Each book has relatively low value as a physical object and can be turned over to the complete control of

---

*Editor's Note: In January 1984 the Supreme Court overturned the Appeals Court decision against Sony Corp. and ruled that consumers do not violate federal copyright law when they use video recorders to tape television programs for their own use.

the user with relatively limited safeguards. Anyone with the ability to read can make full use of these printed materials with limited library staff mediation. Because many different readers need many different books, and the flow of materials from user to library to user is promoted by loan periods, libraries are able to serve thousands of readers at the same time.

Computers change all that. If the same information is in a computer instead of in printed books and serials, the library must buy equipment to make that information available. This equipment must be protected from misuse. The use of the computer equipment requires staff assistance (ironically, using the computer in public service in the library is much more labor intensive than the book). The library can help only those people who have a computer to use, and the institution may not be able to afford enough to avoid queues and waiting lists. Users will have to learn the skill of manipulating a computer or depend on an expert to do it for them. The computer will create a new form of illiteracy and dependency. The computer could also be used to invade privacy or to control information available to certain users. This misuse of the computer would be particularly sinister because it could be done from remote locations and without the knowledge of its victims.

If that sounds alarmist and fantastic, another mechanism introduced by computers is all too real. Computer searches of online data bases cost money. In most libraries, all or part of the fee charged by the bibliographic search service is passed on to the user. This is no procedural aberration or temporary policy, and it threatens to change radically the nature of library service.

The publisher of printed serials is paid largely in advance by subscription. The book publisher is paid as stocks of the book sell—whether anyone reads the book or not. The book and serial publishers are paid when someone acquires the paper copy, not when someone uses it.

The computer works naturally on a different basis. The information in the memory of the computer is not usable until retrieved. The companies controlling the computer information bank receive their money when someone interacts with the computer and retrieves some of the information. With the computer as medium, publishers will expect to be paid for each *reading* of their copyrighted material, not for original purchase. When libraries make information from computer data banks available to readers, publishers think of libraries as retailers of the information and expect payment.

This has become, in the past few years, the cause of considerable controversy among librarians. Many, if not most, libraries do pass on the hookup and printout charges for online computer searches, but not staff time. (Most libraries also pass on interlibrary loan charges initiated by lending libraries.) A vociferous group of librarians has discovered that the fees collected by libraries, no matter how reasonable, or by whom originated, create a new class system of information users and change entirely the relationship of library to user.

Classes of Information Users

Already one can say that three "classes" of information users exist. The "upper" class are those fortunates whose employers provide nearly unlimited access to information through expensive, elaborate, up-to-date computers, word processors and telecommunications. Those people without such an employer but who can themselves afford to pay for home computers and entertainment centers constitute a "lower upper" class. They can or soon will be able to obtain online services and packages. They can buy video tapes, video discs and perhaps even satellite receiving antennas. These are the equivalent of the "idle rich." While they can afford expensive information, they may spend their money on expensive equipment in order to play computer games, or be surfeited with more broadcast options than their friends. The "upper upper" class uses information for its cash value. Such people use the services of professional programmers and computer operators, as well as the latest, most powerful equipment.

At the other end of the scale in our information-rich society is the "lower" class, defined not by automobile, or clothing or access to a bathtub, but by inability to afford an information center. Prognosticators say that in 10 years every home will have its own home computer, just as "nearly everyone" now owns a pocket electronic calculator. But surely some in our society will buy food rather than a computer if they cannot afford both. Some will decline to purchase a computer unless it comes free with a TV set. In one view, these lower class untouchables could also be defined by their use of information. As long as they have use only for entertainment, they will remain lower class.

The middle class, to complete the simile, is the herd of people in between: they want information, but can afford only a limited information center at home. Perhaps they will play recordings on cassette or video disc, but they cannot afford online remote hookups. These are the people who will turn to the library to provide information. They will be able to pay for library services.

The lower class will be shut out by their inability to pay. They are not so destitute now, when much of the information they need is available in the library in printed form at no cost. As printed publications die out and are replaced by electronic ones, the lower class will be impoverished to a greater extent.

This description of social classes defined by their access to electronic information appears to be farfetched. But isn't the library now making a distinction between persons based on their ability to pay? Don't those who cannot pay the fee constitute a "lower" class without the access to information that their "betters" can enjoy?

In the university we already have the class system. Most faculty in the sciences are now upper class, and others are middle class. Students tend to be middle or lower class. If the pay-for-use configuration becomes the rule, colleges and universities might be judged by the percentage of faculty and students who are upper versus middle class information users. (It would, of course, be scandalous to have any lower class users.)

Libraries as Fee Collectors

Libraries may be asked to expand their role as fee collectors. William Koch of the American Institute of Physics wants libraries to be partners in publishing.[2] "Republishers," he calls them. He reviews the tension that exists now between publisher and librarian and locates the problem. It is the librarians' insistence on interpreting the "fair-use" language in the 1976 copyright law as a general principle, not as a rare exception. The solution he finds is for publishers to stop being suspicious and to accept librarians as the necessary distributors of their publications, who broaden their readership and have closer relationships with the readers than the publishers do. The publishers should accept libraries as "republishers" who will furnish readers with copies of their journals for a price and who will turn back a portion of the fee to the copyright owners.

Librarians will see no reason to change their policies toward photocopying printed journals on the basis of Koch's article. Read it again in the light of the electronic journal, and it begins to make a different kind of sense. Libraries collect fees and pay computer data base owners now, don't they? If they arranged for document retrieval, either for a photocopy via interlibrary loan or a facsimile reprint via satellite, they would collect a fee, wouldn't they?

In the latter part of the 20th century, information is increasingly becoming a commodity to be developed, controlled, protected, bought and sold, like wheat, tin and bauxite. The scholarly attitude toward information is that it is beneficial to all mankind and should be freely accessible to all. The new value system, some say, reflects the values of corporations —and in our time more corporations are producing information, not manufactured goods, and use Ph.D.s, not hard hats, as a labor force.

On the other hand, it is precisely *because* information is increasingly important in our society that the fundamental idea of information as property is beneficial to authors and researchers. Their interests are protected, not denied, by the operations of the marketplace. The corporations that employ researchers, and the data bank producers and publishers who disseminate their work, are making money as a result—but how else would the author/scholar be recompensed for his labors? Would we prefer to see a "super foundation," perhaps government-sponsored, supporting our authors and scholars? Would this contribute to freedom of information generation and access? Or would it give rise to the greater threat of information censorship and control?

Some librarians believe that publishers of scholarly journals should think like scholars, not businessmen. But publishers *are* businessmen—and, as we have seen, must be in order to survive.

This realization, however, does not make the library's fee-versus-free services problem any easier to solve. Librarians may believe in free access to printed information, but there is no easy way to avoid fees for computer searches. Suppose that a university analyzes the use of a bibliographic search service and the growth of that service in its library. Let us say that more than 1300 searches were performed in 1980 at an average cost of $10, while 1000 searches were performed in 1979. Let's suppose the library administration decides to put $17,000 in the budget to fund searches without charge to users. The $17,000 allows for growth of the service, inflation and a little over for the unexpected. We can guess that the funds would be expended before midyear. Without the fees to create restraint, users would conduct more and longer searches. It would be like furnishing free Xerox copies. No amount of machines would prove adequate to supply the demand.

The library could adopt rules about the number of searches any user could request per year or the maximum length of printouts, or could pay for the first $10 per search but collect any charges incurred over that. All these rules would help spread the money, but all would impose record-keeping problems and a bureaucratic atmosphere. Some students would contrive to get around the rules. We might also suppose that in 1982, 2000 freshmen would turn up requesting searches after they heard about the service. Would the library have to adopt rules defining what class of student is eligible for the free computer searches? The library could easily find itself in an administrative morass in its attempt to maintain the democratic ideal of free access to all.

Vendors of information have a virtual monopoly, since almost all of it is unique, or at least packaged uniquely. Whereas one entertainment can replace another with little difficulty (does anyone care that "Count Your Dollars" is cancelled and replaced by "Name That Price"?), reports of scholarly research are or should be all unique, if not invaluable. Payment for access is inherently distasteful if some students or scholars are thereby denied access to relevant information, but is there any other way to set up a computer-based information service?

An Electronic Journal by Subscription?

I propose that libraries and publishers should examine this problem and work toward an acceptable alternative to pay-for-each-access. For instance, the publisher could establish an annual fee for an electronic journal. This fee would give unlimited access (including reproduction rights) to the library and its patrons for a year and would be paid in advance. The library could easily cancel at the end of the year and the publisher could set whatever price seemed reasonable for the following year. During a subscription year the library would have access to the current year only, or for a higher fee, could have access to past years as well. If a library cancelled its subscription, it would lose access to the years it had already subscribed to. (Alternatively, the library could purchase permanent access to volumes and still have that access after cancelling its current subscription. It could pull the "volumes" purchased from the publisher's data base and enter it into the library's local online system.)

If the subscription price could be agreed on, this arrangement would have advantages for both. Publishers would have the old advantage of publishing serials—money in advance. They would also have some guarantee that the product would bring in a certain income, rather than worrying about the saleability of each article. Libraries would have the benefit of being able to offer access to anyone and would be in the position of encouraging use rather than discouraging it. Each use would make the subscription a better bargain for the library.

This arrangement would work to the advantage of readers, also, since no artificial barriers would be raised between them and the information they need. Since it would tend to promote a wider audience, authors would benefit also. This arrangement would also work for authors by giving publishers no incentive to seek only popular or "best selling" articles as the other system would tend to do.

STANDARDIZATION

One of the most exasperating problems for librarians is the needless extra work caused by serials with unusual numbering systems, hidden bibliographic information, unannounced title changes, and other vagaries. What may seem a creative solution to a publisher is a headache to librarians and indexers who must deal with thousands of publications and create bibliographic control for them. As long as the serial is viewed by its publisher as a private commodity for sale to the public, the problems librarians have with it are irrelevant. But when the journal is a unit in a national and international system of information exchange, the situation changes. The publisher has an obligation to produce the journal in a format that fits smoothly into that system.

The International Serials Data System has been an encouraging success. International Standard Serial Numbers (ISSN) have been assigned to thousands of serials all over the world, with a high percentage of publishers in England, Scandinavia, other European countries, Canada and the United States participating. The U.S. Postal Service requires that periodicals follow certain rules in order to qualify for second class mailing privileges. These rules have been very helpful to librarians. Because of them we know approximately on what page the bibliographic data will appear. Thus, a well-trained clerk who finds no volume and issue numbers on the cover can usually find them on page 3, 4 or 5 (or 6, 7 or 8) along with the publisher's address, the frequency of publication and the subscription rate.

It would come as a surprise to many publishers (and librarians) that sets of standards exist governing the publication of periodicals. Among existing standards are the "International Standard Recommendation for the Layout of Periodicals," ISO/R8-1954, the "British Standard Specification for the Presentation of Serial Publications, including Periodicals," BS 2509-1970, and the "American National Standard for Periodicals: Format and Arrangement," ANS1 Z39.1-1977.

The last publication is a standard that was first written in 1939 and has been revised several times since then, most recently in 1977. It says about itself: "An American National Standard implies a consensus of those substantially concerned with its scope and provisions. An American National Standard is intended as a guide to aid the manufacturer, the consumer, and the general public."[3]

The recommendations of the standard cover a surprising number of items and possibilities. They can be listed in the following areas:

1. *Title.* Five recommendations (keep it short, unique, "define as precisely as possible the special field of knowledge dealt with," etc.)

2. *Cover and spine.* 12 recommendations ("front cover . . . should contain . . . title, . . . subtitle, if any, . . . number of the volume and number of the issue . . . date of the issue . . . International Standard Serial Number . . . location of the table of contents," etc.)

3. *Table of Contents.* 12 recommendations ("Each issue should contain a table of

contents with . . . bibliographic information . . . information on individual articles," etc.)

4. *Masthead.* 11 recommendations ("Containing . . . title and subtitle, with ISSN . . . publisher with full address . . . editor or editorial staff," etc.)

5. *Pages.* 11 recommendations ("Each double-page spread . . . should carry the bibliographic data necessary for the rapid identification of the periodical issue, . . . including title . . . volume and issue numbers . . . page number," etc.)

6. *Articles appearing in installments.* Seven recommendations (For instance, "all installments of an article should be within a single volume, preferably in consecutive issues.")

7. *Instructions to authors.* Two recommendations ("The location of instructions to authors should be the same from issue to issue," etc.)

8. *Supplements.* Four recommendations ("A supplement should conform in trim size and page characteristics to the parent periodical," etc.)

9. *Volumes.* Eight recommendations ("A volume when completed should include: . . . a title page . . . tables of contents . . . text . . . a volume index," etc.)

10. *Changes or irregularities.* 10 recommendations ("If the size of a periodical must be altered. . . . If the title of a periodical must be changed. . . . If two or more periodicals are amalgamated . . .," etc.)

11. *Translation Periodicals.* One recommendation ("should carry, in addition to the translation title, the title in the original language . . .")[4]

The casual observer is surprised by the variations and possibilities covered. Even the experienced serials librarian is hard put to find problems not covered by the standard. All the problems librarians experience, or almost all of them, seem to be covered.

The ANSI standard on periodicals is gratifying but also frustrating to librarians. The problems would disappear if publishers would only follow the standard—but they don't. The noncompliance of publishers appears to be the standard's greatest weakness. What good does it do if the standard is improved every five years or so but publishers either don't know about it or ignore it?

As a matter of fact, the standard is written with the knowledge that it may not be followed in detail by most publishers. "The existence of an American National Standard does not in any respect preclude anyone, whether he has approved the standard or not, from manufacturing, marketing, purchasing, or using products, processes, or procedures not conforming to the standard."[5] The committee realized in writing the standard that different publishers have quite different needs. ". . . the problems of consumer and trade publications often differ considerably from those of scholarly publications. Rather than present two separate standards, however, the subcommittee agreed that a single document giving detailed and in some cases seemingly repetitive statements would be most useful."

I have never seen a periodical that adhered to the standard in every particular. Most scholarly journals follow almost every recommendation, but will reject (or neglect) one. Few list the page of the table of contents on the front cover. Those that do will leave the ISSN number off of the table of contents page or the masthead or will leave out some bibliographic detail from the running title. None of these cause serious problems to the librarian, the indexer or the reader but it is interesting and significant that few if any publications follow the standard exactly.

Perhaps the next revision (now under way) should make clearer what recommendations apply specifically to scholarly publications, what recommendations apply to consumer and trade publications, and what recommendations apply to all. At least publishers would know better what was expected of them and not reject the whole standard as unrealistic and unworkable.

The standard has foreseen so many possibilities and makes so many good recommendations that it is hard to find suggestions for additions to it. Two recommendations would in my opinion strengthen the code. Scholarly journals should be printed on acid-free paper. It would be advantageous for other serials as well, but the scholarly journal is intended to be available indefinitely, and surely the additional cost of acid-free paper would be a small one among other costs, and one that libraries would gladly pay for.

This is also the time to push for the adoption of a machine-readable label on the front or back cover of all periodicals. Probably this would take the form of a bar code which would include title and/or ISSN, volume and issue number, and date of the publication. Identification of the publication is now the last labor-intensive problem in serial receiving work in libraries. This feature would eliminate almost all the time-consuming problem-solving and would improve the reliability of records and probably reduce claims and other problem correspondence with publishers. It would allow libraries to use automated serials receiving systems much more efficiently and reliably. The actual work of checking in daily receipts could be cut by 75% or more. A library receiving 1000 periodicals a day, could, if all had bar codes, take account of them all in two and a half hours instead of spending 16 hours keying them into an automated system or 18 hours entering them into a manual file.

If a standard were easy to interpret and relatively painless to follow, it could also be easier to promote. The American National Standards Institute does not advertise its standards individually or promote their adoption and use. It compiles them. Its job is to get leading representatives of the industry together to agree on standards of mutual benefit. Librarians and indexers could promote this standard, however, and should. Through associations, librarians could make a much stronger effort to get the standard into the hands of publishers, many of whom have never seen it or heard of it. If 30% or 40% of the periodicals that now follow the standard loosely or not at all would adhere to it as a guideline and general rule, much expensive staff time would be saved in libraries. The investment of effort would benefit the whole information system in many long-lasting and important ways.

Ironically, it may be too late to have an important effect on the information system if the printed journal declines soon, as some predict. Now is a time when standards need to be developed for microfilm, abstract and electronic journals. Standard vocabulary needs to be adopted, and industry-wide agreement is needed on production quality, sizes, format, terms of access and reproduction privileges. Standardization for electronic journals brings up another important consideration for the new media: bibliographic control.

BIBLIOGRAPHIC CONTROL

The computer giveth and the computer taketh away. New electronic technology is making it possible to index, catalog and retrieve everything—everything that is printed, that is. Electronic technology is giving birth to new forms of publication, in particular the electronic journal, but creating new problems for bibliographic control.

One of the so-called advantages of the electronic journal is that an author can revise a paper after it has been "published." Let's say that A. Buchholz writes a paper on causes of inflation in 1982 and it is published in the *Online Journal of Economics.* In 1983 critic Marbury points out a weakness in Buchholz's paper. Buchholz defends his paper but in late 1983 asks his editor for permission to insert a paragraph elucidating a point only touched on earlier, and eliminating another paragraph that he has come to wish he hadn't written. The revision makes the paper much stronger. Editor Winthrop believes the changes are minor and agrees to them. The revised version defuses Marbury's points. What is reader MacArthur to make of the exchange between Buchholz and Marbury when he reads it in 1985 and looks up Buchholz's "original" paper as it exists in the *Online Journal of Economics*?

Another proposal for the computer is to "unbundle" articles. No longer do papers need to appear with volume and issue numbers and dates with other papers. They can be put into the data base at any time and retrieved at any later time. Of course, parts of papers could be retrieved, just as easily—perhaps a graph or a fact or a finding. But this flexibility exposes the information system to great risks. No fact, finding or graph stands alone. There is research and experimentation behind them, establishing them. Taken out of the context of that background the "facts" are meaningless.

Scientific truth is like a master painting. We need to know its provenance. Separated from its origins and history, it is doubtful. In the context of its proof, it remains true until another researcher can disprove it. The method used by a scholar is as important as his conclusion. Until another researcher can achieve the same results with the same methods, the conclusions cannot be accepted. This is obviously a key point in the scientific community, and the electronic journal must not undercut it.

Since the advent of printing, bibliographic control has been possible because all the copies printed in an edition from a printing press are alike. Describe one and you describe all. The electronic journal is different. It exists not on paper but in a machine—a highly flexible machine that allows its data to be manipulated, changed, added to and deleted. How can we establish bibliographic control over such a medium?

I make the following proposals:

1. Attach date of entry and accession number to each paper in the data base.

2. Create an international standard electronic serial number (ISESN) which would uniquely identify each electronic publication and which would be administered by the International Serials Data System or another international system like it.

3. All retrievals of any part of the data base would bear a bibliographic strip containing author, title, name of publication, ISESN, year and number of paper.

4. Any paper could be revised at any time, but the whole revised article or the changes or additions would be entered as a new paper into the data base without altering the original. The new paper would receive its own unique number, but would be connected by cross reference to the number of the original paper, and vice versa. Those retrieving the paper would get the one requested but would also get a citation to the other which would also be available for retrieval separately.

5. The computer is so flexible that an original paper could be altered despite the above rules. The computer is also subject to failures that can damage or lose part of the data in its memory. To guard against both of these possibilities, each electronic journal would have at least two official depositories for paper copies of each item in the data base. One would be its national library, the Library of Congress, British Library, Biliothèque Nationale or whatever. The other would be a research library that would agree to preserve the paper copies and make them available for study by qualified scholars. The data base would name its depositories as part of its official identification—when users sign on—the counterpart of a printed masthead.

Without these five rules or something similar to them, the electronic journal will not be the true counterpart of the printed journal. If it produces information only, and not the means of verifying the origin of the information, it will not serve as the primary communication medium among scholars.

GOVERNMENT REGULATION

The scholarly enterprise depends upon free investigation of truth and free exchange of information. All governments have a tendency to meddle in these processes, but in the western democracies at least, the freedom of the publishing process is a well-established and hard won principle. By moving into electronic media, publishing enters an area that has a slightly different tradition. The government has a history of regulating electronic communications. Most of this regulation involves the medium, but the monitoring of the content of electronic communication is more pronounced than the monitoring of printed material. The regulation of the medium creates problems. The Communications Act of 1934 created a federal policy that awards monopolies in telecommunications, restricting the entry of new companies that could reduce consumer costs.[6]

What is needed in the U.S. now is a national cooperative effort of publishers, information industry, libraries and government to extend First Amendment protection to electronic media, work out copyright problems, ensure public access to government information, and set up guidelines for use of electromagnetic communication that would require the least possible government involvement. Such a national effort is being studied by the Association of American Publishers.[7] Librarians should unite with them in creating the national consensus and policy that will open up electronic communication to its full potential as a cost saving, reliable, permanent form of information exchange as useful for scholarship as for commerce and entertainment.

FOOTNOTES

1. *The New York Times,* Oct. 20, 1981, pp. 1, 31.

2. H. William Koch, "The Effect of the U.S. Copyright Legislation on Authors, Editors, Publishers, and Librarians," *Journal of Research Communication Studies* 3, no. 1-2 (September 1981): 95.

3. *American National Standard for Periodicals: Format and Arrangement,* ANSI-Z39.1-1977 (New York: American National Standards Institute, 1978), p. [2].

4. Ibid., pp. 12-16.

5. Ibid., p. 2.

6. Cf. Lionel Van Deerlin, "Information Overload; What the Congress and Information Professionals Can Do About It," *Special Libraries* 72 (January 1981): 107.

7. "AAP Ponders Creation of Federal Information Plan," *Publishers Weekly* (June 26, 1981): 21.

8

Developing Preservation Programs in Libraries

by Carolyn Clark Morrow

A preservation program should be based on the needs of a specific library. Although preservation has many principles that apply to libraries in general, the emphasis and direction of a program will be determined by a particular library collection, building, organization and history.

THE LIBRARY SETTING

Collection

The collection itself and the use to which it is put will in part dictate preservation goals. Is the collection large or small? Does it contain a larger portion of retrospective or current materials? Is the collection weeded or does the library intend to keep materials indefinitely? Do materials circulate out of the building? Is the collection heavily or infrequently used? Does it serve recreational, informational, instructional or research needs? Who uses the library? In a large library with diverse collections, all of these possibilities can be expected.

The physical condition of the library collections must be documented so that preservation goals and priorities can be discussed. A systematic perusal of the collection will uncover particular problem areas and is a necessary step in planning future conservation activities. The services of an expert consultant in conservation can be useful in conjunction with the investigative efforts of the library staff. A consultant's recommendations and observations will be an invaluable addition to planning, and his or her written report can be used to substantiate requests for improved conditions, additional staff or funds for the preservation program. The consultant may give a lecture or presentation to the library staff to generate enthusiasm and ideas for the incipient program.

Reprinted from *The Preservation Challenge: A Guide to Conserving Library Materials* (White Plains, NY: Knowledge Industry Publications, Inc., 1983).

Building

The library building itself and its internal environment have a tremendous impact on the physical well-being of a collection and thus on the direction of preservation planning. A large research collection housed in an old building and located in an urban area will have preservation problems unheard of at a relatively new, air-conditioned state university library. A building's age, floor plans, shelving and storage, and systems such as heating and cooling, ventilation, and air-filtration will all have had effects on material's preservation. Therefore, before specific planning for preservation can take place, preservation needs must be determined through a thorough examination of the building, environmental conditions and overall physical condition of the collection.[1]

Organization

The organization of a library and its institutional affiliation, if any, will determine what preservation and conservation model is best suited to meeting the needs of a collection. To whom does the head librarian or library director report? How are budget monies allocated? What are the lines of authority and responsibility within the library? Is the collection centralized or are there branch or department libraries? Out of which department are binding and repair activities currently managed? Is there a stack maintenance unit?

History

Any previous and current arrangements for physical treatment and maintenance will affect the subsequent organization and emphasis of an expanded preservation program. What has been the legacy of binding and physical treatment? Has the library had a history of dubious mending practices or benign neglect? Was there always a vigorous library binding program? Did the library purchase microfilm copies of serials rather than bind? Were paperbacks prebound? What has been the policy concerning seriously deteriorated items? Were rare and unique items in need of conservation treatment sent to a qualified outside conservator?

POLICY, STAFF AND ORGANIZATION

Once the needs of a collection have been determined and inadequacies in the building and its environment documented, a library is ready to begin establishing the framework for a preservation program. The plan for the program should take into account the present situation and should set realistic goals for improvement.

A policy statement on preservation can be instrumental in defining preservation principles, listing preservation and conservation activities and designating responsibilities.[2] In order for the policy to be effective, the library's governing group, department heads and staff should all be involved in the policy-making process. To be truly effective, the preservation effort must involve the whole library staff. When people are involved in making policy and understand why a particular policy is important, they will be more likely to be supportive.

A designation of priorities is an important part of the policy statement. Priorities are established based on a particular library, its purpose and the condition of its building and collections. They are needed because the task of preserving library resources is mammoth and never ending. Meaningful priorities for a preservation program can be established by balancing those activities designed to have the most significant and immediate impact on the condition of the collections with those designed to provide the library with a logical, unified and well-organized long-range program.

Organizing a preservation program is often a process of rethinking those library functions that may fall within the purview of both long-term preservation efforts and immediate conservation activities. "Preservation" is usually associated with planning or action that will retard the deterioration of library materials. Such activities as the monitoring of environmental control, the installation of screens to filter ultraviolet light from exhibit cases, the development of a disaster preparedness plan and the production of a staff training film are characteristic preservation efforts. "Conservation" usually implies those activities directly concerned with protective or remedial treatment of the physical item. Conservation includes activities such as protection through binding and enclosure, preventive maintenance through a systematic program of repair or sophisticated treatments such as deacidification. "Information preservation," or preserving the intellectual content of seriously deteriorated library materials, involves reformatting a physical item that cannot or need not be retained in its original physical format or medium.

Depending on the library, preservation activities may be organized into a single unified program, that is, an umbrella for all preservation and conservation activities, or a network of policies and procedures that are carried out by several departments or units within guidelines specified by the preservation policy. The possibilities for an *effective* organization for preservation are probably as diverse as the number of libraries developing such programs.

Whatever the organization, the most *efficient* way to organize a cohesive preservation program is to assign overall authority and responsibility to one person. This is usually impossible in all but the very largest or very smallest libraries because preservation affects so many different aspects of library affairs. Consequently, the authority to impose or enforce preservation policies usually comes from the library administration. One workable arrangement for libraries may be to authorize *preservation* policy (which often crosses departmental lines) through the library administration and assign *conservation* responsibility to an individual qualified to organize and direct conservation activities. This individual could also serve a staff function and advise on matters of preservation policy. The success of preservation (not unlike the success of bibliographic control or reference service) is dependent upon the recognition and support of the library administration. Without commitment, direction and enthusiasm from the top, very little can be accomplished.

The development of a preservation program inevitably involves some reorganization of library functions. Unfortunately, some staff may view change as either threatening or insulting. The library administration should encourage acceptance and cooperation by nurturing a broad base of support for preservation *before* imposing changes.

COST OF A PRESERVATION PROGRAM

A preservation program does not need to cost very much. A modest yet effective effort against the deterioration of library materials can simply be instituting policies consistent with preservation principles.[3]

Actually, most libraries already spend funds on preservation, such as to bind unbound materials, to prepare new materials for the shelves and to "mend" damaged materials. The reorganization of these activities within a single unit often improves efficiency, and provides a base for future development of expanded preservation and conservation activities. A preservation committee with a specific charge to examine conditions and make recommendations can significantly enhance the preservation of the collection if the library administration acts on its recommendations.[4]

Most libraries, however, will aim for a comprehensive program that includes the administrative considerations of preservation or preventive maintenance, as well as a program for actual conservation treatment. The major additional cost that libraries assume when they embark upon such a preservation program is for the staff position necessary to organize and direct conservation activities.

Some libraries assign a vacated position line to conservation. Other libraries redefine the job description of an interested staff member and assume responsibility for retraining. This new position can soon "earn its keep" by improving decision making for contract binding, by increasing the efficiency of materials preparation procedures and by upgrading repair activities.

Other clearly identifiable costs of preservation and conservation may include items such as contract binding, salaries and wages of staff assigned to a conservation department or unit, the cost of purchasing reprints or microfilm copies of brittle books, conservation supplies that are directly used in conservation treatments and new equipment purchased to monitor the environment. Many costs, however, are hidden in other budget lines. For example, the cost of changing bibliographic records to reflect the photocopying and withdrawal of a seriously deteriorated work would be subsumed in the cataloging budget.

Inevitably, the cost of preservation does cross departmental and budget lines; thus unless the entire library staff is convinced of the need for preservation, it may resent the additional time and trouble necessary to shelve books properly, or tell a patron that he or she cannot borrow a damaged item until it is repaired, or catalog a microfilm copy of a deteriorated item. A successful program cannot be imposed by the library administration but must become the goal of the entire staff.

Some of the cost of preserving a library collection may not even be part of a library's budget. Building maintenance, environmental control, fire detection and extermination services are often assumed by a parent institution. If inadequate building systems jeopardize the preservation of the collection, the library may have to alert many people outside the library and convince them about the importance of preservation before conditions are improved. For even though conservation scientists have established that library materials will last significantly longer at lower temperatures, it still may be difficult to convince a centralized physical plant to cool the library building to 70°F during the hot summer months.

Perhaps the most significant aspect of the cost of preservation is the very real cost of *neglecting* the physical collection. For example, an improperly shelved book will require repair or rebinding sooner than a properly shelved one. Libraries that use book drops for book return will be forced to repair or replace a much higher proportion of their circulated items than those that only use the circulation desk for returns. These are practical examples of the cost effectiveness of preventive maintenance. In addition, the neglect of preservation concerns results in incalculable costs of irreparable damage to materials of permanent research value or historic interest. A library collection is an enormous investment for the future, and it deserves to be protected.

Libraries planning to increase greatly the range and complexity of conservation treatments performed in-house or contracted for by a cooperative treatment center or private conservation enterprise will need to increase allocations to conservation. Some libraries seek grant funds to provide for new equipment or to enable the restoration of a valuable special collection. Some libraries transfer funds from other budget lines to make room for conservation activities. The most desirable monies, however, are those received because the library is successful in justifying the need for an increased preservation effort.

Costs for specific treatment options are discussed later in this chapter.

PRESERVATION PROGRAM STANDARDS

Environmental Control

A library is responsible for the preservation of those materials that it acquires, describes and stores for the library community it serves. A library should provide intellectual and physical control to those materials, as well as an optimum storage environment that enhances preservation of the collection. The single most important aspect of preservation is environmental control.[5]

Providing a proper storage environment includes protection against the specific environmental agents that cause library materials to deteriorate.

Recommended standards for the storage of library materials specify 68°-70°F and a relative humidity of 50%. A temperature of 68°-70°F is a compromise between what is comfortable for people and desirable for library materials. Actually, as far as most library materials are concerned, the lower the temperature, the better. There is a point, however (approximately 50°F), when unless special procedures are followed, condensation will form on materials brought out of a cold storage area. The best situation is a building that separates stack and public service areas. Then cooler temperatures that retard deterioration are possible, and people can be made comfortable by regulating the temperature and humidity.

The library climate should be kept as close to constant as possible. Systems controlling humidity are as important as those controlling temperature. It is also important that changes in temperature and relative humidity be held to less than ±5°F and ±6% RH.

A hygrothermograph (center) being using to record the temperature and humidity.

While air conditioning is the norm in newer libraries, most air conditioning (cooling) systems do not specifically control humidity. Some control of high humidity does occur during the summer months when incoming air is cooled. But without a humidification system, humidity levels in the winter months will drop drastically—resulting in desiccation of paper, bindings and plastic films. Additionally, if thermostat systems are not working properly or are not capable of responding to rapid changes in the weather, damaging fluctuations in temperature and humidity will occur. Heating and cooling systems tied to a central physical plant are often particularly slow to respond to changes in the weather. Many libraries connected with a large institution experience rapid and drastic fluctuations in temperature and humidity—especially in the spring and fall.

A system of environmental control for a library building should not only maintain specified levels for air temperature and relative humidity but should also filter gaseous pollutants and particulate matter and circulate the "clean" and "climatized" air. Proper air circulation will prevent pockets of stagnant air or small areas where temperature and humidity levels do not meet standards.

Particulate matter is removed by filtration of incoming air. Common commercial filtration systems employ dry filters, oil bath filters or electrostatic precipitators. Though many libraries operate with electrostatic precipitators, they are not acceptable since they produce ozone, which promotes embrittlement of paper. Oil bath filters may not be advisable because they produce aerosols of their own. Dry filters provide excellent filtering efficiency if the system is properly maintained.

Gaseous pollutants are removed by passage of incoming air through treatment beds in the ventilation system where chemicals can absorb specific pollutants. Before such a system is designed, however, the percentage of specific pollutants must be determined.

Damage caused to library materials by exposure to ultraviolet (UV) light rays in sunlight and fluorescent light can be minimized by providing filters to screen UV rays, lowering light levels and keeping lights off when possible. Windows should have curtains to prevent direct or reflected light from falling on library materials, or a UV filtering screen should be applied to the inside of the glass. In stack areas, fluorescent light levels should be kept as low as possible or incandescent lighting should be used. In a closed-stack library, the stack area can be wired to permit lights to be turned off when they are not being used. When stack and public service areas occupy the same space, fluorescent tubes that contain UV filters can be used. Since these are more expensive than ordinary tubes, an alternative is UV filtering sleeves that fit over standard fluorescent tubes. The sleeves, however, must be tested periodically and replaced when necessary.

If environmental control systems are to function properly, they must be maintained on a rigidly specified schedule. Poor maintenance of air conditioning and humidification systems will eventually lead to water-damaged library materials. The effectiveness of an air-cleaning system is dependent on the timely changing of filters and recharging of the system. Systems should be designed and installed with maintenance in mind. Often a library attached to a parent institution will not directly supervise maintenance crews, and communication and control can be difficult.

Environmental control systems must also be monitored to determine if they are meeting the standards set. Periodic adjustment will always be necessary, and there may be occasions when immediate adjustment is needed. Systems purchased from distant companies can be a problem if there is no one available to maintain them or to solve on-the-spot problems. Each system should be equipped with built-in monitors so that non-maintenance library personnel can check the effectiveness of the system. Independent monitors can be used to periodically check the accuracy of system monitors so that recalibration can be performed when necessary.

Physical Control

The preservation of library materials includes provisions for proper storage, shelving, handling and circulation or use. Different kinds of library materials may require different storage conditions depending upon their physical and chemical make-up, their structure or format and their value or intended use.

Some aspects of the physical storage, handling and use of library materials present areas where the preservation of the collection can be enhanced and damage and deterioration averted. Systematic cleaning and stack maintenance activities can prevent deterioration by removing dirt and grime, and can help detect signs of insect infestation and mold growth, or items needing conservation treatment. Likewise, routine reshelving aids preservation because of the opportunity to shelve leaning volumes or volumes placed on their fore-edges correctly and to designate items for binding or repair. Custom protective enclosures can be provided for individual items during the systematic examination and refurbishing of a special collection.

Shelving and Storage

The purpose of library shelving is to provide ready access to the collection. Libraries with stacks that are closed to the public view shelving as a means of storing the collection when it is not being used, while libraries that encourage browsing see stacks as a continuation of public service areas. Regardless of the viewpoint, shelves function as physical support for books; their structure and arrangement should ensure the preservation and effective use of the collection. The shelving arrangement must be flexible enough to allow for expansion of the collection. Tightly packed shelves lead to damage from wrenching books off the shelf and forcing them back on.

When stacks are meant for browsing, there should be enough room to allow easy access to every shelf. If a patron is cramped, he or she will be unable to handle volumes carefully. A table or empty shelf should be available at regular distances so patrons will not be forced to prop books open against other books or to hold several books while looking for others and consequently drop all of them. Footstools should be readily available so users will not have to perch precariously on tiptoe to jostle a book off a high shelf.

The shelves themselves should be easy to clean and wide enough to provide ample support for the books. The painted surface should be smooth without being slick. There should not be any sharp edges or corners, and every shelf should be equipped with a bookend to keep books upright. Leaning books or shelving casebound books on their fore-edges destroys the shape of the spine, causes the book block to pull away from its cover and breaks or tears the thin cloth and paper in the hinge area. Bookends should provide their greatest support at the base of the shelf. Their sides should be thick enough to prevent "knifing" book pages against the bookends when they are reshelved.

Optimum storage for flat paper materials (prints, maps, broadsides and manuscripts) and oversize materials is flat storage. Thus a library storage environment must include adequate flat storage for both oversize and letter-size materials. Convenient and nondamaging access to the materials, as well as suitable tables for their use, must also be available.

Microforms have many applications in a library—as original documents, as preservation copies of deteriorated or space-taking paper originals, as use copies of fragile materials and as copies of documents owned by other libraries. In all instances, microforms that are used will deteriorate and at some point become unusable. If permanent retention of a microform is intended, use copies must be generated as they are needed from a duplicating master negative. A master should be kept in a rigorously controlled environment, preferably a separate storage room at 60°F and 45% RH.

Rare, unique or special collections are customarily stored and used in a separate area that is subject to more stringent security measures than the rest of the library. Because of the value of these materials, measures for physical and environmental security also frequently exceed those for the general collection. A fireproof vault may be included in a rare book room, or halongenated fire extinguishing systems may be used instead of the less expensive sprinkler systems. However, in research libraries, much of a collection may represent material of permanent research value, and "rare" materials will be found throughout the collection. It is most important to keep in mind that this generation's assignation of "valuable" may not be the same as the next generation's.

Handling

Although a certain amount of wear and tear is inevitable when library materials are used, damage caused by improper handling and use can be reduced in a library where preservation is a priority. Minimizing the inadvertent damage caused by ignorance or carelessness and the deliberate abuse caused by selfishness or maliciousness requires sensible policies backed up by constant and unswerving enforcement.

The attitudes of the library administration are reflected throughout the library. Library staff will respond positively to preservation when they realize that the administration is committed, and library patrons will be impressed by a preservation "atmosphere" in a library.

The process of educating the library staff about preservation may require retraining or raising the consciousness of the existing staff conducting formal orientation and training sessions for new staff, and reminding the entire staff on an informal but continuous basis of the importance of preservation and conservation.

Educating the staff can involve such activities as a lecture by a conservation expert, a video tape that illustrates preservation concerns, or small-group orientation within the library. Staff assigned to a repair unit may attend a conservation workshop with the financial support of the library. A combination of these techniques is probably most effective.

Even the library that systematically exposes its staff to preservation concerns will have problem staff members who continue to treat materials roughly or are obstructive to preservation policy. Carelessness is inherent in some people, and not everyone working in a library behaves in a responsible and professional manner. Some people will need constant supervision and reminding and will inevitably cause damage to library materials. Others will need an occasional reminder from their supervisor.

The problem of educating library patrons on the proper care of library materials is much more challenging than that of educating staff. Patrons do not receive their paychecks from the library, and they cannot be required to view a video tape on preservation. A few may feel a general dislike for the "system"—a feeling that manifests itself as animosity toward the library. Frustration with library services may elicit "revenge" against library materials. Studies of academic library patrons have shown that they do not consider even direct mutilation of library materials a very serious offense.

If a library sets a good preservation example, the work of educating library patrons to preservation concerns is half done. Patrons have an almost universal ignorance of the actual costs of obtaining, cataloging and storing library materials. A preservation public relations campaign will alert patrons to their impact on the physical well-being of a collection and the cost of carelessness or deliberate mutilation.

To be most effective, preservation concerns should be advertised in an appealing manner that gets the idea across without harping. Some patrons will respond to pleas to save library materials for the good of mankind, but pointing out how they are hurting themselves will probably get more of a response. Simple instructions on how to handle and use library materials properly can help prevent damage caused by simple ignorance.

Educating library users is a necessary part of a preservation program and it can help prevent needless abuse. However, the problem of mutilation (like theft) is really not one of preservation but rather a matter for criminal prosecution. Studies have shown that the best deterrent to those who would steal or mutilate library materials is the very real possibility of prosecution. How a library handles mutilation and theft will depend upon the state laws, local laws, the institution and the philosophy of the library administration.

Circulation

Although it is obviously desirable for library materials to be used, most of the direct physical damage that accrues is through circulation and use. The best defense against damage is a collection that is properly maintained. Materials that are not appropriately protected by a binding or enclosure are especially vulnerable to damage. Materials that are already damaged or in a state of disrepair are subject to more serious damage.

The patron using library materials is concerned first of all with extracting information. The potential for damage to materials during use is practically limitless. For example, the emulsion layer of microfilm is very easily damaged and the image obscured by rapid movement through a reader, bindings are easily broken by placing them open and face down to mark the place, and large maps are easily torn when they are dragged out from under other maps. The photocopy machine is a notoriously damaging experience for bound materials, as patrons lean heavily on items to get a good copy.

Circulation of library materials out of the library building by direct patron borrowing or interlibrary loan exposes them to a myriad of hazards. Materials that circulate are often bounced along in a bicycle basket, left on an automobile dashboard in the sun, examined over dinner, read in the bathtub and mauled by eager toddlers or hungry pets. A library

"Save a Book" poster published by the Illinois Cooperative Conservation Program with Library Services and Construction Act funds. Simple, graphic instructions educate patrons on how to prevent damage to books.

that allows, and even encourages, circulation must accept that a certain amount of damage is inevitable. One purpose of special collections is to protect materials that are too valuable to risk the hazards of circulation.

Libraries concerned with preservation may want to consider restrictions on the use and circulation of certain categories of materials. For example, patrons wanting to borrow an item in disrepair may be asked to return for it the next day so that it can receive rush treatment. Circulation, especially of fragile or brittle materials, out of the building may be denied and their photocopying restricted.

108   ISSUES IN LIBRARY MANAGEMENT

Automatic Book Return Systems

Automatic book return systems are not recommended since books are easily damaged by mechanical systems that jostle them about, allow them to bump against one another, permit abrasion of the binding or drop them any distance—however slight. The best method of book return is for items to be returned to the desk where they were charged out. Though it is true that humans can be injurious to books, they can be taught to be careful. On the other hand, poorly designed mechanical or automatic systems, once installed, cannot be reasoned with.

In the case of a public library that emphasizes public service, book "drops" outside the building may be justified—the trade-off for the service is fewer circulations per volume and frequent replacement of volumes as a result of damage from rain, overflowing boxes and vandalism. Inside the library, a slot that opens to a gradual slide leading to a table is acceptable providing the table is emptied *as soon* as it is full.

Some libraries, however, insist on an automatic or mechanical system for the return of circulating materials. When automatic systems are used, the library should (1) ensure that a minimum of abrasion and bumping occurs; (2) determine the maximum capacity of the system and chart it against the maximum possible volume of book return within the max-

Book "drops" often result in damage to volumes from rain, overflowing boxes and vandalism.

imum time the system would be unattended; and (3) visit another library where the system is used to see it in operation.

DISASTER PREPAREDNESS

The purpose of disaster preparedness is to maximize preventive measures that can be taken to protect an existing library building and collection from devastation resulting from fire, flood, tornado, earthquake, a building system's failure, etc. Preventive measures include a written plan of action outlining salvage procedures to minimize damage to a collection in the event of a disaster.

Fire

The protection of library collections from fire is complicated by the nature of the materials themselves and the way they are stored and used. Library materials are in many cases irreplaceable and in most cases uninsured. Libraries contain highly combustible, compact fuel that will feed any fire that manages to get started. Detection is a problem because there are many remote areas; in a large library the staff is unable to supervise the entire stack area. To make matters worse, water from high pressure hoses used in fire-fighting causes additional serious damage—bindings warp, colors bleed and pages stick together. Salvage operations are complicated when damaged buildings cannot be entered immediately, since wet paper is subject to mold growth almost immediately.

Two major considerations for the protection of a library building and its contents from fire include (1) construction features, and (2) arrangement of the functional areas and utilities within the building. (Of course, site location is also an important factor to consider.) These factors are important regardless of the method of fire detection or the building's extinguishing system. If a building was constructed with the fire hazard in mind, then a possible fire may be prevented or, if a fire is started, it may not spread uncontrollably.[6]

Building Construction

A building constructed of "fire-resistant" materials is not necessarily "fire proof." It may be that the contents of the building will burn completely, but the building itself will remain standing. In any case, all materials, even fire-resistant materials, will burn and/or disintegrate if the fire is hot enough.

In order to fight a fire effectively, the building must allow for access by the fire department. A complete plan of the building indicating stack areas, aisles and entrances, windows and knock-out panels, utilities and priority collections, catalogs and records must be available. The fire hazard exists around the clock, not just during library hours; a fire-fighting force without a plan for access wastes valuable time in forceable entry.

The physical security of collections should not hamper either fire fighting or safety for staff and patrons. Requirements for exits are outlined in local building codes, but many libraries channel all traffic from the stacks through a single circulation desk and a single exit. Neither collection security nor people security need be jeopardized if the fire alarm system is integrated with exit systems.

Arrangement of Areas

The principle of compartmentalization is perhaps the single most important aspect of fire-prevention planning. In the past, construction of tier upon tier of self-supporting metal stacks created a chimney effect, encouraging the spread of fire. This type of construction has been rejected, except in cases where aesthetic considerations unwisely outweigh fire safety. In fact, any vertical opening that allows passage of flames between floors is inadvisable. Compartmentalization will confine fires to the areas in which they start. Stacks separated by fire-resistant floor construction and further compartmentalized by fire doors, resist the spread of fire. Stairways, elevators and pipe shafts should be enclosed. Service areas should be compartmentalized and/or separated from stack areas because they are high-risk areas for fires. Stacks separated from public service areas and used only for storage can receive maximum fire protection.

Heating, electrical and air-conditioning systems should be installed and maintained so that they will not increase the fire hazard. Boilers and furnaces can be cut off from the rest of the building by a fire resistive enclosure and/or installed in a separate structure. Heating and air-conditioning ducts and pipe shafts should prevent the passage of flames between floors. Inadequate maintenance of utility systems within library buildings has been the cause of numerous fires. Preventive maintenance performed periodically and according to systems specifications can lessen fire risks.

Automatic Extinguishing Systems

Even if a library building is constructed of fire-resistant materials and has fire doors, compartmentalization and the services of a good fire department, it still should be furnished with automatic systems for fire detection and extinguishment. Automatic detection systems operate by sensors which, depending upon the system, respond to a temperature change, the light flash of a fire or the presence of smoke or invisible products of combustion. To be effective, every detection system should be able to notify the local fire department, trigger an alarm in the building, indicate the location of the fire, shut down the ventilation system and recall elevators.[7]

An automatic extinguishing system will contain a fire or put it out. Extinguishing systems for libraries use either water or gas. Although water can cause extensive damage to library materials, it has been repeatedly proven that modern automatic sprinkling systems can effectively suppress fires with minimum water damage to collections. When sprinkler heads operate independently, water is discharged only from those sprinklers activated by the detection system. Recent developments in the salvage of water-damaged library materials are a further incentive to installation of sprinkler systems.

Gas systems for the suppression of fire use either carbon dioxide or halon (a halogenated hydrocarbon). Carbon dioxide will extinguish a fire by smothering flames, but it is not recommended for libraries because of the great and immediate danger to people.

Halon is a liquefied, compressed gas that extinguishes a fire by interfering with the combustion cycle. It is harmless to people in exposures up to five minutes. Halon is very effective and particularly advantageous for libraries because it does no damage to books and manuscripts. However, it is an expensive system relative to automatic sprinklers; a false discharge may cost as much as $30,000. The use of a dual detection system—where two separate sensor systems must be triggered to activate the extinguishing system—will prevent expensive false alarms. Automatic detection systems, like all other building systems, should be periodically checked to be sure that they are operating properly.

Water Damage

Almost all disasters involving libraries result in water-damaged materials. Storms, floods, tornadoes and high winds bring water; water is used by fire fighters to extinguish fires; and earthquakes cause broken water pipes. Man-made calamities usually involve water from overflowing cooling or humidification systems and leaky plumbing or bursting pipes. Damage caused by the water from natural disasters is increased by the accompanying dirt and debris.

Special precautions should be taken by libraries located in areas where frequent storms or flooding occur. Libraries with recurring water problems should not store library materials in the basement, or at least not place materials on the bottom shelves. Water detection devices can be installed, and the water sensing unit can be connected to a central alarm system. However, large-scale damage can happen almost instantly if water pipes above shelving break. Likewise, dripping from an overflowing humidification system can go undetected for long periods and ruin important materials before the problem is even noticed.

A well-maintained building will prevent many conditions that can lead to a disaster, but only good luck can protect a library for all time from all potential calamities. It is imperative that every library be prepared to act quickly to salvage irreplaceable library materials in the event of a major or minor disaster.

Preparedness for Salvage Operations

Disaster preparedness includes an assessment of the existing library building to determine potential hazards. The building and its detection and alarm systems, fire extinguishing systems and climate control systems should be examined and problem areas noted. Areas such as the roof, physical plant, duct-work, food service or lounge, shipping and receiving and conservation treatment facility can present special hazards. A schedule for periodic inspection and monitoring should be instituted.

Development of a written disaster preparedness plan will enable a library to act expediently and react appropriately to a disaster.[8] The disaster plan should include the designation of key staff members who would authorize and supervise salvage operations; the identification of priority collections for immediate protection and salvage; lists of necessary services, equipment and supplies; and a step-by-step procedure for salvage operations.

The designation of a disaster "team" to organize and supervise salvage operations should include someone, usually an administrator, who can authorize expenditures, cut through red tape and elicit cooperation from all those involved. If a library is part of a larger institution, there may already be a procedure for responding to a disaster and a designated safety or security officer. However, the library will also need to designate specific staff members and delineate responsibilities. If no specific person has been assigned preservation responsibility, a small disaster preparedness committee can be charged with developing a written plan. A large library may have a building manager who is knowledgeable about the building and its systems and can direct efforts to stabilize the environment, ensure the safety of workers and reduce the danger of rampant mold and mildew growth. Such a person can also act as a liaison with central janitorial services, electricians and plumbers, and assemble necessary equipment and supplies. Local sources of equipment and supplies should be listed in the disaster plan so that salvage efforts can proceed with a minimum of confusion and delay.

A specific person, most logically a librarian with preservation responsibilities, can become expert in the salvage and restoration of water-damaged library materials. The development of staff expertise in this area is vital if *additional* damage to affected materials as a result of improper handling or treatment is to be averted. This person would be responsible for obtaining current information on the treatment of water-damaged library materials, devising a salvage procedure and establishing contact with services for freezing, vacuum-drying, fumigation, photographic processing and smoke and soot removal. If additional technical information is needed, this person can contact conservators and others who have had experience in the salvage and restoration of water and/or smoke-damaged materials.

Subject librarians, department heads, bibliographers and curators should be responsible for assigning priority ranking to collections. In the event of a disaster, these priority collections would be salvaged first. The list of priority collections should be keyed to *exact* locations and become a permanent part of the disaster preparedness plan. Actual floor plans that include shelving and storage arrangements can be appended to the plan and updated as necessary.

A major disaster will necessitate the involvement of volunteers or temporary paid help. Because wet materials can be easily damaged, it may be best to identify library staff members who would volunteer to help in salvage operations. To minimize confusion and coordinate efforts, volunteers at the disaster site can be organized into "work teams" with a group leader or be supervised by a member of the library's disaster team. Salvage can be exhausting and depressing work, and supervisors should arrange for refreshments, rest periods and regular relief by fresh workers.

Responding to a Water Disaster

A typical procedure for responding to a disaster involving large-scale water damage follows.

1. Establish the safety of the affected area.

2. Stabilize the environment. The temperature and humidity should be kept as low as possible. The season, weather and condition of the building systems will affect how quickly temperature and relative humidity can be controlled. Mold will flourish at 70°F and 70% RH even on "dry" materials. The usual rule is that wet materials are subject to mold growth after 48 hours.

3. Assemble necessary equipment and supplies.

4. Assemble the work teams.

5. Remove water-damaged materials that will be frozen from the affected area.
   a. Remove wet materials by a human "chain."
   b. Pack materials for freezing as close to the disaster site as possible.
   c. Pack the wettest materials first.
   d. Materials that will be frozen will be packed in plastic milk crates and coded as to location.
   e. Transport materials to a freezer facility.
   f. Transport frozen materials to a facility for vacuum drying and, if necessary, fumigation.

6. Wet photographic materials should be kept wet and cold and moved immediately via a refrigerated truck to a photographic facility for reprocessing.

7. Remove water damaged materials that will be air-dried from the affected area. (Coated paper cannot be air-dried or the pages will "block"—stick together in one mass.)
   a. Set up the area for air drying well away from the affected area if control of temperature and humidity will be a problem.
   b. Cover large tables with unprinted newspaper. Use fans and dehumidifiers to circulate the air and keep temperature and humidity down.
   c. Remove damp materials via book trucks to the drying site.
   d. Place damp books upright and open the covers slightly. Do not fan the pages open. Support the book block with small squares of book board so that the contents will not sag forward and pull out from the cover and the spine will retain its shape.
   e. Just before drying is complete, lay books flat with the spine hanging over the edge of the table and weight them with paper-covered bricks.
   f. Fumigate the materials after they are completely dry.

8. Clean and sterilize the affected area.

9. After air drying and fumigating damp materials, arrange for necessary repair, rebinding and restoration.

10. After vacuum drying frozen materials, acclimate dried materials for a period of six months to restore moisture equilibrium. Arrange for necessary repair, rebinding and restoration.

CONSERVATION TREATMENT OPTIONS

Environmental control, physical control and disaster preparedness are activities central to a comprehensive preservation program. Their implementation will significantly enhance the overall condition of a collection and will help prevent large-scale damage from occurring. There are, however, deteriorative processes over which libraries have no control, such as the deteriorative processes that weaken bindings during routine use and embrittle paper during aging. These require the intervention of conservation treatments (see Figure 8.1).

The decision making that accompanies the selection of a conservation treatment is part of collection development. By allowing materials to deteriorate beyond the point of usability, libraries limit access to information and frustrate users. By altering the physical item through the intervention of treatment, libraries may alter the bibliographic item.

For the purpose of developing a rationale for treatment decision making, conservation efforts can be divided into (1) maintenance activities (for new materials being added to the collection or those materials still in reasonably good condition) and (2) the disposition of deteriorated items that have been designated for long-term retention. Eventually, many items being maintained will also have to enter the decision-making routine for long-term retention. The reevaluation process for long-term retention is necessary if collections are to be *dynamic* rather than static and are to serve patrons by being responsive to their needs. Few libraries will be able to afford the luxury of preserving, in their original state, everything they have ever accessioned or cataloged.

Preventive Maintenance

Preventive maintenance is as important a concept in library preservation as it is in automobile maintenance or health care. The protection afforded by environmental control, proper shelving and handling practices, and the more active maintenance procedures of selective binding, mass deacidification, proper storage containers and timely repairs can significantly reduce the need for later restoration or replacement. Thus, in the entire scheme of library operations, maintenance of the physical collection is cost effective. Central to a maintenance program is the deliberate protection of items *prior* to their being made available for use, through conservation treatments such as mass deacidification, library binding, and the use of protective jackets, folders and boxes.

Mass Deacidification

Chemical stabilization of acid book paper by mass deacidification will prevent subsequent weakening and embrittlement of the paper from acid deterioration. *Paper that has already become brittle, however, will not be restored to former strength and flexibility through deacidification.* In an ideal maintenance program, each paper item being added to the library's permanent collection would be tested and those items with an acid pH would be deacidified. Arranging for treatment would involve (1) contracting for the service; (2) screening and testing incoming materials and designating them for treatment; (3) transporting materials to the treatment facility; and (4) keeping accurate records

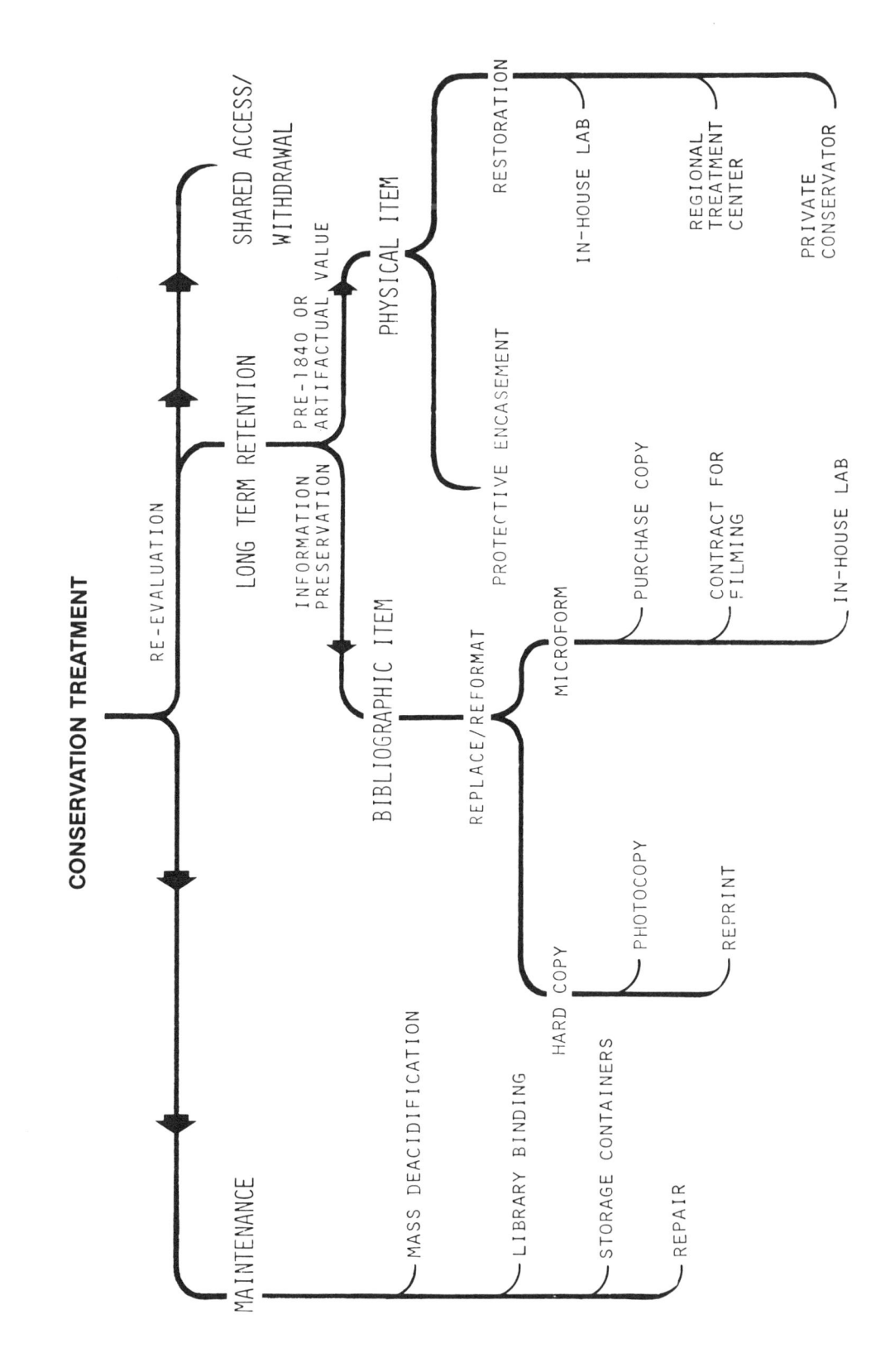

Developing Preservation Programs in Libraries   115

Figure 8.1   Conservation Treatment

CONSERVATION TREATMENT

- MAINTENANCE
  - MASS DEACIDIFICATION
  - LIBRARY BINDING
  - STORAGE CONTAINERS
  - REPAIR
- RE-EVALUATION
  - BIBLIOGRAPHIC ITEM
    - REPLACE/REFORMAT
      - HARD COPY
        - PHOTOCOPY
        - REPRINT
      - MICROFORM
        - PURCHASE COPY
        - CONTRACT FOR FILMING
        - IN-HOUSE LAB
- LONG TERM RETENTION
  - INFORMATION PRESERVATION
  - PRE-1840 OR ARTIFACTUAL VALUE
    - PHYSICAL ITEM
      - PROTECTIVE ENCASEMENT
      - RESTORATION
        - IN-HOUSE LAB
        - REGIONAL TREATMENT CENTER
        - PRIVATE CONSERVATOR
- SHARED ACCESS/WITHDRAWAL

on items sent and returned. Realistically, the addition of a deacidification step to the already cumbersome routines of acquisitions, cataloging, binding and marking would even further delay the process of making information available to patrons. Further, the expense of deacidification would have to be added to today's frozen or even shrinking budgets for new materials. On the other hand, if the technology is available to ensure that acid paper will be made permanent if deacidified, then libraries should take advantage of the treatment for their permanent collections. If materials destined to deteriorate are knowingly added to "permanent" collections, then libraries must hope that in the future it will be technologically, financially and practically feasible to convert deteriorated materials to other media that can conveniently and satisfactorily transmit information to users.

Library Binding

Library binding is the most common, and often the only, conservation activity routinely practiced by libraries. It is the responsibility of the library to communicate product specifications to the library binder. In order to make appropriate decisions on the suitability of library binding for certain types of materials, staff must be familiar with every aspect of bindery production. This usually means periodic trips to the binder's premises.

A contract for library binding should do more than specify prices; it should clearly state acceptable binding methods and materials and delineate responsibilities. For example, a library should always reserve the right to choose the method of binding. Some issues to consider are: the initial and projected condition of the book paper; method of sewing (including oversewing, machine through-the-fold sewing, hand sewing, and adhesive binding); margins; trimming; rounding and backing of spines; and types of covering material.

Storage Containers

Proper storage containers for unbound paper materials, maps, manuscripts, microforms, photographs, phonograph records, magnetic tapes and discs and for items with unusual formats are important for preventive maintenance. To meet conservation standards, a container must provide protection against mechanical damage caused by movement; physical damage caused by particulate matter, abrasion or pressure; and chemical damage caused by the migration of impurities from adjacent materials or the container itself. Depending on the structure, containers can also serve as buffers against fluctuations in temperature and humidity and protection from ultraviolet light rays and some atmospheric pollutants. Examples of common containers are map folders, manuscript storage boxes, microfiche envelopes and motion picture film cans.

Repair

An active and well-organized book repair program is a vital maintenance activity. Since 1840, libraries have not only seen a sharp decline in the quality of paper, but in the quality of book manufacture as well. The inadequacy of publishers' bindings has meant that libraries are forced to repair volumes, or have them rebound by a library bindery, almost as soon as they are used. Since a library binding for every new acquisition is out of the question, the maintenance of a collection depends on the development of a series of simple in-house repairs.[9-11] An ideal program would include periodic, systematic perusal of the shelves for materials in need of repair. The need for repair can, of course, be greatly diminished by proper storage, shelving, handling and use.

Long-Term Retention

Since libraries will not want to retain unusable materials, items that are seriously deteriorated must enter a decision-making process for long-term retention—to determine if they should be withdrawn, restored or reformatted. The following questions will need to be asked about every item: Should this item be kept in the collection? Is the paper brittle? Can it be commercially rebound or repaired in-house? Would a protective box be appropriate? How is it used? How often is it used? Does it have value as an artifact? Does it need to be in hard copy format? Is a commercial reprint available? For how much? Is a commercial microfilm copy available? Has another library filmed it? Are they planning to? Is it too long to photocopy and bind? Should the original be discarded after replacement? How much would it cost to have it restored?

The answers to these questions are not always simple. There may be disagreements about issues such as what should be kept, how many copies should be kept, what constitutes brittle, the advisability of binding or repair, the quality of a reprint and the choice between film stocks and formats. There is also the consideration that when money is spent on replacement, it cannot be spent on new books. Finally, library staffs may not want to make these decisions, or simply may not have the time to make them.

TREATMENT: THE DECISION-MAKING PROCESS

Even with all the issues and controversies, libraries are still left with the primary consideration—can this item be used? If it cannot and it is kept without restoring or reformatting, then the library must restrict or deny its use. This results in what many libraries euphemistically refer to as "restricted access" or "storage." Not restoring or reformatting is a type of decision making since, left alone, a deteriorating item will eventually turn to dust. Are libraries wise to expend huge sums for online bibliographic control of their resources if significant portions of the collections are physically disintegrating? Can libraries justify the retention of materials that cannot be used? Clearly, this is where an overall collection development policy that includes preservation must enter in.

Preserving Intellectual Content

Fortunately, not all library materials need to be kept in their original state, or even format. If appropriate to the individual item and its projected use, the information contained in the item can be preserved by replacement in microformat. This is not a panacea, however, or even a simple option.[12] Some types of information would be lost by reformatting; information is sometimes dependent upon the original format; microfilm is not the preferred format for some items; microfilm is only "archival" if it is the right film, filmed correctly, processed correctly and stored and used properly. After all, there is no point in substituting one impermanent medium for another. Additionally, not every deteriorated title is available commerically, and in-house labs and contracts for outside filming are both complicated undertakings. Even with all the problems, microfilming is still the foremost preservation tool for deteriorated paper stock. In fact, the vast number of items that have *already* deteriorated make microfilming the *only* option in many cases. Coupled with cooperative filming programs among libraries, microfilming is an impressive treatment option for preserving and sharing information.

Preserving the Physical Item

What if a library is compelled to retain a seriously deteriorated book physically—because it has artifactual value or the content is dependent on its original format? For example, half-tones, color reproductions, etchings and other illustrations are not very satisfactorily microfilmed or photocopied. If the paper is brittle, each page can be laboriously deacidified and strengthened by lamination and the book rebound. Such a process is expensive, and skilled services are difficult to obtain. A protective box would buy some time, which is the rationale behind the Library of Congress's Phase Box Program. Damaged items are boxed and their characteristics and condition noted so that they can be retrieved and grouped for treatment in the future.[13] For example, the treatment for an ordinary 18th-century volume with a damaged binding, but strong paper and the sewing still intact, would usually be leather treatment and boxing. If the paper quality permits and the expense is warranted, the book could be rebound and the new binding executed to be compatible with the period of the book's production. This is an especially appropriate treatment option for important books that are not in their original bindings.

Choosing the Treatment

Who in the library will make the difficult decisions about treatment options?[14] Subject specialists and bibliographers are in the best position to know an item's informational value, instrinsic value, value to the collection as a whole and expected use. Reference librarians who act in a collection development capacity are also concerned about the disposition and treatment of deteriorated items. Treatment options, in general, are based on what is technologically, financially and practically feasible. The option for a particular item is based on what is appropriate in terms of its condition, value to the collection and present and projected uses. Not all items in the same condition warrant the same treatment. Even the determination of "condition" may be a matter for some deliberation.

In a library with a comprehensive preservation program, decision making is best accomplished through liaison between the subject specialist and the preservation librarian or conservator whose job it is to be knowledgeable about treatment options. The selection of a conservation treatment is a collection development decision. There are reasonable shortcuts to this process. A philosophy and framework for decision making in individual libraries can be developed to expedite routine decision making while ensuring that impor-

Custom-made protective enclosures for rare/fragile materials.

tant decisions are made by the appropriate people. The determination of categories of items for treatment can simplify decision making by setting parameters for treatment options. For example, new paperbacks that are sewn in signatures rather than adhesive bound might constitute one category of materials. In this case the library might make the unilateral decision always to retain the signature format by providing a hard cover casing rather than choosing the less-expensive option of an oversewn binding. A group of items that constitutes a discrete collection is another case when decisions can be made en masse. This kind of decision making does *not* ignore the fact that each individual item may be a separate and unique problem. However, it is safe, for example, to make the decision to provide acid-neutral envelopes for all the thin pamphlet material in a discrete collection without going through the process of making individual decisions. If libraries are to expect results, then it is imperative that they recognize and apply practical solutions.

The intelligent use of conservation treatment options requires coordination throughout the library of all the processes that affect the physical item and all the people who are involved in making treatment decisions—including decisions concerning withdrawal or reformatting. Trained and experienced paraprofessionals and conservation technicians can do an excellent job making decisions for maintenance, library binding, routine repair and protective encasement—providing that a framework for decision making has been developed and professional librarians are available for advising on bibliographic matters, and collection development and budgeting.

Costs

How much will treatment options cost libraries? Maintenance activities, although they initially cost money, will save money in the long run. If, for example, it costs $7 (including transportation, treatment, in-house processing and record-keeping) to have a book deacidified before being used, then it may be wise to spend the money on treatment now rather than wait for the book to deteriorate and be forced to spend $20 to $30 to replace it or reformat it and change the bibliographic record. Likewise, a simple remedial repair executed in time may eliminate the need for a costly repair later.

Unfortunately, many libraries have a history of inappropriate maintenance activities, such as leather volumes that were "treated" with shellac, books that were "mended" with surgical tape and photographs that were "protected" by being mounted on acid mat board with rubber cement. The costs of unsuitable practices and inappropriate treatments are difficult to calculate. At the very least, the useful life of materials is considerably shortened. And it is a sad fact that the bulk of most conservators' work is repairing damage that could have been avoided—time that could have been spent treating items worn out through normal handling and use or providing protection for vulnerable items.

Replacement of a badly deteriorated item takes time and costs money. An initial search must be made to check holdings, to locate missing volumes or other copies or editions, and to determine replacement options and costs. It takes time to make a final decision and acting on that decision takes more time. Reprints are not cheap, and a single title wanted in microform may be buried in an expensive microfilm series. An in-house lab represents a major expense, yet a librarian may spend months working with a commerical filmer before a quality product is produced on a regular basis. If the library intends to retain the *physical* item, a protective box made in-house may cost anywhere from $4 to $25, or more. Custom commercial boxes start at $20. A simple cased rebinding for an ordinary book would take even an experienced technician approximately eight hours to execute. A typical restoration job by a conservator may cost $150 to $300.

Within the limitations of a library's particular preservation options, it is desirable to determine the estimated cost of each particular option. Such cost figures are an integral part of decision making. For example, if a library determines that the average unit cost of repairing a book in-house is cheaper than sending it for a new library binding, it may decide to increase its capabilities and do more book repair. Likewise, certain rules can be established for decision making based on a library's experience with costs. For example, it may be cheaper to search for and purchase a microform copy than to arrange for the filming of the library's own deteriorated item.

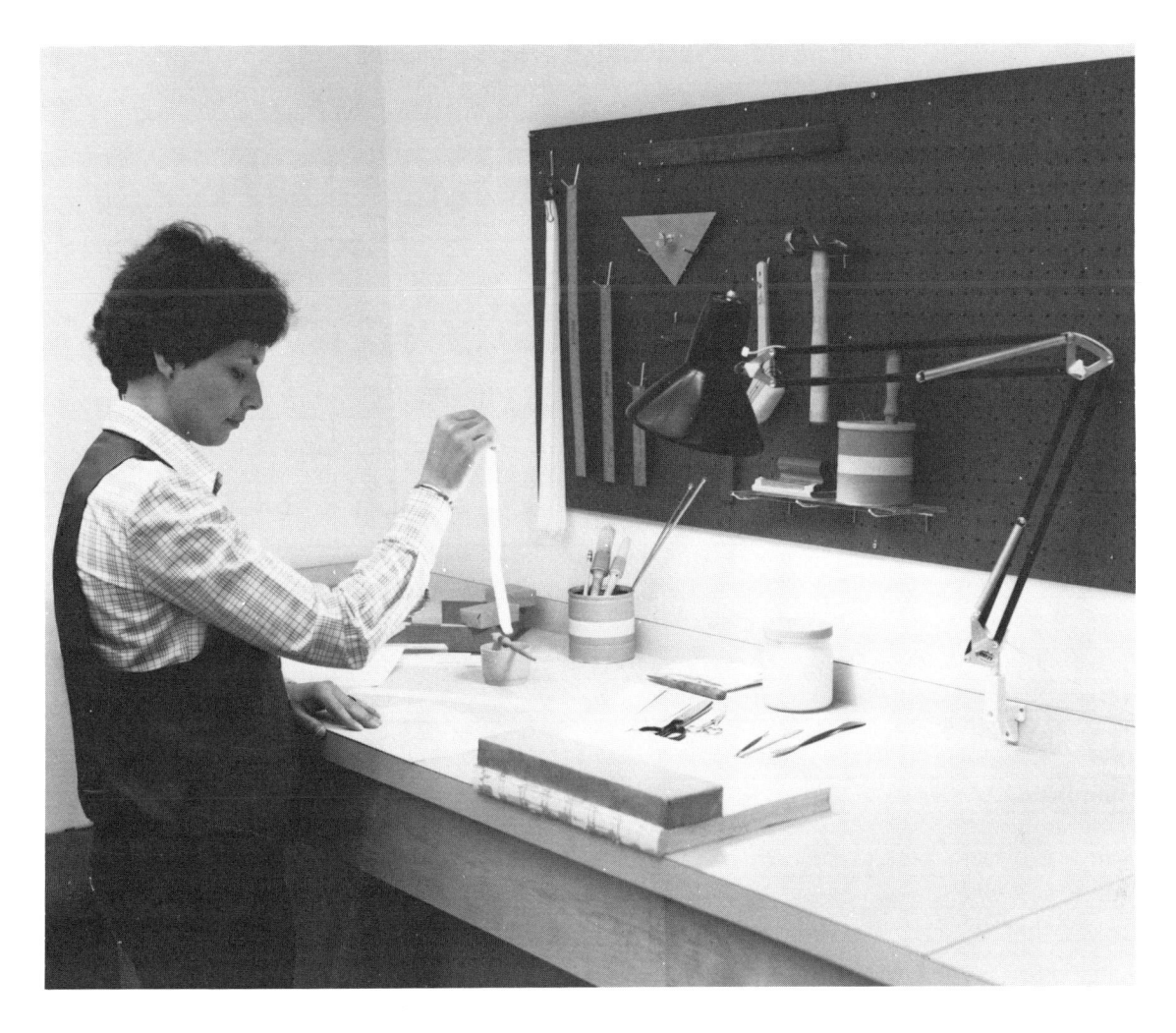

Routine book repair station, Morris Library, Southern Illinois University at Carbondale.

Librarians must consider responsible custody of their collections as part of their professional responsibilities. By taking an active role in conservation treatment decision making, librarians will ensure that they continue to be directly involved in the composition of their collections.

MODELS FOR ORGANIZING PRESERVATION PROGRAMS

The following (see Figure 8.2) are models for organizing preservation programs in a range of library sizes and types. Every library collection is unique and most libraries will not *exactly* fit one of the five levels of preservation organization suggested by the models; however the models can be used as a guide for organizing preservation and conservation activities.

Figure 8.2 Preservation Program Models

PRESERVATION ACTIVITIES Level*	1	2	3	4	5
○development of a preservation policy statement		x	x	x	x
○development of a disaster preparedness plan	x	x	x	x	x
○standards for environmental control	x	x	x	x	x
○monitoring the environment		x	x	x	x
○information preservation program including withdrawal or replacement of brittle books	x		x	x	x
○cooperative filming projects				x	x
○microfilming contract with a commercial firm					x
○cooperation with reprint and microform publishers				x	x
○library binding specifications and contract	x		x		x
○mass deacidification specifications and contract				x	x
○preservation responsibility for certain subject areas in agreement with other libraries					x
○microfilming of rare/fragile materials to reduce handling of originals		x			x
○standards for handling and use, loans and exhibits	x	x	x	x	x
○education programs for staff and patrons	x	x	x	x	x

CONSERVATION ACTIVITIES Level	1	2	3	4	5
○fumigation		x		x	x
○storage containers	x	x	x	x	x
○exhibit support design and installation		x		x	x
○marking	x		x		x
○preparation of materials for library binding	x		x		x
○pamphlet binding	x		x		x
○simple book repair for general collections	x		x		x
○extensive book repair for general collections			x		x
○leather treatment	x	x	x	x	x
○simple protective folders		x	x	x	x
○protective encasement		x		x	x
○arranging for treatment of artifacts not within the conservator's area of expertise		x			
○stabilization of book structures		x		x	x
○selective in-house binding of new acquisitions				x	
○deacidification		x		x	x
○restoration of original bindings				x	
○conservation rebinding				x	x
○treatment documentation and fragment files		x		x	x
○arranging for sophisticated scientific support/ analytical services				x	x
○arranging for custom protective encasement and occasional sophisticated conservation treatment	x		x		
○simple flat paper repair and encapsulation	x		x		
○flat paper repair, encapsulation, matting and mounting		x		x	x
○conservation/duplication of photographic images		x		x	x
○conservation/conversion of plastic base materials		x		x	x

*Level refers to type of library and collection, explained further below.

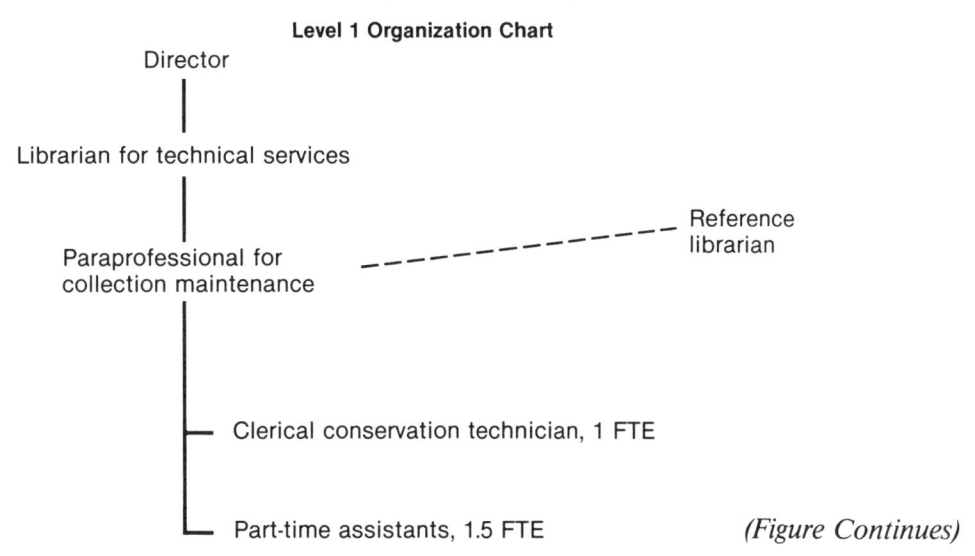

Figure 8.2 Preservation Program Models (Cont.)

STAFF (FTE)	Level	1	2	3	4	5
professional librarian		.2		1.0	1.0	1.0
professional conservator			1.0		4.0	1.0
paraprofessional, library		1.0		2.0	1.0	3.0
clerical		1.0		2.0	2.0	4.0
conservation technician			2.0	1.0	6.0	2.0
part-time assistants		1.5		4.0		8.0
volunteer			1.5		2.0	
	Total	3.7	4.5	10.0	16.0	21.0

SPACE (square feet)	Level	1	2	3	4	5
office/s			120	120	300	500
processing		500		750		1500
workshop/laboratory		225	625	625	1500	1200
	Total	725	745	1495	1800	3200

Level 1:

Small college library or large public library with a heavily used core collection of standard works and current resources and a small retrospective collection. Includes a small collection of rare books, manuscripts and unique local history materials.

Level 1 Organization Chart

Director
|
Librarian for technical services
|
Paraprofessional for collection maintenance — — — — — — Reference librarian
|
├─ Clerical conservation technician, 1 FTE
|
└─ Part-time assistants, 1.5 FTE

(Figure Continues)

Figure 8.2 Preservation Program Models (Cont.)

Level 2:

Historical society library or discrete historical collection pertaining to a particular geographic region or specific subject, person, topic or time period. Includes original documentary resources and artifacts, as well as secondary research materials and reference works in support of the collections. Collection includes a wide variety of artifacts not limited to books and flat paper materials. Active exhibition and education programs.

Level 2 Organization Chart

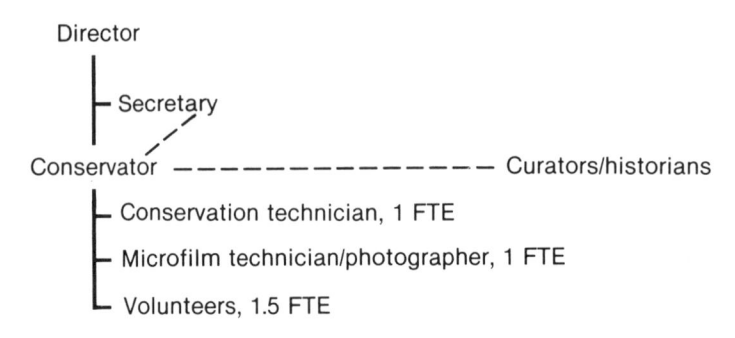

```
Director
   ├─ Secretary
Conservator ──────────── Curators/historians
   ├─ Conservation technician, 1 FTE
   ├─ Microfilm technician/photographer, 1 FTE
   └─ Volunteers, 1.5 FTE
```

Level 3:

University or large college library with a heavily used core collection of standard works and current resources and a moderately used retrospective collection. Includes several small branch or department libraries and a small separate collection of rare books and manuscripts.

Level 3 Organization Chart

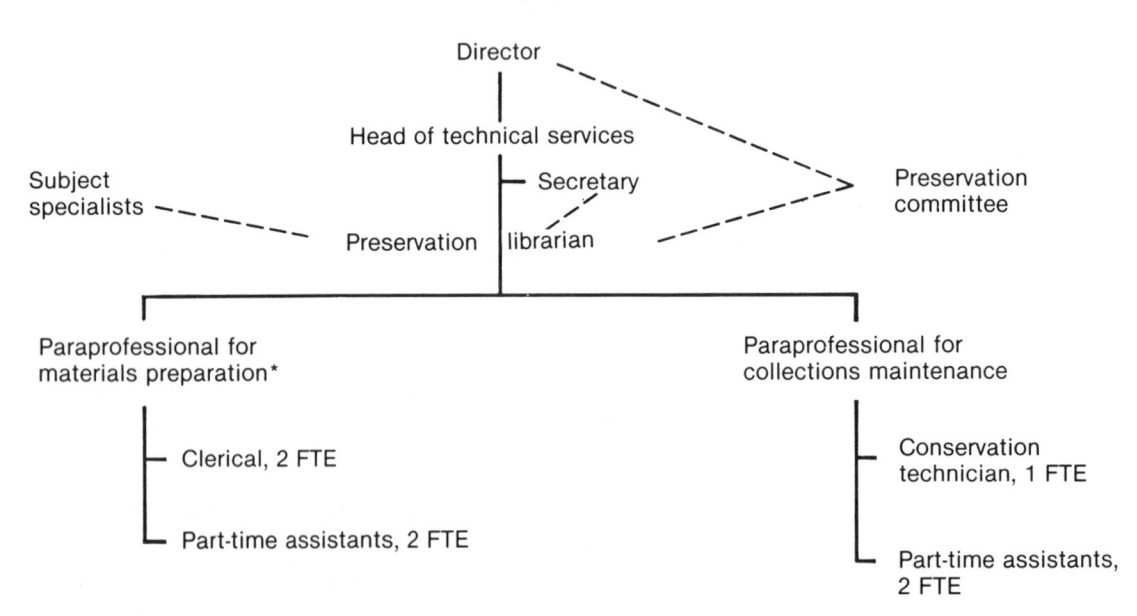

```
                        Director
                           |
                Head of technical services
                           |
Subject                  ┌─ Secretary          Preservation
specialists ─────── Preservation librarian ─── committee
                           |
        ┌──────────────────┴──────────────────┐
Paraprofessional for                    Paraprofessional for
materials preparation*                  collections maintenance
        |                                       |
        ├─ Clerical, 2 FTE                      ├─ Conservation
        |                                       |   technician, 1 FTE
        └─ Part-time assistants, 2 FTE          └─ Part-time assistants,
                                                    2 FTE
```

*Includes binding preparation and marking.

Figure 8.2   Preservation Program Models (Cont.)

Level 4:

Specialized research library or separate special collections library associated with a large research library. Includes collections of rare books, manuscripts, photographs, ephemera and other unique materials pertaining to one or several particular fields. Includes secondary research materials and reference works in support of the collections. Active exhibition program and popular collections that are heavily used.

Level 4 Organization Chart

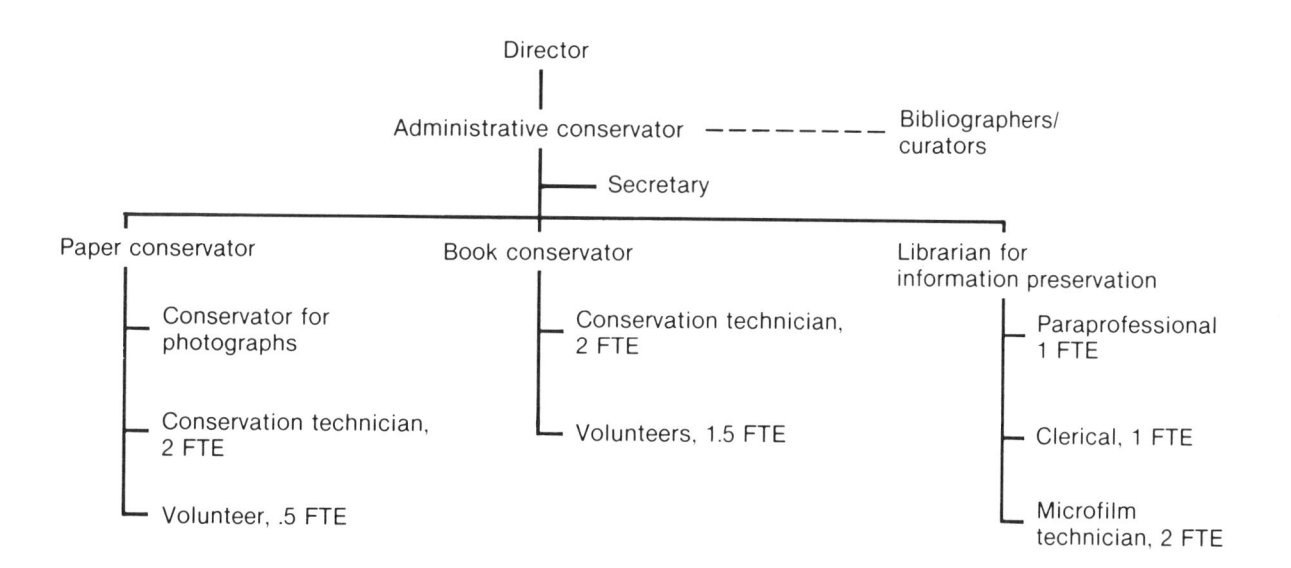

```
                          Director
                             |
         Administrative conservator — — — — — — — Bibliographers/
                             |                     curators
                             ├── Secretary
    ┌────────────────────────┼────────────────────────┐
Paper conservator      Book conservator         Librarian for
                                                information preservation
  ├── Conservator for      ├── Conservation technician,   ├── Paraprofessional
  │   photographs          │   2 FTE                      │   1 FTE
  ├── Conservation         └── Volunteers, 1.5 FTE        ├── Clerical, 1 FTE
  │   technician, 2 FTE                                   └── Microfilm
  └── Volunteer, .5 FTE                                       technician, 2 FTE
```

(Figure Continues)

126   ISSUES IN LIBRARY MANAGEMENT

Figure 8.2   Preservation Program Models (Cont.)

Level 5:

Large research library with diversified collections organized into one central or main library receiving moderate use and numerous branch or departmental libraries receiving heavy use. Includes a large separate collection of rare books, manuscripts and photographs.

Level 5 Organization Chart

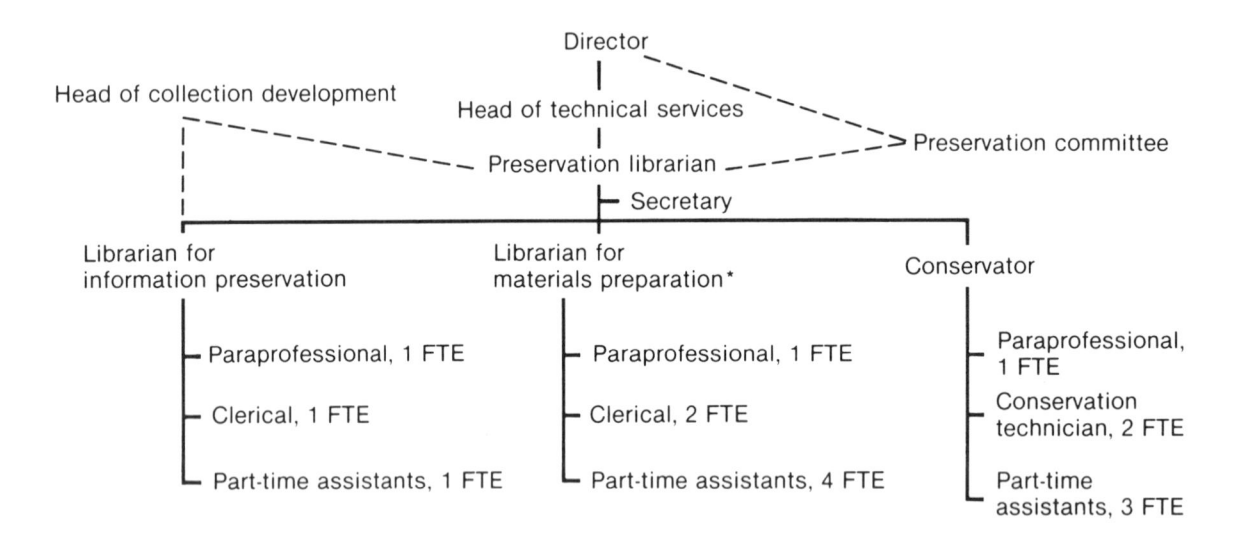

```
                              Director
                                 |
Head of collection development   |
              ------- Head of technical services -------
             |                   |                       > Preservation committee
             |         ---- Preservation librarian ----
             |                   |
             |                 Secretary
             |                   |
    Librarian for          Librarian for              Conservator
    information preservation  materials preparation*
                                                      
    - Paraprofessional, 1 FTE   - Paraprofessional, 1 FTE   Paraprofessional, 1 FTE
    - Clerical, 1 FTE           - Clerical, 2 FTE           Conservation technician, 2 FTE
    - Part-time assistants, 1 FTE  - Part-time assistants, 4 FTE   Part-time assistants, 3 FTE
```

*Includes binding preparation, marking and preparation for mass deacidification.

FOOTNOTES

1. George M. Cunha, *What an Institution Can Do To Survey Its Conservation Needs* (New York: New York Library Association, Resources and Technical Services Section, 1979).

2. Carolyn Clark Morrow, "A conservation policy statement for research libraries," University of Illinois, Graduate School of Library Science *Occasional Papers Series,* no. 139 (July 1979).

3. Pamela W. Darling, " 'Doing' preservation, with or without money: a lecture on carrying on a preservation program," *Oklahoma Librarian* 30 (4) (October 1980): 20-26

4. Robert H. Patterson, "Organizing for conservation: A model charge to a conservation committee," *Library Journal* 104 (10) (May 15, 1979): 1116-19.

5. Paul N. Banks, "Preservation of library materials," in *Encyclopedia of Library and Information Science, Volume 23,* eds. A. Kent, H. Lancour and J.E. Daily (New York: Marcel Dekker, 1978), pp. 180-222.

6. National Fire Protection Association, *Recommended Practice for Protection of Libraries and Library Collections* (Boston, MA: National Fire Protection Association, 1980).

7. Timothy Walch, *Archives and Manuscripts: Security* (Chicago, IL: Society of American Archivists, 1977).

8. Hilda Bohem, *Disaster Prevention and Disaster Preparedness* (Berkeley, CA: University of California, April 1978).

9. Jane Greenfield, *Wraparounds,* 1980. *Tip-ins and Pockets,* 1981. *Paper Treatment,* 1981. *Pamphlet Binding,* 1981. *The Small Bindery,* 1981 (New Haven, CT: Yale University Library).

10. Carolyn Horton, *Cleaning and Preserving Bindings and Related Materials* (Chicago, IL: American Library Association, 1969).

11. Carolyn Clark Morrow, *Conservation Treatment Procedures: A Manual of Step-by-Step Procedures for the Maintenance and Repair of Library Materials* (Littleton, CO: Libraries Unlimited, Inc., 1982).

12. Pamela W. Darling, "Microforms in libraries: preservation and storage," *Microform Review* 5 (1) (April 1976): 93-100.

13. Margaret Brown, Donald Etherington and Linda McWilliams, *Boxes for the Protection of Rare Books:Their Design and Construction* (Washington, DC: Library of Congress, 1982).

14. Robert DeCandido, "Preserving our library material: preservation treatments available to librarians," *Library Scene* 8 (1) (March 1979): 4-6.

9

Basic Publicity Techniques for Public Libraries

by Benedict A. Leerburger

There are probably as many varieties of public libraries as there are villages, towns and cities. Each library must consider itself unique; each serves a specific type of patron. However, all libraries, regardless of size or clientele, have common bonds. All are concerned with their relevance in the community and must fulfill their purpose as information centers. Many also serve as centers of recreation. All libraries must concentrate their efforts on a single key element: *service*. Without it there is no need to market the library.

The variety of services a library has to offer must be known to as many people in the community as possible. Edward J. Montana Jr., of the Boston Public Library, put it this way: "Keeping the library in the public's mind continually by fostering community relations and a steady build-up of goodwill among the various elements of a community by telling the 'library's story,' to use a hackneyed phrase, will do much to ensure not only its widespread use but also widespread support when it is needed."[1]

WHO HANDLES PUBLIC RELATIONS?

It is generally agreed that one staff member should be assigned the overall responsibility for public relations. In most smaller libraries, the individual chosen knows little about the specialty but has the desire to learn. For the larger public library, particularly in urban areas, a professional public relations specialist should be seriously considered. The PR manager should have an understanding of the workings of the system but does not need a degree in library science. Remember, he or she must wear two hats: as the public's representative on the library staff and as the library's representative to the public.

The basic qualities required of the public relations specialist are the same whether the individual is an outside professional or a staff member. Selling in all forms is a people-related activity; the PR specialist must like people and have the ability to get along with them. Meeting a deadline, dealing with printers and mailers, listening to an irate patron who

---

Reprinted from *Marketing the Library* (White Plains, NY: Knowledge Industry Publications, Inc., 1982).

"deposited the book in the book drop last week despite what they say at the circulation desk" can be harrowing. The job is not for a lover of the tranquil.

Of course, the public relations individual should be sincere and able to stick with an assignment even if it becomes unpleasant. The ability to write well, quickly and on schedule is important. There are many intangibles that separate a good PR person from an ordinary one: the ability to recognize a story, to "sell" news of the library to the media, to know that a forthcoming library event will catch the public's attention, to identify a potential problem before it becomes a public nuisance. The PR person should have a wide variety of interests and be able to accept new ideas and radical solutions.

Previous experience in journalism, publishing or the social services is a real plus. In many communities a volunteer with previous public relations experience can be found through an ad in the local newspaper. An experienced volunteer has the advantage over a staff member assigned to the task because the volunteer is usually able to devote time *solely* to the public relations function; the individual, if properly selected, knows the ways of the community; and, best of all, the price is right.

THE LOCAL NEWSPAPER

To keep the community aware of library activities and policies, the PR individual must take advantage of the local organs for information dissemination. Perhaps no single source can provide such widespread coverage of library events, news and policy changes as the local newspaper.

In large cities, the so-called local paper is primarily national in scope and finds it easy to relegate library releases to the back pages or the trash can. However, even in major metropolitan centers, there are many local newspapers aimed at a select audience. They may be neighborhood papers, foreign-language papers, or special-interest papers with an emphasis on food, real estate, etc. Each of these local papers reaches members of your library community, but rarely are these publications considered a viable means of selling the library. However, a creative public relations individual can use them effectively. A Spanish-language paper, for example, might be interested in stories about the library's collection of materials in Spanish or on Hispanic subjects. Columns devoted to reviews of new books, travel information or exhibits with a particular ethnic angle are welcomed by editors eager to serve their special audiences.

Making the Initial Contact

Most small circulation newspapers rely heavily on the editor in chief for suggesting story ideas and managing the newsgathering activities. The editor is easily accessible and eager for new ideas. Better yet, if you can provide a complete story that needs only minor editing, you have saved the editor's time. It is most important to meet the editor and cultivate an ongoing relationship. Often you may discover that the editor has assigned a cultural affairs editor or community news editor to monitor the library along with a shopping list of other potential news areas within the community.

The initial contact with the editor will enable you to identify the person responsible for library coverage and set up a meeting. A joint meeting with both the editor and the reporter covering the library can provide an even stronger liaison. There are a few simple "do's" and "don'ts" that should be observed during this first meeting.

• Do come prepared with specific suggestions. These may be ideas for periodic columns such as a book review column, children's reading list, activities column, etc.

• Don't ask the editor what he or she may like in the way of library coverage. If the editor had library stories in mind you would have heard about it. Remember your job is to sell, not shop.

• Do learn as much as you can about the newspaper and its audience before you meet the editor. You don't want to suggest subjects that might be taboo to a newspaper's special audience. On the other hand, by knowing the paper's typical reader you are in a much stronger position to suggest a weekly column geared to the interests of that audience.

• Don't assume that the library is going to provide the paper with front page news. You represent a service organization. The product you have to sell is service.

• Do ask the editor how you may submit written copy to make the editor's job simpler. Although there is a standard way to write a news story or press release, some editors prefer copy typed to fit certain specifications.

• Don't assume that all editors believe in the First Amendment and will rush to fly the banner of controversy. Your library's recent lecture on sex education in the schools might be of major interest to you, but the paper may not want the story if it feels the subject is too hot to handle.

Preparing a Press Release

The basic way to submit material to the newspaper is through a written press release. It is possible that your local editor or reporter is willing to take a story over the phone; however, there are potential problems in this method. Too often facts are garbled. And the slant that you would like the story to take is often lost. It is better to submit a formal release, and then allow the editor to get back to you with any unanswered questions or problems. A sample press release is shown in Figure 9.1.

The press release need not be a formal document but it should follow some simple, basic guidelines. Here are a few of the basics:

• Type all your communications. You are a professional organization and all material coming from your library should have a professional appearance.

• The name of the issuing body should appear on your press release. This may simply

Basic Publicity Techniques for Public Libraries 131

Figure 9.1 The Press Release

From: The Administrative Offices
  Baltimore County Public Library
  320 York Road
  Towson, Maryland 21204

You don't need special press release paper. This is enough.

For Release: Monday a.m. Papers, February 13, 1978

Essential. Editor looks at this first.

APPLICATIONS FOR SENIOR CITIZEN DISCOUNTS

Story in a nutshell useful for headline writing.

Applications for senior citizen discounts cards, issued by the Baltimore County Commission on Aging, are now available at all 18 branches of the Baltimore County Public Library.

The essentials of the story. Can be used as a spot as is on the radio.

Eligible for the cards are all (ciitzens) of Baltimore County sixty years of age and over. The applications can be filled out at the library, which will forward them to the Commission on Aging, or they can be mailed by the applicant to the Commission. Application forms may also be taken by family members and friends to give to older citizens.

When this happens, don't worry.

A Directory of Aging Services in Baltimore County, which has been developed by the Baltimore County Commission on Aging, is also available in limited quantities at branches of the Baltimore County Public Library.

Keep paragraphs short.

This directory lists the services and programs available to older adults in the County, including discounts, education, employment, financial aid, health, housing, legal, nutrition, recreation and volunteer organizations, social services and home care, telephone reassurance and transportation.

An "add on" story related to the first part of the release.

The directory is available, while quantities last, free of charge. In the event that free copies for distribution have been exhausted, library patrons can see the branch library copy, which is retained at the branch for reference.

# # #

For Further Information Call:
Geoffrey W. Fielding
Special Projects Officer
Telephone: 296-8500

Essential — in case of questions.

Double space all releases. Triple space between paragraphs so "breaklines" can be written in. Use one side of sheet only.

Source: Baltimore County Public Library. Reproduced with permission.

be the library's name and address, but it might also be a committee or subcommittee working within the library.

• Also provide the name of an individual who can supply additional information, and be sure to include a telephone number. Some organizations provide both the library number and the individual's home number. The concept being conveyed is that you're giving the paper a news story that has a sense of immediacy. If the editor has a need to reach you quickly, you're available. The individual's title or area of responsibility should also be stated on the release.

• The subject or lead is usually typed in capital letters and centered across the top of the release. This brief heading provides the essence of the story and also gives the editor a basis for composing the actual headline that will appear in the paper.

• Include a release date. There is rarely a need to release a library story at a specific time. However, since you may be sending your release to both weekly and daily papers it is better to date your release to conform to the needs of the weekly paper. If it doesn't matter, simply state, "For Immediate Release." The problem you can encounter is that the weekly paper, knowing it will be beaten by the daily, will ignore your story.

• A coded reference number is sometimes useful. Although smaller libraries do not have the problem of filing and recording releases, many PR organizations will code the date or internal number of the release. This code usually appears on the last page of the release in the lower right hand corner. (For example, July 14, 1982 would appear as 071482.)

• Use only one side of the page. Special paper isn't necessary; however, some libraries do use printed or mimeographed sheets with the library's name or logo on the sheet. The advantage of this is primarily one of identification. The newspapers that receive your releases know immediately that you have a message for them. Larger papers in urban areas receive so many press releases each day that a means of immediate identification is most helpful for the editors.

• Double space all press releases and leave a triple space between paragraphs.

• The first paragraph of your press release should contain all the elements of your story. Remember the basics of journalism: who, what, when, where. Your first paragraph should be structured to stand alone. (It can also be sent to the local radio station and can be used as a spot news announcement without rewriting.)

• Tell your story completely, but don't embellish it. Editors are used to "pap." They see it every day. The library doesn't have to prepare a feature article under the guise of a press release. Although some editors claim that they would rather see more than less in a release, don't include more information than is really necessary.

• Either photocopy or multilith your press releases. Don't use carbon paper or send an original to one paper and a copy to another. You can count on the second paper finding out that its competitor received the original. You need friends, not enemies.

- Maintain a consistent style. Paragraphs should not be divided from one page to the next unless absolutely unavoidable. Number all pages, and use the word "more" at the bottom of a page if the copy continues. Leave generous margins. Choose a standard style book (e.g., *A Manual of Style,* published by the University of Chicago Press) and stick to it.

- Have someone else proofread your press release. Writers are not effective proofreaders of their own copy.

What Is News?

The subject of your press releases should vary as the services and activities of the library vary. Basically, your release must do two things: educate and inform. If there is to be an event (for example, a speaker) at the library, the release should provide all pertinent information. In addition to the basic "who, what, when, where," it should offer information to stimulate interest in the subject of the talk. As a librarian, there is no one better to do research on a subject than you. Do your work thoroughly. Include some interesting details. Of course, a description of the speaker is a must. If the individual is listed in one of the standard reference works, your job is much simpler. Don't be afraid to write or call the speaker and request biographical information for the press. If the library has a few basic books on the speaker's subject, these can be mentioned at the end of your release.

Write your release with the assumption that the reader knows little about the subject. Don't write down, but don't assume the reader is an expert. Informing or educating the public about new library features can be particularly difficult—and important—as electronic technology in libraries becomes more prevalent. An educational program can be developed initially through a series of press releases announcing the new system, describing its advantages and possible difficulties, and explaining how it will benefit library users. Follow-up releases, displays and seminars in the library are well worth considering.

The question of "what is news?" is a valid one in promoting library services. From the library's point of view, news is simply information not known to the general public. Interpreting the news or evaluating an event to determine whether or not it is newsworthy is another matter. The acquisition of a new book may be a "news event" but certainly not worthy of a press release. However, the acquisition of a major work is well worth a press release. For example, if your reference department has just received the 1980 edition of the 20-volume *New Grove Dictionary of Music and Musicians,* a release stating only that the book is now in the library probably will never see print. However, a description of the massive work's history, scope and value to the community could make an interesting news or feature story.

Many local papers are interested in publishing a library column (see Figure 9.2). This column can be devoted to a review of a major book, a listing of important acquisitions, a roundup of recent library events and planned future activities or, for the weekly paper, a box, "What's Happening at the Library," in which future programs are listed.

134 ISSUES IN LIBRARY MANAGEMENT

Figure 9.2 Clippings from *The Cairo Messenger* Weekly Library Column

Source: *The Cairo Messenger*, Cairo, GA. Reproduced with permission.

A follow-up release describing a lecture or concert that has already occurred may well be worthy of a news item. A portable tape recorder is an excellent way to preserve a speaker's words. Permission to record a speaker should be obtained in advance and, wherever possible, direct quotes should be checked with the speaker before submitting them to the press.

Photographs

Photographs are also welcomed by local papers. Most newspapers require black-and-white glossies and do not accept color photographs. Although some papers will accept Polaroids, reproduction quality is better if 8-inch by 10-inch non-Polaroids are submitted. The size can be smaller but it is better to check with your local editor before submitting pictures. Often, the paper will assign a staff photographer to cover a specific assignment if the subject matter warrants it. Again, when selling your story it doesn't hurt to sell the idea that the story can be improved with pictures. You must, however, exercise some judgment. Don't try to heavily promote a story that isn't worth it. Your credibility with editors is very important. Protect it!

A legal point should be raised in conjunction with the use of photographs. If you ask a subject to pose, or film an individual in action, have the person or persons sign a "no payment rights" form to protect the library from a commercial rights claim. The form should make it clear that your subject has no objection to being photographed and allows the library to use the photograph in any and all ways the library chooses. Another legal consideration is the use of existing photographs, art work or video tapes that may be in the library's collection. Although the library may own the actual material, it may not own the rights to reproduce the work. A call to the town's legal officer or to a local attorney should give you a quick answer.

CONSIDER THE AIR WAVES

The printed page is only one way to spread your message. The local radio and TV stations can be extremely valuable assets in your marketing campaign. With the rapidly growing acceptance of cable television, the opportunities for libraries to take advantage of air time is better than ever.

In evaluating the best media for your library's marketing effort, it is important to place your news item or public service message in proper perspective. The announcement of a coming book fair could be covered in the spot news segment or as a public service announcement by your local radio station, but might not warrant consideration on television. The actual event, however, could make an interesting television spot. Thus, planning is an important element in deciding on the proper media for coverage and in designing the message itself. Broadcasting, like print journalism, offers several avenues of approach: the basic news story, public service announcement, longer broadcast "specials" devoted to a specific subject or format, and the visual story.

The major difference between broadcast news and print journalism is the depth of coverage. While print people usually include details in their reportage, the person behind the microphone has time only for the highlights of the story. Newsworthiness is the key when submitting a release to the broadcaster. The news release you send your local paper probably will not do. It should be shorter, more to the point and, if possible, written for a newscaster to use as a script.

The Public Service Announcement

For information concerning the library, the public service announcement is most appropriate. This brief message, designed to fit into a 15-60 second slot on radio or TV, can alert members of the community to an event, service or activity being planned by the library. The public service release is not a news story, a paid ad or an ongoing broadcast. It is simply a message that the local station may use at its discretion at various times during the broadcast day or week. (See Figure 9.3.)

Usually, the decision to use your release is made by the station manager. Thus, it pays to make contact with this person. A visit to the local station enables you to meet the station manager and discuss ways in which you can work with the station. As an information agency within the community you have a lot to offer the station. For example, your library's

Figure 9.3 Special Event Public Service Announcement

Subject: Movie ("Desk Set")
Public service announcement to be used
Monday, May 7th through Tuesday, May 16th

Organization
and address: _____

Contact:
(include your title
and phone number) _____

MOVIE: DESK SET, MAY 16th @ 8:00 P.M.

Announcement Time: 20 seconds
Number of Words: 51

ARE YOU A NOSTALGIA FAN? REMEMBER THOSE GREAT SPENCER TRACY, KATHERINE HEPBURN MOVIES? ONE OF THE BEST OF THEIR OLDIES—"DESK SET"— WILL BE SHOWN AT THE ROCK CITY PUBLIC LIBRARY ON TUESDAY EVENING MAY 16TH AT EIGHT IN THE EVENING. JOIN THE LOVERS OF YESTERYEAR AT THE MOVIE, "DESK SET."

reference department can provide background details to radio or TV reporters about events, or your library may contain a hard-to-find phonograph record that the station wants to use. Cooperation is an important element in developing an outlet for your message.

Your meeting with the station manager should provide information concerning format of releases and the type of material most likely to be broadcast. A tour of the facilities will give you a deeper insight into the workings of the station and emphasize your interest in a cooperative relationship. Assuming the role of listener or viewer, you can become familiar with the type of programming, the audience approach and the general character of the station.

When preparing your own public service announcement for the station, keep in mind what the listener or viewer can retain in 10, 20, 30 or 60 seconds. Limit your message to no more than two basic points. The rule of thumb for translating words into seconds for a radio announcement is:

10 seconds = 25 words	30 seconds = 75 words
15 seconds = 37 words	60 seconds = 150 words
20 seconds = 50 words	

When you write a public service message, it helps to use your library stationery. Use one sheet per release. Be sure your name, address and phone number are on the page. Include time limitations on the announcement. (You don't want a meeting announced the day after it is held.) Also, it helps to tell the announcer how many seconds the release will run when read on the air. Double or triple space your announcement.

In writing for the radio, keep in mind a few basic rules:

• Keep your sentences simple and your words descriptive.

• Stay away from words that are tongue-twisters or alliterative.

• Avoid long, no-pause sentences. Announcers like to breathe.

• Your initial words should be grabbers. Get the listener's attention first, then present the details of your message.

• Choose an informal and conversational style. Avoid being stiff or pedantic.

• If possible, repeat your message at least twice, using the same key words. A commercial for skin moisturizer repeats the name of the product eight times in 60 seconds.

• Don't overwrite. "Say it tight and make it right."

Finally, read the announcement to yourself—out loud. If you have a tape recorder, tape it and listen to the playback. Ask a colleague to comment on the message. Don't be afraid to rewrite, reread and retime until you have a script that delivers the message the way you want it.

138   ISSUES IN LIBRARY MANAGEMENT

Public service announcements are effective for promoting general library services, as well as specific events. Because they are not tied to a particular happening, they can be used at any time. Figure 9.4 illustrates sample messages of this type.

Figure 9.4   General Public Service Messages

20 seconds; 50 words
IF YOU'VE GIVEN UP READING BECAUSE BOOK PRINT IS TOO SMALL, LOOK AGAIN. YOUR LIBRARY HAS BEST SELLERS AND OLD FAVORITES IN THE LARGE PRINT FORMAT. AND YES, THEY'RE AS LIGHT IN WEIGHT AS REGULAR PRINT BOOKS. FOR YOUR READING PLEASURE VISIT THE PUBLIC LIBRARY FOR BOOKS IN LARGE PRINT.

10 seconds; 26 words
FIND OUT ABOUT BOOKS BY MAIL, A FREE SERVICE FOR PEOPLE LIVING IN RURAL AREAS. REGISTER AT YOUR NEAREST PUBLIC LIBRARY AND RECEIVE BOOKS BY MAIL.

15 seconds; 37 words
ENJOY VISITING MUSEUMS? EXTEND THE PLEASURE TO YOUR HOME, AT NO COST, BY BORROWING FRAMED ART REPRODUCTIONS FROM YOUR PUBLIC LIBRARY. REMBRANDT, CHAGALL, PICASSO, WINSLOW HOMER AND MANY OTHERS ARE WAITING FOR YOU. AT YOUR PUBLIC LIBRARY.

Source: Reprinted by permission of the author and publisher from Rita Kohn and Krysta Tepper, *You Can Do It: A PR Skills Manual for Librarians* (Metuchen, NJ: Scarecrow Press, Inc., 1981.) Copyright © 1981 by Rita Kohn and Krysta Tepper.

Preparing a Television Spot

If your community has a local broadcast or cable television outlet, another dimension is added to your library message—visual impact. This extra dimension means extra care has to be given to the choice of the message as well as to the method in which the message is presented. Obviously, a public service announcement with no visual impact potential should be avoided. Don't give up on television too quickly, however. A strong imagination can do wonders in developing visual images.

In most cases your message will not be a live or videotaped presentation, unless your library has access to video equipment and can produce its own tapes. A number of libraries own their own equipment, which they use for a wide variety of educational, informational and cultural programming; the same equipment may be used for public relations as well. In communities with cable TV franchises, libraries have access to use of one channel and often may receive instruction in the use of television equipment (see below).

However, still photos or color slides can also sell your message in a professional manner, assuming they are well shot and effectively organized. The most important aspect is still the message. Again, a tour of the local station and a meeting with the station manager or producer will open doors and provide you with information about the needs of the station. Don't be afraid to ask for help from station employees when you design your presentation.

There are a few basic differences between script preparation for radio and TV. The copy you write to accompany the visuals should be paced more slowly than radio copy because the viewer coordinates two senses—sight and sound. Thus, the ratio between words and seconds tightens. The TV ratio becomes:

    10 seconds = 20 words
    20 seconds = 40 words
    60 seconds = 125 words

The script must be closely coordinated with visuals, but your copy must not simply duplicate what is shown. The exception is when you are illustrating an address or phone number. Music can be used providing it is well chosen. Background sound must not interfere with the basic message you are delivering. In selecting music, it is a wise idea to first check with the local station. Since recorded music is copyrighted you may discover that a fee may be due ASCAP (American Society of Composers, Authors and Publishers, 1 Lincoln Plaza, New York, NY 10023).

Using Cable TV

The laws pertaining to cable television are in a state of flux. At present, the cable company that has a franchise to operate in your area must provide a public access channel and a local government access channel. The library qualifies for use of the government channel. Groups or organizations that use the library's facilities for their own presentations qualify for public access use. In either case, local cable air time is readily accessible and offers the creative librarian the opportunity to take advantage of programs presented by others in the library or to actually produce library programs for the community.

Cable television requires some knowledge of equipment and TV technology. Many cable companies, as part of their franchise agreement with the city, are committed to educating the public on using video equipment. Thus, an individual or two, selected by the librarian, has the opportunity to take courses in TV operation. Often the franchise agreement also states that company equipment may be borrowed by trained individuals. Television tapes must be purchased by the library and, like audio tapes, can be used many times. Tape cost, however, is substantially higher—as much as $40 for a two-hour tape, compared to about $6 for an audio version.

Kinds of Programs

Types of programs that can be presented via television are as varied as the interests of the library's patrons. Programs may include story hours for children, public debates on community issues, panel groups discussing new books, instructional courses (these can cover cooking, languages, exercise, auto repair, estate planning—let your imagination be your guide) and, of course, interviews.

When selecting individuals for an interview or for potential course instructors, look to community resources first. It is always possible to go outside the community to hire people, but chances are your community has plenty of home-grown talent available. Keep a card file of residents and their special talents and interests. This is a good way to keep track of potential "guests." In most cases your speaker will volunteer his or her services at no cost. If the library is in a university community or within driving distance of a college, there will be a wealth of talent covering special disciplines. Don't forget to check with your local school system for possible topics and guests.

Another source of guests is the book publisher. All major publishing houses want their authors to receive publicity and often arrange speaking tours that take authors to nearby communities. A letter to the publicity director stating your plans to tape author interviews may well bring you an unexpected guest.*

Conducting a TV Interview

As for the interview itself, there are a few basics to consider. The odds are that your library staff contains neither a Barbara Walters nor a Mike Wallace. However, the individual you select as an interviewer must have many of the same qualities as a network star. Looks aren't important; confidence in oneself and an awareness of the subject under discussion are. The following guidelines may help.

• Do your homework. If you're talking about a book be sure you have read it. Some things can't be faked.

• Know the person you're interviewing. Some personal insights not only enable you to frame your questions more succinctly but also generate an aura of friendliness between interviewer and interviewee.

• Use graphics when possible. Television is a *visual* medium and two people sitting around a table talking can become dull unless the subject is extremely interesting. When interviewing an author, you must have a copy of the book. If you are dealing with a subject that can be illustrated (travel, current events, movies, art, etc.) try to obtain either still photographs or slides that can be used during the interview. Don't try to incorporate film footage unless you have the expertise to do so.

• Decide well before the interview what format you want to follow. Jot down both subject areas and specific questions. If you plan a half-hour interview have enough material prepared to cover an hour. However, once you start your interview allow the topic under discussion to lead you in your questioning process. There is nothing worse than reading a series of questions, many unrelated, and expecting the individual being interviewed to provide continuity for you. Your program will sound and look like a press conference. You can be assured that the interviewee will provide an answer that will enable you to follow up with a

---

*Publishers' names and addresses can be found in *Literary Market Place* (NY: R.R. Bowker & Co., annual) and *U.S. Book Publishing Yearbook and Directory 1981-82* (White Plains, NY: Knowledge Industry Publications, Inc., annual).

question not on your list. This is fine and provides the spark of spontaneity that holds an audience.

Interactive Television

The development of two-way, or interactive, cable television has considerable potential for libraries. Through such systems, coupled with computers, home viewers can have direct access to library information resources. Although few applications exist as yet, the Qube system in Columbus, OH, has been in operation since 1977. Using Qube, the Public Library of Columbus and Franklin County has produced a monthly television program, "Home Book Club," which allows viewers to "talk back" and respond to discussions of current bestsellers. At the end of each show, readers/viewers may participate in selecting the next book for discussion. Through the same Qube system, viewers can also request that the next book be mailed to their homes.

Ultimately the library plans to make a variety of information services, including reference materials, community information files and data bases, available to Qube subscribers. The opportunity for enhancing a library's service to and image in the community through such programming is enormous.

MAINTAINING GOOD PRESS RELATIONS

The library's relationship with newspapers, radio and television is a two-way, continuing process. The media are looking for news, the library for publicity. The library PR individual must not only make a good initial contact with an editor or station manager, but must maintain a cooperative association. Two long-established, productive relationships may illustrate this point.

The Roddenbery Memorial Library in Cairo, GA, has offered a Saturday morning "Pied Piper Story Hour," with stories told by staff members or college students, on local radio since 1948. The library also works hard to maintain a cooperative association with the local newspaper. Librarian Wessie Connell reports:

> We go the extra mile and initiate activities which engender good will. . . . For example, with our newspaper, we furnish extra columns or fillers not merely on library news but on things of interest to the entire area. When the annual Rattlesnake Round-Up is held in a neighboring community in February, the editor is furnished a fact sheet on snakes by the library, and in the fall during the hurricane season, fact sheets on weather and cyclones are furnished the paper. Occasionally we list titles of relevant books.[2]

Another example of well-maintained media relations comes from the experience of W. Best Harris, city librarian in Plymouth, England:

> We started our program at Plymouth with the one effective tool we had, a good local history department. We used this material to produce at least one weekly story for one or more of the local newspapers, stories not concerned with the functions of the library but with the contents of the library.

We made it our business—as we still do—to keep local reporters informed of such things as anniversaries of local events and personalities; of anything on the local history scene that was unusual, especially if it could be illustrated by an old print or photograph; and of any new acquisition of local flavor. Over a period of the first two years we got to know many of the local reporters, and through them we learned what constituted a story, and what a journalist would be looking for. Equally important, we gained their confidence and started the process of making them believe that libraries offered good copy from time to time. We backed up these local history press stories with illustrated lectures offered free to any organization anywhere in the city.[3]

These examples point up another aspect of marketing the library through the media: events do not have to be specifically library-oriented to be part of the library's PR effort. As the information service agency in your community, your mandate is very broad. By keeping aware of community activities and working with the media, the opportunity to spread the library's message widely, inexpensively and frequently is ever present.

THE NEWSLETTER

Newspaper, radio and television publicity represents an outsider's reportage of library activities; the newsletter represents the voice of the library. Many items not covered by the press can be dealt with in considerable detail in the newsletter. In large libraries, there may be a variety of in-house published newsletters, some aimed at library patrons, others at the library staff.

In the case of library systems, newsletters can be used to communicate to member libraries. In early 1980, for example, the Public Libraries Section of the New York Library Association initiated a quarterly newsletter, *Public Relations Plus,** to share public relations ideas, successes and failures. In its first issue the newsletter described how the Mamaroneck (NY) Free Library distributed paperbacks to motorists waiting in gas lines, how another library helped to save the local newspaper and other activities.

In-house newsletters can also assist in educating staff members, informing them of changes in the library, policy matters and technical data. When the Chicago Public Library was in the process of converting to an automated circulation system, it launched a newsletter, *Data Processing News,* to keep staff members up-to-date on the progress of the switch-over as well as its implications. The newsletter is described as "a forum for communication, information, and problem exchange, new ideas and solutions." The library plans to keep publishing not only for the duration of the project but "for as long as we are growing and evolving into new and different forms of computer-assisted information access."[4]

Newsletters designed for the community must be informative, attractive and nontechnical. Avoid library jargon and the common buzz words so familiar to the professional librarian. Staff news should be omitted. Details on the workings of the library are also inappropriate, unless there is a change that will have a direct effect on the patron.

---

*Available free from: Public Information Department, Mid-Hudson Library System, 103 Market St., Poughkeepsie, NY 12601.

Before starting a newsletter, there are a few basic questions that should be considered:

• Assuming you have a need to communicate more effectively, is a newsletter the answer?

• If you are planning an in-house newsletter, will it be cost-effective?

• Will the information provided by the newsletter supplant or complement staff meetings?

• Is there enough money in the library budget to cover the cost of a newsletter? Are outside funds available to help defray costs?

• Is there enough information to justify a newsletter on a continuing basis?

The Role of the Editor

Once the decision is made to commit library or outside funds to a publications program, the next major decision is who will be responsible for overseeing the project. Someone who is interested, motivated and able to do the best job possible is needed. This individual, or editor, must have the full support and backing of the library director. Although the editor is usually a staff member, there is no reason why a reliable volunteer couldn't handle the job. The duties and responsibilities of the editor must be clearly understood by the director as well as the other librarians. The editor's job description must provide the responsibility and *authority* to set deadlines, solicit articles, arrange for photo sessions and make final decisions. Since money must be spent the editor must have a budget and the authority to use it.

The same qualities specified for the public relations specialist are needed by the newsletter editor. The editor must oversee, compile, write, edit, type and be prepared to be directly involved with the printing or mimeo process. A lot of busy work is involved: folding, stapling, stuffing envelopes, taking material to a printer, post office or film lab. In other words, the editor, too, wears many hats and is involved in many activities never suggested at library school.

The type and quality of information included in the newsletter demands an open-minded editor who understands the needs of the community and the library. As editor, the material covered must interest you or it won't interest others. An editor who concentrates on human events and activities is in a better position to capture the interest of the audience. Whether editing for an in-house audience or a large community one, the editor must have a clear picture of the audience.

Some specific story ideas that can be included in a newsletter have been suggested by Sally Brickman, of Case Western Reserve University Libraries:[5]

• Getting to know you—highlight staff and its accomplishments.

• Meetings and programs—when they are, who will speak, what issues. Follow-up in the next newsletter.

• Building plans.

• Book reviews, new and old books, book sales and interlibrary loan.

• What's new in library literature, organizations, papers and people.

• Letters from happy patrons and their suggestions; columns by the director and a roving reporter.

• Policy changes and new services.

• Consumer education, how-to articles, legislation.

• Special services: microfilm, microfiche, equipment available for rental, video tape programs, etc.

• *Avoid* personal issues about staff and patrons.

Budget Planning

Before starting a newsletter, determine well in advance the size of the newsletter, amount of copy or pictures required, the cost of printing or using the mimeograph machine and the cost of distribution. These elements will enable you to plan a budget. It's a good idea to add at least 10% to the final budget figure to cover inflation. In particular, the price of paper is rising at a rapid rate.

A hidden cost that many people erroneously consider part of the printing process is that of typesetting. Professional typesetting charges vary enormously; a minimum is about $15 per page. Some libraries own word processing equipment with typesetting features or may have access to word processors owned by other local organizations. The use of word processors simplifies editing and produces a professional looking newsletter at considerable savings. However, libraries without such equipment can still produce attractive and interesting "typography" by using a typewriter with interchangeable heads.

The format of the newsletter—physical size and number of columns—can vary according to the tastes of the editor. Most newsletters use an 8½-inch by 11-inch page. This will provide two columns of approximately 3¼ inches each or three columns of about 2¼ inches each. Photos can be contained in a single column or spread across several columns depending on the layout of the designer. Major stories can be run in two columns (using a three-column format), giving added importance to your message. If both sides of a standard 8½-inch by 11-inch sheet are used, there is room for about 1200 to 2000 words of copy (depending on type size), a logo or masthead and a blank one-third page for affixing an address and postage. If the newsletter is not to be mailed, this third of a page is used for additional copy.

With a printed newsletter, you can double the size without doubling the cost (although some increased cost will be incurred). To produce a four-page publication, each page 8½ by 11 inches, the printer uses a single sheet of paper measuring 8½ by 17 inches. The sheet is printed and folded in half. It is usually folded again in the shape of a folded business letter. The final publication can now be mailed in a standard number 10 envelope or used as a self-mailer.

Printing costs vary, of course, but are based on several factors, including the size of the newsletter, the quality of paper selected, the number of copies desired, and the number of colors used. When photographs are used, a glossy paper is more desirable than the less expensive bond. Newsprint is the least expensive. In estimating costs, the printer uses a fixed standard for his setup charges. These include making plates, preparing photos, inking the press and cleaning up the press after the print run. These setup charges are constant regardless of the number of copies run. Therefore, it is cheaper, on a per unit basis, to print a large number of copies.

Before choosing a printer, shop around and obtain comparative prices. The cost of printing varies greatly by regions as well as by individual printers within the same region. Table 9.1 reflects typical costs for printing an 8½- by 11-inch sheet of 20 pound white bond paper.

Table 9.1 Typical Newsletter Printing Costs

Number of Copies	1 color 1 side	1 color 2 sides	2 color 1 side	2 color on 1 side & 1 color on reverse side
1,000	$ 28	$ 51	$ 60	81
5,000	92	151	171	227
10,000	171	287	302	401

Source: Based on author's survey of printers in the New York area, June 1981.

One possible way to save money once you have decided on a printer is to offer to buy a six month or one year supply of paper in advance. Not only do you offset the increase in future paper prices, but you may get a discount by buying paper in bulk. These cost savings, however, must make up for the potential loss of income incurred by tying up your assets for this period of time.

Newsletter Design

The design of the newsletter is another important element. Since the newsletter is the representative of the library, it must portray the library in its best light. The newsletter must strive to obtain its own identity. This can be accomplished by the use of a well-designed masthead or logo. An eye-catching design is not easy to achieve. A simple, uncluttered look works best. Often, a local designer can be asked to develop a newsletter design on a voluntary or low-cost basis.

Instead of a formal design used as a logo, consider a photo or drawing of the library, an open book, the initials of the library arranged in an interesting pattern, etc. If an attractive masthead is used, there is no reason why a logo has to be included. The prime purpose of the design element is to draw attention to your product (the newsletter) and to assure recognition.

The use of a colored ink is another way to reinforce recognition, and the cost of colored ink is minimal. One major consideration, however, should be kept in mind: any photos used in the newsletter will appear in the same color as the ink selected. Also remember that certain colors have a negative effect on readability. Avoid reds and light colors against a white paper. Consider using color to highlight your logo and masthead—then print your body copy (including photos) in black. Keep in mind, however, that a two-color selection will increase printing costs since each sheet must be fed through the press twice—once for each color.

The masthead should include your library's name, location, volume, number and date. The newsletter title (*Library Views, Book News, Bookmark,* etc.) should be given the most prominence. (See Figure 9.5.)

If an experienced designer is not available, experiment with several styles and layouts before committing yourself to a final format. Try different arrangements incorporating boxes, borders, symbols and pictures. Drawings can be used as well as photographs. If you do select photographs, make them interesting. Show people in action. There is nothing duller than an individual standing next to a stack of books.

In preparing copy, apply the same basic rules for writing a press release. Start off with a catchy lead sentence. Get the reader's attention with your initial paragraph. Keep your paragraphs short, and try to eliminate unnecessary words. A headline, written as a complete sentence, is another attention getter. It's a good idea to read your own copy first, but another proofreading should be done by someone else. Check spelling, grammar and punctuation. A dictionary and thesaurus are good companions. A style manual is also helpful.

Distribution

In the original newsletter concept you undoubtedly had a specific audience in mind. Reaching that audience and delivering the finished, printed newsletter is another matter.

Distribution methods depend on the type of newsletter, size of the library budget and the nature and size of the community. A newsletter need not be mailed; personal distribution in the library can work very well. There should be a central distribution point where newsletters and other printed material (book marks, film schedules, policy statements, schedule of coming events, etc.) are readily available and highly visible. The circulation desk is an excellent place to distribute printed material. Often the librarian checking out books can sug-

Figure 9.5 Newsletter with an Eye-catching Masthead from the White Plains (NY) Public Library

DIRECTIONS

NEWS OF THE WHITE PLAINS LIBRARY **SUMMER 1981 / NO. 16**

The Pied Pipers!

Children love the warm and welcoming place that is the Children's Library, a world filled with books, records, toys to borrow, magazines and special things to do. What draws them back again and again is the unique group of people that makes up the staff — special people who are their special friends.

Sara Miller, who for eight years has been the head of children's services, is the catalyst that sparks this group. She has received professional recognition for her knowledge of children's literature and recently served a term as a member of the prestigious Newbery Medal Committee, which each year selects the best in children's books. She gives classes at Pace University and Manhattanville's Graduate School. Sara received her MLS from Columbia, and worked for several years at New York Public Library, serving a valuable apprenticeship with their eminent children's coordinator, Augusta Baker. She takes special pride in the "Alice Room," a research collection for serious students of children's literature, teachers, authors and illustrators, which houses landmark and prize winning children's books and reference material. Among her pet projects have been workshops on successful parenting and introducing children to books. Schoolchildren welcome her class visits, as she brings the many aspects of the Library to life and tells about the many marvelous activities she and the staff plan and present. "But" she says, "all these extras are icing on the cake, planned with only one goal in mind — to put a child and a book together!"

Librarian **Florence Modell** has that special flair for putting a child with just the right book. She received her MLS from Queens, after taking time out to raise her family, worked for a time as a school librarian and came to White Plains thirteen years ago.

(l-r) Sandy Sivulich, Gigi Avitabile, Lee Palmer, Jo Carpenter, Sara Miller (not pictured, Florence Modell, Edith Carpentieri).

Her love of children's books is contagious and she is as thorough as she is enthusiastic. A youngster who has an assignment on the Soviet Union will be led to books on Russian art, music, folklore and cooking, as well as fiction and background. Her "specialty" is books for the very young. She tells us, "Nothing is too good for a child. The best picture books are a blend of fine art and rhythmic prose." Among her "must reads" are the classic *Goodnight Moon* by Margaret Wise Brown, Beatrix Potter's *The Tale of Peter Rabbit* and Maurice Sendak's *The Nutshell Library.*

The newest member of the Children's Room Staff is **Sandy Sivulich**, who joined us as a part-time librarian in 1979. She received her MLS from Rosary College in River Forest, Ill., and worked in the Chicago area where she was active in professional library associations. Sandy, who has also served on the Newbery Medal Committee, taught children's literature and did hospital storytelling and library consulting in Erie, Pa., before moving here with her husband and small daughter two years ago. She particularly enjoys traditional storytelling, and has given workshops for parents, nursery school teachers and weekend storytellers in games, fingerplays and storytelling. Her Sunday Story Times, where youngsters bring teddy bears, rag dolls and stuffed animals are weekend highlights. A perennial favorite is her own version of *I'm Going On A Bear Hunt* (published by E.B. Dutton in 1973) where the youngsters "swim," "row" and "climb" with her through rough terrain to find that bear!

When youngsters enjoy our popular puppet shows, they are entertained by a talented team who, it's hard to believe, have 43 years of Children's Room experience among them!

Author and puppeteer **Lee Palmer's** job title reads "Storyteller," and she is the only official staff storyteller in Westchester. Young alumni of her popular Story Times who meet her in the supermarket or on the street are amazed to realize she doesn't live in her special purple chair in the Story Room, picture book in hand. Fifteen years ago, while working as a PTA volunteer in the Ridgeway School Library, she took a storytelling course at the Library and was asked to come on staff for "twenty minutes

(Pied-Pipers, continued p 2)

gest that the latest newsletter or other pertinent piece of literature be taken along with the armload of books. Another common location to distribute literature is at the library's entrance. A large slotted stand or table can be placed there to attract the attention of all who enter and leave the library.

On the other hand, selective mailings are very effective and increase the community's awareness of the library. Selecting the mailing list requires judgment. The cost of mailing is the single most expensive item in most newsletter publishing ventures. Even though the library qualifies for a special, nonprofit postage rate, bulk mailing still costs a few cents per recipient.

There are a few individuals and groups who should definitely be on your list. Certainly, any individual who specifically requests a copy should be included, as should members of a Friends of the Library organization. It is also a good idea to add key individuals in the community whose influence is important to the library. These should include all local government leaders, officers of local civic organizations, other libraries (including school, corporate and private) in the community and regional library organizations. Make sure all members of the library staff receive their personal copy—public relations begins at home.

It is a good idea to consider at least one community-wide mailing a year. If the community is a small one then you probably will be sending your newsletter to every family. In large cities and towns, this will probably be too expensive. However, by using a coupon or return card you can test local interest in your newsletter. Simply request those who want a free subscription to return the coupon. Coupons should also be easily accessible in the library.

Your list of subscribers should also include all cardholders. One problem is that there is usually more than one cardholder to a family. Sending multiple copies of the newsletter to a single address is expensive and can create a negative image. If possible, a special mailing list of cardholders should be prepared annually with the newsletter addressed to the "Smith Family."

Lists can be typed on special forms which, when used in most duplicating machines, will produce pressure-sensitive labels. Although this method requires a great deal of hand labor, it is probably more cost-effective than using computer-generated labels. If you plan to use several lists, be sure to code them to avoid duplication of mailings. For community-wide mailings, it is usually too expensive to prepare a special list of all families in your area. A call to the town, village or city clerk's office should let you know whether the list you need is already available. Since all municipalities have their own lists for tax purposes, it is possible to borrow or rent a computerized set of labels.

Locating apartment dwellers is another matter. Companies that sell mailing lists may be able to assist in assembling names of community members not available through the clerk's office. These list brokers will charge from $40 to $75 per thousand names. Often you may acquire a list of apartment houses by zip code rather than individual names. The list broker may suggest that the slug "occupant" or "resident" be used. These slugs are also computer-generated and can be included in the standard price, or are available at a slight additional charge.

Scheduling

Consideration must also be given to timing publication and mailing. If a special event is planned at the library, you should plan your mailing to assure maximum publicity. You should avoid sending your newsletter in the midst of the Christmas season, for example, when it can easily be lost under a pile of greeting cards. The summer is another time to avoid if many members of the community are away on vacation. In many areas of the country the first week of a month is "bill week." The psychological disadvantage of having your newsletter delivered with a host of bills should also be considered.

Once the decision is made as to the frequency of publication, it is important to hold to your schedule. If people know when to expect the newsletter they will begin to look forward to receiving library information on an established schedule. Scheduling also makes it much easier for the newsletter's editor to assign articles, edit and plan printing and mailing.

Funding the Newsletter

Funding the newsletter is always an important consideration during these times of tight budgets and high interest rates. Consider community fundraising efforts for the sole purpose of publishing a newsletter. Money from a library book fair, sale of books that have been weeded from the collection, or library special events for which an admission fee is charged are other possible fundraising options. Perhaps the most common source of funds for newsletters is a Friends of the Library group.

Before seeking money from the Friends, the community or any civic group, it is important to determine in advance a full year's costs. A full budget, with costs spread out on a month-by-month basis, should be prepared. Since there will be little, if any, editorial costs involved, major expenditures will be for printing and mailing. These costs can be estimated quite accurately once you have established the number of copies to be printed and the number to be mailed. These amounts won't be identical since you will want a supply of newsletters in the library to be used as handouts. Include in your cash estimate the following costs: list rental, indicia (plus annual mail permit), envelopes if a self-mailer is not used, mailing house charges for affixing labels and stuffing envelopes, postage and a miscellaneous category that covers items such as film, pencils, pens, typewriter ribbons, photocopying charges, posterboards for preparing mechanicals, etc.

THE ANNUAL REPORT

Another publication that enables the library to get its message across to the public is the annual report. Its purpose, design, theme and audience vary greatly. For some, the annual report is published for the edification of a specialized public—trustees, library staff and legislators. For others, the report is another way to reach patrons and nonlibrary users with the message that the public library is a community resource operated by a dedicated group of information specialists. In addition, the report serves as a vehicle of accountability to the public.

What is the library doing with public funds? How is the taxpayer benefiting? The report gives the library the chance to pat itself on the back. In the process of telling the public what a good job the library is doing, the report can also increase staff pride in its work.

Establishing a Theme

Many annual reports contain basic circulation data from the previous year, number of new library cards issued, reference calls received, etc. However, there are also many annual reports that are based around a central theme. A new building addition, an important anniversary, the retirement of a major community public figure, or the need for new services or important equipment can serve as themes. Other themes cover goals and accomplishments of the previous year or aspirations for the forthcoming year, recent major acquisitions, new programs, community involvement, etc. The theme should be expressed by the title, and carried out consistently throughout the text.

Some interesting themes have been found in the annual reports of public libraries in recent years. The Public Library of Youngstown and Mahoning County (OH) published an annual report entitled "Thanks to Everyone," basing its theme around a successful library fundraising effort. A report published by the Hunterdon County Library, Flemington, NJ was entitled "Yours for only $2.38." The theme referred to the per capita tax revenue spent by community members on library services.

It is helpful to review what other libraries are doing, so send for copies of annual reports published by neighboring libraries as well as libraries of comparable sizes in other parts of the country. Also look at the annual reports published by business organizations. Obviously, the public library can little afford the luxury of a lavish, four-color report like those produced by IBM, General Motors or Eastman Kodak. However, the ideas expressed in both style and coverage may be worth considering. For example, the Harland Co., which supplies checks and checkbooks to bank customers, designed its annual report in the shape and format of a wallet-sized checkbook. A library's annual report can show the same imagination. The New Orleans Public Library, in a city renowned for its French restaurants, recently designed its annual report to resemble the menu of an elegant New Orleans restaurant. (See Figure 9.6.)

Most library public relations specialists have developed the theme of an annual report well in advance of production time. Ideas can spring from meetings with staff members, the director, trustees, Friends or from reports published by other libraries. It helps to develop an idea file or folder in which you can place random bits of useful information accumulated over the year. Collect attractive layouts from brochures and pamphlets, unusual reference questions, letters or phone calls from patrons that highlight various aspects of library services, library statistics, photographs taken in the library, etc.

The annual report should emphasize the major aspects of your library's services—the collection, personnel, individuals and groups served, special events and activities. When you mention staff, board or community participation in library activities, you are emphasizing community awareness of the library and the services it performs.

Figure 9.6 Front Cover and Sample Page from the New Orleans Public Library Annual Report

Figure 9.6 Front Cover and Sample Page from the New Orleans Public Library Annual Report (Cont.)

MENU

APPETIZERS

Art Exhibit Quiche
Central Library and branches showcase original work by artists in the community, providing an outlet through which patrons can become familiar with the art and culture of their communities.

Women's Night Canape
A weekly forum addressing women's issues and interests through programs of cultural, political, social and personal significance. Both men and women are invited to participate.

Tossed Afro-American History Month
This Bicentennial February exploded with a Black Experience Film Festival at four library locations, a lecture series at one branch, Dashiki and Free Southern Theatre performances, and Danny Barker and his jazz band at all library locations.

Securities and Investing (in season)
Popular lecture and discussion series conducted by local stockbrokers held at various library locations.

Lump Open House Cocktail
The Central Library opened its doors one Sunday in May to an afternoon of continuous programming on all three floors simultaneously. This event was designed to highlight, through live presentation, the varied resources of the NOPL.

Marinated French Arts Festival
Algiers Regional Branch hosted a month-long festival of weekly films, concerts and slide-lectures, immersing patrons in the historic culture of France.

Films du Jour with Chitterlings
Full-length Shakespeare films, The Six Wives of Henry VIII, The Spoils of Poynton, a weekly lunch hour film festival at Central, and films for children were offered throughout the system.

Producing the Report

The production schedule for the annual report will be determined mainly by the intended date of publication. This is often timed to coincide with the library's annual meeting or the beginning of a fiscal year.

The amount of time required to produce the report will vary with the number of staff members available to work on the project, the size of the report and the budget. The Public Library of Cincinnati and Hamilton County (OH) starts two months prior to publication date. The production of the Lorain (OH) Public Library annual report takes Betty Piper, public relations specialist, about "one month, from my conference with the director to finished copy. But I work on other things between times too."[6]

The size, design and number of copies produced will depend in large part on the size of your budget. Often the Friends or a business organization in the community will sponsor the annual report. If these outside funds are not available, costs must be paid from the library's public relations budget. The same cost considerations that apply to newsletter production, previously discussed, apply here. Remember that the message is most important and that a simple report can serve the purpose. It isn't necessary to produce an annual report in the style of A.T.&T.

In designing the annual report, keep in mind that a cluttered page will lose your audience quickly. Keep your presentation uncomplicated. A simple cover and brief headlines with a few large illustrations may be all that is required to capture the reader's attention. Avoid in-house library jargon such as loan transactions, search techniques, interlibrary loan, COM, LC, etc. By preparing the copy in advance, it is much easier to plan a layout. Cutting material if the layout is too tight is simpler than adding "puff" that fools no one and will dilute your message.

Distributing the Report

A good looking annual report has little, if any, impact if it is not distributed to the core audience that is so important to the library. This group should include members of the library board, city council or other local government officials, advisory committees, Friends, staff and, of course, your users. Other groups to consider include community leaders, state and federal legislators, executives of major corporations in the area, and representatives of local schools and other educational institutions. Since the individuals on your core list may fluctuate periodically, your list should be reviewed each time your annual report is published.

In addition to supplying information to the core group and community, the annual report also provides an excellent opportunity for press releases to local papers and radio/TV stations. A copy of the report should accompany the release, and it should be stated that extra copies of the report are available at no charge from the library. It is also possible to increase public awareness of the report and the library by offering extra copies of your annual report to such individuals and organizations as clubs, supermarkets, banks, doctors and local realtors. If your community has a Welcome Wagon, copies of the annual report, as well as other library publications, should be made available.

CONCLUSION

The library's marketing specialist must take advantage of all available resources to communicate with patrons and all members of the community who influence the library's future. The use of press releases, newsletters, radio and TV announcements and annual reports are among these resources. Although cost must be a factor in deciding how best to spread the word, the cost to the library of failing to sell its services may be far higher.

FOOTNOTES

1. Edward J. Montana Jr., "Public Relations for the Metropolitan Library," in *Public Relations for Libraries*, ed. Allan Angoff (Westport, CT: Greenwood Press, 1973), p. 19.

2. Wessie Connell, "Public Relations in the Small Public Library," in *Public Relations for Libraries*, ed. Allan Angoff (Westport, CT: Greenwood Press, 1973), p. 78.

3. W. Best Harris, "Public Relations for Public Libraries," *Assistant Librarian* 64 (February 1971): 18.

4. *Library Journal* 105 (February 15, 1980): 2370.

5. "Prepare: The Library Public Relations Recipe Book," mimeographed (Preconference publication of the Public Relations Section, Library Administration Division, American Library Association, 1978), p. 9.

6. Ibid., p. 41.

10

Marketing Academic and Special Libraries
by Benedict A. Leerburger

Academic libraries and the host of libraries serving the needs of business, government, research organizations and other special-interest groups have many of the same marketing needs and problems as the public library. The need for funding is ever present, as is the need to educate the "community" (e.g., students and faculty, managers, researchers) that the library is its vital information center.

Although many of the same problems exist in both public and nonpublic libraries, there are elements unique to the nonpublic library. The constant threat of loss of tax revenue from a municipal government is absent. (Government libraries and public colleges, however, are concerned about financial aid from government coffers.) The potential problem of community pressure groups is usually lacking. Although the academic library will undoubtedly feel pressure from various school departments to enhance a special collection or subject area, in many cases these pressures are not only manageable but should be encouraged. Faculty are likely to better appreciate the importance of the library if they work with librarians to develop acquisitions policies that meet the needs of their departments.

Nonpublic libraries have their own financial pressures. While academic libraries do not have to prove the necessity for their existence (one could hardly run an educational institution without a library), they do have to compete with other educational resources for steadily eroding funds. Special libraries, or information centers, in profit-making organizations must compete with other departments for the company dollar. And the costs of operating a library or information center are rising rapidly, particularly in institutions that offer sophisticated computer services.

Thus nonpublic libraries must pay attention to marketing. They must increase their level of service to their institutions and must ensure that their parent organizations recognize their value and respond to their needs. In an academic setting, this means communicating with faculty, administration, governing boards and alumni, as well as students. In

---

Reprinted from *Marketing the Library* (White Plains, NY: Knowledge Industry Publications, Inc., 1982).

other special libraries, it means gaining the ear of top management, as well as researchers and other personnel who make more direct use of library services.

BASICS OF ACADEMIC LIBRARY PROMOTION

The academic library should develop the same type of public information program as the public library. However, since the academic library's "patron" can be more clearly defined, the question "Who should I tell my story to?" becomes much simpler. For example, it is obvious that the school administration—the group that pays the bills—must know whenever the library prepares an important new exhibit or display, publishes a major bibliography, acquires special equipment or receives a bequest. Similarly, the faculty (often drawn to a school or university because of the resources of the library) must be kept informed. George S. Bobinski, of the School of Library Science, University of Kentucky, suggests that "Academic librarians could well use the mail to welcome incoming new faculty—even before they arrive on campus. They could be provided information about the library and asked for reading lists and other library needs months in advance of their arrival on campus."[1]

The largest patron group, of course, is made up of students, and the best way to communicate with them is through the school newspaper. A periodic column written by a library staff member or public information specialist can be very effective. A meeting between the library director and the editor of the school paper may lead to the assignment of a student reporter to cover library affairs. Having a reporter include the library as part of his or her beat will help to spread news of library activities still further.

The campus radio and television station are other outlets that should be investigated by the aggressive library public information specialist. Book reviews, author interviews, literary discussions or debates involving students and faculty, new book announcements, etc., are all items that lend themselves to an audio or visual format.

The library director should assign a staff member the responsibility of working with the various campus media outlets. The individual must be knowledgeable about student and faculty interests and problems, as well as about library operations. Often the choice of a student aid (perhaps one majoring in communications) can work in the library's best interest.

Reaching Faculty Members

With the continued development of new technologies, it is increasingly important for the academic librarian to develop marketing programs directed toward faculty members. For example, many scholars, used to old-fashioned research techniques, are totally unaware that their own library has a computer-based information retrieval service that can create a tailored bibliography in hours instead of months. Some schools have adopted the position that library skills are as important an element in a student's total education as any major course of study. Although this trend is not catching the imagination of many educators, a good library-faculty liaison can encourage integration of library skills as an instructional element.

Developing a formal program to establish a liaison between the library and academic departments has been tried successfully at several institutions. Dr. Laurence Miller, who established a liaison program while director of the University Library, East Texas State University, defines liaison work as:

> ... a formal, structured activity in which professional library staff systematically meet with teaching faculty to discuss stratagems for directly supporting their instructional needs and those of the students. Such individual conferences can be general in purpose or have a specific objective such as orientation to a new service. Liaison work can be a part-time or full-time activity. In either case it differs fundamentally from the patterns of occasional contacts that have always been made and sometimes initiated by librarians.[2]

Developing a liaison program does require a library staff with able personnel and, perhaps more importantly, personnel interested in the program. The staff must have the time to devote to the function. Since in many cases time can be equated with money, some libraries are unable to devote as much effort to such a program as they would like.

The librarian serving as a liaison must do more than use the opportunity to "sell" the latest in library services. It is just as important to listen to comments, complaints, requests and general suggestions that may lead to improved library service. Once these suggestions have been voiced, it is equally important for the liaison person to report them to the appropriate person within the library. To be told by the chairperson of the psychology department that increased acquisitions of psychology periodicals should be a top priority, and to let that request be ignored, will result in counterproductive public relations. The request should be passed on to the serials librarian for evaluation. A letter or memo from the serials librarian to the chairperson of the psychology department, acknowledging receipt of the request, would serve to improve the library's image. Even if all requests cannot be honored (and it's safe to assume that they cannot), an explanation as to why a certain request cannot be granted and an invitation from the librarian to keep the dialogue flowing will show the library's interest in maintaining communications.

To assure a smooth liaison effort, it is also most important that the library's internal communications are open. The liaison librarians must be kept informed of activities occurring in all parts of the library. According to Miller,

> Liaison work is one of the few potential effective methods we have to make an impact on the problem of the nonuser. At the same time, it can assist in maintaining the library's viability as the primary campus information agency. It is, however, a method that is vulnerable and one that requires continuous follow-up, excellent internal communications between those who are involved and those who are not, sustained interest, and a willingness to share and learn from experience within a given academic setting.[3]

David Taylor, director of the Robert B. House Undergraduate Library, University of North Carolina, Chapel Hill, has taken the concept of keeping the faculty informed a step further. During the school year the library publishes a monthly newsletter directed to the faculty. (See Figure 10.1.) Articles are devoted to two broad library-related areas: specific information about the school library and general information about national library trends,

Figure 10.1 University of North Carolina Library — Faculty Newsletter

LIBRARY NOTES

University of North Carolina Library

Chapel Hill   27514
ISSN: 0468-5725

June, 1981   No. 406

The Information Explosion and the Library

The Least Publishable Unit

The Least Publishable Unit (LPU) is a phenomenon only recently encountered in scholarly literature, especially in medicine and biology. LPU is a name given to a tendency of authors to fragment a piece of research into the maximum number of articles. These may be a short article on a project with preliminary results followed soon by a final report. Or a study of several variables relating to a disease may be separated into three or four papers and published in different journals.

The cause of the LPU appears to be the "Publish or Perish" syndrome. The more published articles that can be gotten out of a research project, the better for the author. But not the better for the library and the indexer and the reader.

As William J. Broad explains in the March 13 issue of Science, "This fragmentation contributes to a host of problems, not the least being the sheer growth of the literature. One estimate holds that Index Medicus for 1985 will weigh more than 1 ton." (Science vol. 211, 13 March 1981, p. 1137) It certainly makes the work of the researcher more difficult when he must run down several references only to find that many duplicate the data of others. It makes the job of the teacher and the student more difficult when several articles with only shades of different information must be read and digested to understand a mechanism that might have been documented in one well-rounded article.

Robert W. Buddemeier and Jesse Roth, writing in the May first issue of Science, point out other factors causing the LPU. Some funding agencies dictate time tables for research projects, including publication of results. As journals and fields proliferate, authors who want diverse specialists to read their research must publish in different journals catering to those specialties. The journal editors themselves may contribute to the LPU because of their rigid impositions of space limitations. (Science vol 212, 1 May 1981, p. 494)

Suggestions for curing the LPU do not sound encouraging. Careful reviewing could abort an article that is only slightly different from one already published, but how can every reviewer know all the literature that intimately or be aware of manuscripts accepted but not yet published by another journal? Reviewers could also be sensitive enough to see that a paper was not a complete report of a research project and send it back to the author, but that is even less likely to be one hundred percent effective. Committees reviewing credentials could also take developments, new technology and information that could affect the faculty. During the summer, the library publishes a single issue, usually devoted to a single topic or theme, e.g., "Services to Support Teaching."

Reaching the Students

A library can devise many special programs to make students more aware of library services and needs. Sometimes a program can involve a large portion of the student body. For example, George Bobinski writes of a college library director who persuaded student leaders to help the library raise funds for books and staff.

> A special student library committee was formed, and they in turn persuaded a student body of 3000 to assess themselves $10 each toward the library book budget. The result was not only an additional $30,000 for library books, but also convincing and embarrassing evidence to local college officials and the state legislature that more money had to be found for all state university library units. The following year it was found.[4]

One imaginative program, based on a concept tested successfully at Colby College in the 1950s, also involves the entire student body. In this project, a library-student-faculty committee selects a basic list of about six books (classics or contemporary titles) and urges all students to read them. Students can then elect a single title as the following year's "Book of the Year." Teachers in relevant departments might integrate the book into the curriculum. If the author is living, he or she may be invited to the campus. The publisher's representative might also be asked to speak about the work. The library, naturally, becomes a focal point in these programs. Other works by the author may be displayed, and a special bibliography on related subjects may be prepared.

This kind of program is obviously most suited to a small college. Larger institutions, however, have many other opportunities for creative marketing to students. Two notable programs are those of the Robert B. House Undergraduate Library at the University of North Carolina and the Milton S. Eisenhower Library at Johns Hopkins University.

In addition to its faculty newsletter, mentioned above, the Robert B. House library publishes a student newsletter. If there is a story the director feels should also be covered by the student daily newspaper, a call to the editor usually brings a student reporter. (Unlike many student newspapers, the paper at the University of North Carolina will not accept press releases. The paper serves as a training tool for journalists, and the editors believe that the best stories are obtained by having reporters do their own fact-gathering.)

Like many colleges, the University of North Carolina includes a brochure about the library in the orientation packet distributed by the student government. North Carolina, however, does considerably more. All students enrolled in a freshman English program, for example, go to the library during a class period for a formal slide presentation and a tour of the library's facilities. Uses of reference materials, periodicals, search services and special collections are explained. The students are also taught how to use the stacks. (*Playboy Magazine* has singled out the library at the University of North Carolina as "the best place to meet students of the opposite sex." Another interesting way to market the features of an academic library?)

One of the more interesting services of the Robert B. House Library is its Term Paper Consultation Program. Any student preparing a research paper can sign up for a one-on-one session with a reference librarian to discuss the student's project and specific reference needs. A student learns how to prepare his or her own bibliography, how to locate specific periodical citations and, in general, how to take maximum advantage of the resources of the library. The individual clinic serves to build a student's confidence in accomplishing library-related work and to erase the age-old stigma of the library as a stuffy place containing books that nobody can find. Most important, by bringing students and librarians together in the freshman orientation program (which reaches about 90% of all freshmen) or the Term Paper Consultation Program, the library is making its presence felt on campus and convincing students and faculty that it is indispensable.

The Milton S. Eisenhower Library at Johns Hopkins University takes a different approach in marketing its services. In addition to preparing standard descriptive material for the university handbook given to all faculty and students, Susan K. Martin, the library's director, has turned to paid advertising. The library bought a two-page center spread in the student paper to describe the features of the library, outline the many services available and publicize the hours of operation. The Eisenhower Library also sends press releases to the student paper, but the two-page paid spread is far more eye-catching than an editorial column.

Library Director Martin is considering other marketing techniques aimed at students. On the drawing board is a special reception designed for incoming freshmen and new transfer students to meet the members of the library staff and learn about the library's vast resources. Ms. Martin is also considering a self-guided tour of the library in which new students would be given maps containing information about the library's highlights. Numbers on the map would correspond to numbers placed in key areas within the library.

The library currently provides basic library orientation for all freshmen through a student group. Unfortunately, according to Ms. Martin, most freshmen have already visited the library during their initial visits to the university and believe that when they begin school "they know all about the library and what we can offer them." Marketing the academic library to the student body is a most difficult chore when dealing with ambivalence or a know-it-all attitude. Thus, there is an attempt to involve student leaders in the library's marketing campaign through orientation programs involving upperclassmen, the use of the student newspaper and the involvement of student library aids who maintain a positive attitude about the library and its services.

Reaching the Library Staff

A successful marketing effort begins with the library's own staff. According to Eli Oboler, "What should be the most common and important regular publication of any academic library with at least five staff members is a regularly issued—preferably monthly —staff bulletin. It can be an invaluable adjunct to library public relations."[5]

The use of staff newsletters will serve the library in many ways. In a panel discussion at the American Library Association's 1980 annual conference, Sally Brickman, of the Case Western Reserve University Library, identified two basic purposes of the newsletter: It informs the staff of current library happenings, new developments and news directly related to library personnel, and it provides a permanent record of library events and developments. Each issue of her newsletter contains an interview with a library employee, thereby adding a more personal note.

Ms. Brickman, who reports to the library director and acts as an unofficial liaison with the staff, believes the newsletter meets four basic objectives:

• Creates an awareness of the library's goals.

• Keeps the library staff informed of library-related events within the library and outside.

• Increases the effectiveness of staff members, resulting in increased productivity.

• Encourages a favorable staff attitude towards the library as well as fellow staff members.

Joanne R. Euster, director of the San Francisco State Library, has analyzed the role of staff public relations in a way that should be of interest to academic librarians. Ms. Euster defines three basic functions of a staff public relations program: 1) To provide feedback to the library or organization from the staff; 2) To help the organization determine what it must do to obtain the goodwill and cooperation of all members of the staff; 3) To plan and implement means of achieving that goodwill and cooperation.

> People should feel good about their work. However, to do their job well employees need enough information to understand their individual job and also to know how that job fits into the overall job of the library or organization. . . . [Staff public relations] is in part an activity and in part an organizational style and philosophy. The underlying principle to make staff public relations work must be a certain permeability of the organization; a basic assumption that the sharing of information and knowledge is good for the library. This is, in large part, a matter of leadership style.[6]

To ignore the staff in favor of full concentration on selling the library to patrons and potential benefactors can be a disastrous road to follow. Keeping staff members fully informed and enthusiastic about current and future library developments will assist the director in the overall marketing program.

DISPLAYS AND EXHIBITS

Creating displays and exhibits is an essential element in promoting the academic library. Current topics or celebrations of events such as United Nations Week, the 250th anniversary of Haydn's birth, the centennial of the state, city, school, etc., are ideal opportunities for a display. There are several excellent sources for finding appropriate dates:

A. Black and C. Black, *Writers and Artists Yearbook* (Boston, MA: Writer, Inc., annual).

William D. and Helen M. Chase, comps., *Chases' Calendar of Annual Events* (Flint, MI: Apple Tree Press, annual).

Miriam A. DeFord, *Who Was When?*, 3rd ed. (Bronx, NY: Wilson, 1976).

Linda Millgate, *The Almanac of Dates* (New York: Harcourt Brace Jovanovich, Inc., 1977).

Some examples of displays presented by the Idaho State University Library may be of interest to others in planning:

Tomorrow's Careers
Western Books
That's a No-No! Drugs, Liquor, Marijuana and Tobacco
The Defense of America
The Arts in Flux; Art, Drama, Music, Film, Television
The End of the Empires
The British Museum and Its Publications
Prehistoric Fauna and Flora
Brazil: A World in Itself
America the Un-Beautiful: Why Conservation?

The American University Today
Christ and Revolution
Books from Down Under
America's Black Writers
The Sea: Its Poetry and Practicality
Gems, the Uncommon Stones
Law Enforcement
Japan in the World Picture
New Life for American Cities
Help for Small Business
The Challenge of Crime
100 Years of the Weather Bureau

Staff and Student Resources

In developing a topic for display, it is wise to consult department chairpeople to determine areas that may be of special interest and to solicit materials that may be held by individuals. A professor who has a private collection of books, artifacts, art objects, etc. is usually delighted to lend his collection for a library display. Often special departmental libraries (located apart from the general university library) will contain materials that should be included in a major library exhibit. Museums in various academic departments contain items that should be considered as well.

Naturally, the school's art department should be consulted on topics that involve art or graphics, or for assistance in designing the exhibit. Talented art students may be available as contributors. For example, Sterling Memorial Library, Yale University, takes frequent advantage of its students' artistic output. Drawings or book illustrations created by students are often shown in a display case adjacent to rare book illustrations borrowed from Yale's Beinecke Library (rare book and manuscript collection.) Many libraries use student artists to create posters to advertise and supplement a display.

The technique for planning and undertaking an academic library display will not vary too much from the basic format of planning and carrying out a public library exhibit. There are a few differences, however. The availability of student talent, mentioned above, is one. Also, in most cases, the academic library will have greater resources at its disposal to combine various materials into a fairly elaborate and unified display. Finally, faculty consultation makes it easier to obtain accurate and interesting signs and other informative notices to accompany an exhibit.

Publicizing the Exhibit

Publicity is as important to an exhibit in the academic library as it is in the public library. Many of the techniques described for public libraries are applicable and should be used to communicate with campus media. If you wish to attract visitors from outside the school, be sure to include local papers and broadcasting stations in your promotion effort. A notice should also appear in the campus weekly calendar. Posters or mimeographed announcements should be placed on the main student bulletin board (usually located in the Student Union), fraternity and sorority houses, dormitories, dining rooms and other campus buildings that provide bulletin board space for general announcements. Posters and announcements should also be displayed in prominent areas in town. Local bookstores, for example, are often eager to cooperate with academic libraries. Consider developing a special format for posters (such as The XYZ Library Presents . . .) to provide a recognition factor.

Whenever possible, a schedule of forthcoming exhibits and displays should be distributed to school and town media. Let the various news outlets have the opportunity to plan to cover your exhibits. You may be requested to provide background information, including pictures, concerning the development of a particular show.

Exhibits and displays serve as attractive, decorative show pieces, as well as educational aids. Most important, they bring people to the library. By preparing a book list or suggested bibliography, the librarian is ready with necessary back-up material for the individual who gets "turned on" by the display and wants to know more. By getting the right book in the hands of the right person, the library is accomplishing one of its primary goals.

ACADEMIC FRIENDS AND ALUMNI GROUPS

Developing good public relations can also be accomplished through an academic Friends of the Library group. Not only do Friends help to promote library events, but they can be most influential in periodic fundraising efforts. According to Eli M. Oboler,

> Perhaps the zenith in American "Friends" groups is the one at Brandeis University, which for many years, through various schemes for raising money, has provided practically all the regular book purchase support for the library there. But this is an unusual, probably unique, situation, not likely to be a national model. Still, it indicates just how far such a group can go if it is dedicated.[7]

Usually, Friends organizations are composed of alumni who try to locate special collections or individual books that are needed by the library but are hard to acquire through regular acquisition channels because of their high cost. Keeping alumni aware of the library's special interests is one way to build the collection. Another is to publicize any major gift of an individual's papers, thereby encouraging other donations.

In soliciting a gift of an individual's papers, be careful not to suggest that the gift may represent a substantial tax savings. While the donation of stocks, bonds, works of art, etc. may have an exact value placed upon them that is acceptable to the Internal Revenue Service, placing a dollar value on personal papers for tax purposes can be difficult. The library should suggest that the gift of manuscripts or personal papers be made with proper legal consultation and accompanied by the necessary legal papers. In addition, certain gifts of private papers are closed for a period of time, at the donor's request, to protect the privacy of the giver or contemporary associates. These various caveats should be clearly spelled out and, of course, observed.

Friends and other academic groups or alumni associations can also be very helpful in fund raising. All college alumni are familiar with the annual letter appealing for funds. Rarely does the library become involved in a direct appeal to alumni for funds. Often a separate appeal by the library can muddy the waters when the various alumni associations are campaigning for the college. Usually, funding for the library from alumni sources should be coordinated with the university's alumni office and not conducted separately.

Alumni-organized book sales have been popular methods of raising money for the library. Perhaps the largest academic book sale is the annual event conducted for the libraries of Brandeis University. The annual sale is held under two large circus tents in a shopping center parking lot in Wilmette, IL. The sale, organized by members of the North Shore Brandeis National Women's Committee, raised nearly $150,000 in May 1981. More than 25,000 book buyers flooded the area, looking for that rare first edition or simply to pick up last year's best sellers for under a dollar. A Hemingway first edition was sold for $3, a complete encyclopedia for $25.

Volunteers prepare for next year's Brandeis sale the day following this year's sale. Books are stored and sorted in a rented warehouse during the year and placed in predetermined aisles well in advance of the first customer's entrance. Maps are printed to assist the bargain hunters find their way among the books. The sale, first held in 1958, attracts people from miles around. One 1981 buyer, Phyllis Erickson of Bettendorf, Iowa, owns her own book store. She acquired 250 books to help boost her store's stock. Said another book sale patron, "This thing's a fixture. You can't walk through the tent without seeing someone you know."[8]

SPECIAL COLLECTIONS

The acquisition of manuscripts, rare books, papers, photographs, etc., is a constant goal of academic libraries. As noted above, Friends' groups can be helpful in acquiring additions to a collection. Sometimes a more elaborate marketing effort is needed, particularly if a collection is of broad scope. A particularly interesting example of a special collection that was made possible by aggressive marketing is the oral history collection at Columbia University, in New York.

The concept originated with Columbia historian Allan Nevins, who in 1948 started to build his own private oral history collection of major figures in the arts, government, sciences, education, business and other areas. Eventually the project became too big for one person. With the aid of funds from the Lucius N. Littauer Foundation, plus full cooperation from the university, an important research center began. Today Columbia's oral history collection is the largest and, perhaps, the most important in the world. Yet no funding came from the general income of the university. Gifts and bequests from individuals, grants from public and private agencies, plus support from the library's Bancroft fund underwrote the project (now the Oral History Research Office, Columbia University).

It took a massive public relations effort to convince foundations, individuals and the university that an oral history collection was a worthwhile undertaking. The promotional campaign was organized by the project's late director, Dr. Louis M. Starr. It received a significant boost when Dr. Starr sold the rights to distribute microform transcripts of the collection to the New York Times Co. Royalties from this arrangement continue to help the project to operate.

Special collections themselves can be viewed as a marketing tool. A major collection will draw researchers from many other institutions and will be publicized in scholarly journals and via word of mouth. The library can benefit greatly from this exposure.

Leading academic libraries have numerous special collections. At Harvard University, for example, the central collection alone (that is, not including library divisions serving primarily the schools of business, divinity, medicine, architecture and others) includes the Hofer Graphic Arts Collection, the Keats Memorial Collection, the Theodore Roosevelt Collection, the Trotsky Archive, and more than 50 author collections ranging from Aristophanes to Thomas Wolfe.

Smaller libraries also have special collections that bring them wide recognition. Many collections reflect the interest of a university department or the history of the region. For example, the libraries at both Haverford and Swarthmore colleges have built extensive book and manuscript collections on the history of the Quaker movement, which has been important in that area of Pennsylvania. Similarly, the William Bennett Bizzell Memorial Library at the University of Oklahoma has developed one of the nation's finest collections devoted to American Indians.

Academic libraries sometimes work with other institutions, particularly state libraries, to develop complementary special collections. To complement the University of Oklahoma's American Indian collection, for example, the state library in Oklahoma City has built upon the university's collection and the Oklahoma State Historical Society has accumulated many unique documents relating to the American Indian. (Its collection of Indian constitutions, for example, is extremely rich.)

One of the nation's finest state historical libraries is the State Historical Society Library in Madison, WI, which has a world-famous collection of materials on labor history and social action groups. Several hundred yards from the State Historical Society Library is the University of Wisconsin–Madison Memorial Library. Rather than develop competing collections, these two superb facilities work in unison to develop collections that supplement each other. Thus, each library's financial resource is used to the maximum extent, and each library builds its own identity.

MAKING MONEY WITH YOUR COLLECTION

Using the library's collection for commercial purposes is being tried more readily by more libraries. Several decades ago a library approached by a commercial publisher with the request to borrow a rare edition almost universally honored the request without question. The reprint book business was built upon the generosity of librarians who felt that their wares were public and should be made available to all who asked and promised the books would not be damaged.

By the mid-1970s, however, library directors realized that their valuable resources were providing healthy profits for the reprint houses with little return to the library. Several of the large university libraries became mass suppliers, first to reprinters, then to micropublishers. Under the guidance of Eugene Powers, a brilliant business leader and library benefactor, University Microfilms, Inc. was founded in Ann Arbor, MI. It was not a coincidence that the University of Michigan's University Library was located in the same city. For years, the University of Michigan Libraries supplied many of the materials that were committed to microform and sold to other libraries throughout the world.

When library directors understood that their wares were serving a commercial purpose with little return to the library, lending policies began to change. Whereas a scholar could borrow material without charge, a commercial firm that wished to use material either to reprint or commit to microform was charged a fee of approximately $25 per volume. The firm was required to return the material either re-bound or in the same condition it was in when it left the library. Many libraries also requested a complimentary copy of the publisher's edition.

The next step in developing a working relationship with publishing concerns was to enter into contractual arrangements involving fees, royalties and advances against royalties. A library with a unique collection learned that micropublishers were glad to film the collection at the publisher's expense, pay the library a royalty or fee, and supply a microform edition to the library. Thus, original, rare and often fragile manuscripts and documents could be kept in an archival chamber while scholars used the microform editions for their research. This arrangement served to improve the library's income but also served to enhance the importance of the library's collection as more and more people learned of its existence. Another, perhaps more valuable purpose was also accomplished. Many libraries had important collections of rare periodicals with some issues missing. The micropublisher was able to locate the missing pieces at other university libraries, film them and provide a complete edition of a single title.

One of the most ambitious undertakings involved a small, but highly successful micropublisher, Research Publications, Inc. (Woodbridge, CT), and two of the world's finest business libraries: the Goldsmith Library at the London School of Economics and the Kress Library at Harvard University's Graduate School of Business Administration. By combining both collections a unique microform library of business and management was published. The result is probably the best collection of historic business materials ever assembled. Both libraries share in royalty payments and both have profited substantially from sales.

Not all libraries have a collection that justifies a commercial micropublisher's effort and investment. For the library that believes it has a unique collection it would pay to write to several major micropublishers (see *Guide to Microforms in Print,* published annually by Microform Review, for listings) and describe the collection. A micropublisher will need to have a description of the collection, rough number of pages, format of the collection (i.e., books, manuscripts, letters, newspapers, etc.), physical size of the material, and an estimate of the condition. If a micropublisher is interested, he will either request that you send your collection to his laboratory for filming and processing or, if this is not possible, make arrangements to film on site. Since the cost of on-site filming is considerably higher, a publisher may be discouraged if you insist that material cannot leave the library.

If a micropublisher agrees to film your material, the library usually receives a royalty ranging from 8% to 15% of publisher's net receipts. In addition, the library should receive a complimentary copy of the film. Naturally, material borrowed from the library must be returned in good condition. Often old volumes will require rebinding after filming. This is done at the micropublisher's expense.

MARKETING SPECIAL SERVICES

Marketing special services can present problems if the staff is unfamiliar with the service or if there is not a well-orchestrated promotional campaign. The rapid growth of technology in the library requires particular attention. Automated circulation systems, electronic security systems, computer-based catalogs and online information retrieval services are becoming commonplace in libraries, particularly in academic settings. Both staff and patrons must be educated about the features and value of these devices. There is little doubt that technological innovations are turning the library of the future into the library of today. A library that fails to comprehend and communicate the importance of automated services may well find itself the library of the past.

According to Alice H. Bahr, project librarian/government publications at the Muhlenberg College Library, "The reluctance of some librarians to actively promote online services reflects a healthy concern that staff might be inundated with more work than it can handle, but it also reflects an unwillingness to accept the fact that such services redefine the nature of reference work."[9] This comment underlines the need to promote new services to staff as well as patrons, particularly when the service involves what many consider complicated electronic equipment.

Thus, the initial step in marketing a special service is to acquaint the staff fully with the system, its potentials and possible pitfalls. "There is little likelihood that promotional materials and activities will reflect system capability if staff members aren't given sufficient time to exploit the system. To allow staff to become comfortable with equipment, most libraries use a system a few weeks or months before publicizing it."[10] The Computer Based Information Center Staff at Philadelphia's Free Library spent three months working with the New York Times Information Bank before announcing the service's availability. The staff at Lehigh University's library spent a month testing its online equipment before promoting it.

Marketing special services to patrons uses the same basic techniques as for other library services. Posters, press releases, special displays and group meetings all serve to inform the public. Fortunately, some vendors of specialized services or equipment supply free materials for promotional purposes. Major vendors of online services (Lockheed, SDC Search Service and BRS) will supply libraries with posters or other promotional pieces, including ads, to assist in a marketing campaign. Many of the vendors of online services also allow libraries a reduced connect rate when the libraries are providing demonstrations to students, faculty and fellow librarians. By promoting a special service, such as the online service, many librarians have discovered that patrons become aware of other library services as well.

PROMOTING THE SPECIAL LIBRARY

Marketing the special library, particularly in a corporate setting, often requires a different set of guidelines. Rarely, for example, does the library serve the public as, to a limited extent, do most academic libraries. In fact, many special libraries make it a policy to deny the public access to staff or materials. By its very definition, the special library is designed to provide maximum service to the specific audience that has created the library and, in most cases, pays the bills. Marketing to this audience becomes much easier when it is possible to define, almost to the individual, who will be using the library's services.

Elizabeth Ferguson, former librarian of the Institute of Life Insurance, lists promotion among the basic functions of an outstanding special library:

1. The library provides the material for essential research in the conduct of a business.

2. The library provides reference service to assist in essential research.

3. The library *promotes its services* so that employees look to it for assistance.[11] (Italics added.)

Ms. Ferguson also writes: "It is not surprising that one often hears special librarians say that their major problem is to 'educate management.' I submit, however, that there is a most unattractive air of superiority in this phrase, and I would like to see it eliminated from our public relations vocabulary. *Inform, interpret*—yes—but not *educate*."[12]

Special libraries vary widely in size and services. Many are very small, staffed by a single librarian with perhaps a clerical assistant. Others have hundreds of thousands of volumes in their collections and comparably larger staffs. Some large companies with multiple locations have separate libraries, or "information centers," as they are increasingly being called, in different facilities. Usually these satellite libraries specialize in the particular area of research at that facility. A Union catalog usually unites the corporate collection.

In most corporate libraries, the library director is responsible for the development and implementation of a library marketing program. Funds are generally taken from the overall library budget. The library director may report directly to top management or to a department head, such as the chief of administrative services, research and development, public information, or information systems, if the library is a unit of that department.

Whatever its size and place within the organization, the special library must begin its marketing effort by informing all potential users of the library's existence, its location, its telephone number(s), and an overview of the many services offered that will save both time and money. Many corporations include a discussion of library services during the period of new employee orientation. Some organizations provide printed handouts containing pertinent information about the library. Unfortunately, since the new employee is also burdened with handouts from every other company service ranging from insurance and retirement benefits to profit sharing and stock options, it is more than likely that the library's brochure will receive too little attention. It becomes necessary, therefore, for the special library to develop an ongoing and continuous program to inform its patrons of its services.

Examples of Corporate Library Marketing

McGraw-Hill, Inc., a company with several corporate information centers serving its various divisions, has a fine central library that distributes a monthly bibliography of recently received materials to key corporate personnel. The bibliographic listing is organized by subject and contains titles of both books and periodicals. Executives who are interested in receiving one or more of the listed titles simply check off the name(s) and return the bibliography to the library; the requested material is then forwarded to them. Noncirculating reference material is starred on the bibliography and is available for use only within the library. The system keeps employees aware of the library's continuing effort to acquire current material and also assures employees that they will be kept abreast of important professional developments.

At Exxon, the information center is part of the company's administrative service division. The manager of administrative service reports directly to the corporation's secretary. Thus, the information center is highly visible from the top of the corporate ladder. Like many other large corporate libraries, Exxon's information center provides all company employees with a publication (published semimonthly) that details current library-related developments. A video tape explaining library services is available to all employees and is shown to all new employees. A separate brochure explaining the center's available data bases is also produced. The director of Exxon's information center, Mary Rizzo, is responsible for public relations.

At the Seattle–First National Bank, the manager of the library is a corporate assistant vice president, Jeannette Privat. She believes that special librarians should "quit talking to ourselves and begin talking to others." Ms. Privat has elevated her library to an essential element in the bank's operations. To communicate with management, the library publishes a quarterly report on departmental operations. In addition, the library produces an annual usage questionnaire for major departmental users. (See Figure 10.2.) This enables the library to get some feedback on the quality of its services, to obtain information on user plans for the coming year, and to remind users that "they are getting a lot of service from the library."

Other promotional activities include a "How to Use the Library" talk at departmental and branch staff meetings; presentations at regional managers' meetings; slide-tape presentations at branch staff meetings; a section in the bank's "Business Service Package Operating Guide" on methods of obtaining information for officer calls; and announcements and articles in the bank's newsletter and magazine. Library services are mentioned in new employee orientation programs, and individual tours are given to new employees, particularly officers and researchers.

At the General Foods Marketing Information Center, manager Lois Seulowitz begins her "selling" program by providing new employees with a brochure listing samples of typical questions the information center is prepared to handle. As part of the general orientation for new employees, a film strip explains the information center and its many services. Articles on recent technical developments related to General Foods' operations, along with current bibliographic information, appear in the company's newspaper and in appropriate corporate bulletins aimed at a specific audience. When a new periodical is received by the information center, the table of contents is photocopied and distributed to approximately 700 employees who have asked to receive information in their special field of interest. Visitors or employees passing through the General Foods lobby can see an attractive display describing the information center and the various ways it is being used. (At General Foods, the public can use the company information center by appointment.)

Bell Telephone Laboratories Inc. has developed a networking information resource that is being shared by the company's 22 libraries. Eight separate computer systems now can access more than 200 data bases around the country. "The image we had in mind when we decided to pool our resources was a library without walls," says Robert A. Kennedy, director of Bell Labs' libraries and information center. Marketing the features and advantages of this vast resource is accomplished through articles in company newsletters, descriptive brochures and individual demonstrations.

A Special Library in a Not-for-Profit Agency

There are, of course, many special libraries that are not part of profit-making organizations. They include libraries at foundations, museums, research institutes, associations, unions, etc. Nina Root, director of the library of the American Museum of Natural History, believes that the best way to show the importance and strength of her library to the individuals responsible for its support is to maintain a high degree of visibility. "I am very active in many professional organizations and I encourage other members of our library staff to be active as well." Ms. Root writes articles for both library and museum publications, thereby keeping her library and the museum in the spotlight.

The library uses various other marketing techniques. In October 1981, for example, Ms. Root organized a conference in Philadelphia on the "Bibliography of Natural History." Attendees included librarians from U.S. and foreign museums, as well as scientists interested in learning about research tools available to them. The library also produces a column, "Recent Publications in Natural History," which is published in the museum's regular publication, *Curator*. The bibliography contains full citations for new materials organized into 12 separate categories. In addition, the library selects at least one major new title and obtains a detailed review from one of the museum's curators for publication in *Curator*.

Since the museum's library is also open to the public, the library maintains a permanent display case in the public viewing area. Called Library Gallery, the case often shows rare books from the library's extensive collection or photographs taken by explorers or naturalists that may never have been previously exhibited. The library has a policy, shared by many other not-for-profit special libraries, of lending material to other libraries or organizations for display. Thus, artifacts from the museum's library can serve as "public relations representatives" when they are on loan.

MARKETING TIPS FOR THE SPECIAL LIBRARIAN

In order to provide good services and, in turn, to promote them, special librarians must above all keep abreast of developments in their patrons' area of interest. Often this requires reading technical literature, taking special courses (usually reimbursed by the company or organization), attending meetings and briefing sessions and becoming familiar with the organization's business. If the librarian is not interested in electronics then he or she will have a serious problem marketing the services of a library serving a company in the electronics field. "A sharp librarian can make as good a vice-president as can a sharp salesman moved up from the ranks, but he must know more than how to classify and arrange information. He needs to be indispensable to the company and to thoroughly understand management, planning, operations research, the company's special field *and* public relations."[13]

Herbert S. White, dean of the Indiana University Graduate Library School and former president of the Special Libraries Association, comments:

> Libraries must recognize that the organization has its own needs and the successful library will develop its plans to satisfy those needs. Developing relationships with individuals who, in turn, will broadcast the library's value and importance is but one way to improve the library's image. Too often, libraries have tried to serve the needs of all segments of the corporate or public community and, as a result, have failed to serve any of the needs successfully. The successful library is an aggressive library. It will search out and locate its clientele, then state: "It's my job to help you. What are your problems?" Perhaps Donald Urquhardt (former director, British National Lending Library) said it best: "McDonalds did not get rich selling hamburgers to vegetarians."[14]

Figure 10.2 Seattle-First National Bank's Library Usage Questionnaire

INTER-OFFICE CORRESPONDENCE

To _____ From Jeannette Privat
   _____   Assistant Vice President & Manager
   _____   Library
                                   HOB -12

Subject Library Usage   Phone 4056
                                                Date   10/14/80

During the last year, your area was a frequent user of Library services. To help us meet your future needs, we would appreciate your taking a few minutes to answer the attached questions which pertain to your expected usage in 1981.

If possible, we would like to have the questionnaire returned by October 22nd. Thank you for your assistance.

Library Usage Questionnaire

Please check the appropriate boxes which pertain to your expected level of usage in 1981. For reference, your approximate level of usage in 1980 is listed in the second column.

Service	Your Area's Approximate Level of Usage in 1980*	Expected Level of Usage of This Service in 1981				
		Much Higher	Higher	Same	Lower	Much Lower
Research Services		☐	☐	☐	☐	☐
Ordering Publications		☐	☐	☐	☐	☐
Routing Periodicals		☐	☐	☐	☐	☐
Renewing Subscriptions		☐	☐	☐	☐	☐
Photocopying Articles,		☐	☐	☐	☐	☐

Comments: _____

*Because of the record-keeping expense, we don't keep complete statistics but have approximated the usage. Numbers are based on 9 months of actual data.

Figure 10.2 (Cont.)

Additionally, to help us serve you better, we would appreciate your answering the following questions concerning the quality of our existing services.

	Very Good	Good	Needs Improvement*
Research Services	☐	☐	☐
Comments:			
Ordering Publications	☐	☐	☐
Comments:			
Routing Publications	☐	☐	☐
Comments:			
Renewing Subscriptions	☐	☐	☐
Comments:			
Photocopying Articles,	☐	☐	☐
Comments:			

Thank you for your responses. Please return the questionnaire to:

        Jeannette Privat
        Library
        HOB - 12

*If you have checked "needs improvement" in any area, please indicate in the comments section what aspect concerns you.

Source: Seattle-First National Bank. Reprinted with permission.

Marketing special libraries means keeping a constant lookout for another way to get the message across. If the organization publishes a newsletter or company paper, the librarian should talk with the editor and request a special column for library news or suggest the use of fillers prepared by and attributed to the library. If the organization is involved in an acquisition, the library is a natural source of information about the acquiring or acquired company. A well-written, interesting article will inform all company personnel and also show that the library is in the forefront of news and information gathering. The library can organize a regular book review column on works of particular interest to personnel. Facts and figures concerning the corporation can be sent regularly to certain managers, e.g., those responsible for stockholder relations.

A few large corporations have an external house organ. The library can help the editor as well as itself by suggesting stories or supplying information on a regular basis. A memo to the corporate public relations department suggesting a series of articles on the history of the organization or on the special field in which the organization is involved will undoubtedly mean the library will be called upon to assist in locating information, photographs, etc.

Some companies are particularly interested in preserving and promoting their history. Companies that maintain extensive corporate archives should work directly with the library. An aggressive librarian might suggest that the history-minded company take a few steps beyond maintaining files. Should select corporate material be preserved on microfilm? If so, the librarian should become involved in the selection and indexing process.

How about oral histories? Many corporations have already started an oral history collection covering both company history and the development of a specific industry. For example, Federated Department Stores has an extensive collection covering company policies, methods, changes in consumer tastes and buying habits, etc. The Weyerhaeuser Timber Company has developed an oral history program detailing lumbering practices, labor problems, immigration and corporate developments involving Weyerhaeuser as well as many of its competing firms. The special librarian should become involved in this kind of information-gathering program.

Suggesting new programs to management shows the library as a vital, active part of the organization and not simply an information storeroom. If management is favorably impressed with the suggestions offered by the special librarian, it is likely that a request will be made for a more detailed action plan complete with budgetary projections. Thus, the librarian becomes involved in basic management techniques. Most important, by promoting the special library to those individuals who are responsible for its future, the librarian serves the interests of the parent organization and also assures that the library will not be ignored during budget time or periods of general business unrest.

A final word on marketing the special library and one that is applicable to all library promotion efforts: Word of mouth is often the best public relations tool. Find that elusive fact or citation for a patron once, and you can be sure that a positive image of the library will result. Or, as Holgar J. Johnson, former president of the Institute of Life Insurance put it, public relations is "90% doing a good job and only 10% telling about it, important though that is."[15]

FOOTNOTES

1. George S. Bobinski, "Case Studies in Library Public Relations," *Kentucky Library Association Bulletin* 34 (April 1970): 16.

2. Laurence Miller, "Liaison Work in the Academic Library," *RQ* 16 (Spring 1977): 213.

3. Ibid., p. 215.

4. Bobinski, op. cit., p. 13.

5. Eli M. Oboler, "Selling the Academic Library," in *Public Relations for Libraries,* ed. Allan Angoff (Westport, CT: Greenwood Press, 1973), p. 147.

6. Joanne R. Euster, "Staff Public Relations is Not a Newsletter" (Paper delivered at the American Library Association Annual Conference, July 1, 1980).

7. Oboler, op. cit., p. 142.

8. *The New York Times,* June 1, 1981, p. 7.

9. Alice H. Bahr, "Promotion of Online Services," in *The Library and Information Manager's Guide to Online Services,* ed. Ryan E. Hoover (White Plains, NY: Knowledge Industry Publications, Inc., 1980), p. 161.

10. Bahr, op. cit., p. 163.

11. Elizabeth Ferguson, "Creation and Development of an Insurance Library," in *Public Relations for Libraries,* ed. Allan Angoff (Westport, CT: Greenwood Press, 1973), p. 188.

12. Ibid.

13. Josephine Raburn, "Public Relations for a 'Special' Public," *Special Libraries* (December 1969): 650.

14. Telephone interview with author.

15. Ferguson, op. cit., p. 182.

Selected Bibliography

"AAP Ponders Creation of Federal Information Plan." *Publishers Weekly* (June 26, 1981): 21.

Allen, Thomas J. *Managing the Flow of Technology: Technology Transfer and the Dissemination of Technological Information Within the R&D Organization.* Cambridge, MA: M.I.T. Press, 1977.

Allman, Katherine; Wing, Paul; and McLaughlin, James. *A Proposed Taxonomy of Postsecondary Education Subject Matter Areas.* (Preliminary Draft). Boulder, CO: National Center for Higher Education Management Systems at Western Interstate Commission for Higher Education, 1975.

American National Standard for Periodicals: Format Arrangement. (ANSI Z39.1-1977) New York: American National Standards Institute, 1978.

Angoff, Allan, ed. *Public Relations for Libraries.* Westport, CT: Greenwood Press, 1973.

Annual Report of the Library, 1947-48. Chicago, IL: University of Illinois, Chicago Circle, 1948.

Bahr, Alice Harrison. "Promotion of Online Services." In *The Library and Information Manager's Guide to Online Services.* Edited by Ryan E. Hoover. White Plains, NY: Knowledge Industry Publications, Inc., 1980.

Banks, Paul N. "Preservation of Library Materials." In *Encyclopedia of Library and Information Science, Volume 23.* Edited by A. Kent, H. Lancour and J.E. Daily. New York: Marcel Dekker Inc. (1978): 180-222.

Baumol, W.J., and Marcus, M. *Economics of Academic Libraries.* Prepared for Council on Library Resources by Mathematica, Inc. Washington, DC: American Council on Education, 1973.

Becker, Joseph, and Hayes, Robert M. *Handbook of Data Processing for Libraries.* New York: John Wiley & Sons, 1970.

Bobinski, George S. "Case Studies in Library Public Relations." *Kentucky Library Association Bulletin* 34 (1970): 13-16.

Bohem, Hilda. *Disaster Prevention and Disaster Preparedness.* Berkeley, CA: University of California, April 1978.

Bowen, D.H. Michael. "The Economics of Scientific Journal Publishing." *Journal of Research Communications Studies* 3 (1981): 172.

Bradford, S.C. *Documentation.* London: Crosby Lockwood, 1948.

Broad, William J. "The Publishing Game: Getting More for Less." *Science* 211 (March 13, 1981): 1137-39.

Brown, Margaret; Etherington, Donald; and McWilliams, Linda. *Boxes for the Protection of Rare Books: Their Design and Construction.* Washington, DC: Library of Congress, 1982.

Brown, Norman B., and Phillips, Jane. "Price Indexes for 1981, U.S. Periodicals and Serial Services." *Library Journal* 106 (July 1981): 1387-93.

Chait, R. "College Mission Statements." *Science* 205 (September 7, 1979): 957.

Chomet, S., and Nejman, E. "The Economics of the Physics Journal." *Journal of Research Communications Studies* 3 (1981): 194.

Clapp, V.W., and Jordan, R.T. "Quantitative Criteria for Adequacy of Academic Library Collections." *College and Research Libraries* 26 (September 1965): 371-380.

Cunha, George M. *What an Institution Can Do to Survey Its Conservation Needs.* New York: New York Library Association, Resources and Technical Services Section, 1979.

Darling, Pamela W. "'Doing' Preservation, with or without money: a lecture on carrying on a preservation program." *Oklahoma Librarian* 30 (October 1980): 20-26.

_____. "Microforms in Libraries: Preservation and Storage." *Microform Review* 5 (April 1976): 93-100.

DeCandido, Robert. "Preserving Our Library Materials: Preservation Treatments Available to Librarians." *Library Scene* 8 (March 1979): 4-6.

DeGennaro, Richard. "Escalating Journal Prices: Time to Fight Back." *American Libraries* 8 (February 1977): 69-74.

Easton, David. *A System Analysis of Political Life.* New York: John Wiley & Sons, 1965.

Economics of Scientific Publications. Washington, DC: Council of Biology Editors, 1973.

Elton, Martin, and Vickery, Brian. "The Scope for Operational Research in the Library and Information Field." *ASLIB Proceedings* 25 (August 1973): 305-319.

Euster, Joanne R. "Staff Public Relations is Not a Newsletter." Paper delivered at the American Library Association Annual Conference, July 1, 1980.

Evans, Glyn. *Development of a Responsive Library Acquisition Formula.* (Final Report). Washington, DC: U.S. Department of Health, Education and Welfare, Office of Education, Office of Libraries and Learning Resources, 1978b.

Evans, Glyn; Gifford, Roger; and Franz, Donald. *Collection Development Analysis Using OCLC Archival Tapes.* (Final Report). Washington, DC: U.S. Department of Health, Education and Welfare, Office of Education, Office of Libraries and Learning Resources, 1977.

Fry, Bernard M., and White, Herbert S. *Economics and Interaction of the Publisher-Library Relationship in the Production and Use of Scholarly and Research Journals.* (NTIS PB249 108) Washington, DC: National Science Foundation Office of Information Service, 1975.

Gardner, Jeffrey, and Webster, Duane. *The Formulation and Use of Goals and Objectives in Statements in Academic and Research Libraries.* Washington, DC: Association of Research Libraries, Office of University Library Management Studies. Occasional Papers #3, April 1974.

Gertsberger, P.G., and Allen, T.J. "Criteria Used by Research and Development Engineers in the Selection of an Information Source." *Journal of Applied Psychology* 52 (August 1968): 272-279.

Gold, Steven, "Allocating the Book Budget: An Economic Model." *College and Research Libraries* 36 (September 1975): 397-402.

Greenfield, Jane. *Pamphlet Binding.* New Haven, CT: Yale University Library, 1981.

_____. *Paper Treatment.* New Haven, CT: Yale University Library, 1981.

_____. *The Small Library.* New Haven, CT: Yale University Library, 1981.

_____. *Tip-ins and Pockets.* New Haven, CT: Yale University Library, 1981.

_____. *Wraparounds.* New Haven, CT: Yale University Library, 1980.

Gross, J., and Talavage, J. "A Multiple-Objective Planning Methodology for Information Service Managers." *Information Processing and Management* 15 (1979): 155-167.

Hamburg, Morris, et al. "A Systems Approach to Library Management." *Journal of Systems Engineering* 4 (January 1976): 117-129.

Hamburg, Morris; Clelland, Richard; Bommer, Michael; Ramist, Leonard; and Whitfield, Ronald. *Library Planning and Decision-Making Systems.* Cambridge, MA: M.I.T. Press, 1974.

Harris, W. Best. "Public Relations for Public Libraries." *Assistant Librarian* 64 (1971): 18-19.

Harvey, L.J. *Managing Colleges and Universities by Objectives.* Littleton, CO: Ireland Educational Corporation, 1976.

Herner, Saul. "System Design, Evaluation and Costing." *Special Libraries* 58 (October 1967): 576-581.

Horton, Carolyn. *Cleaning and Preserving Bindings and Related Materials.* 2nd ed. Chicago, IL: American Library Association, 1969 (Library Technology Program Publication No. 16).

"Journal Costs Alarming Scholars." *Chronicle of Higher Education* 11 (November 17, 1975).

Kantor, Paul B. "The Library as an Information Utility in the University Context: Evaluation and Measurement of Service." *Journal of the American Society of Information Science* 27 (March/April 1976a): 100-112.

Kates, Jacqueline R. "One Measure of a Library's Contribution." *Special Libraries* 65, no. 8 (August 1974): 332-336.

Kent, Allen, et al. *Use of Library Materials, The University of Pittsburgh Study.* New York: Marcel Dekker Inc., 1979.

King, Donald W. *The Journal in Scientific Communication: The Roles of Authors, Publishers, Librarians, and Readers in a Vital System.* Rockville, MD: King Research, Inc., 1979.

King, Donald W., et al. *Statistical Indicators of Scientific and Technical Communication (1960-1980).* vol. 1-5. Rockville, MD: King Research, Inc., 1976-1979.

Koch, William H. "The Effect of the U.S. Copyright Legislation on Authors, Editors, Publishers and Librarians." *Journal of Research Communications Studies* 3, no. 1-2 (September 1981): 95.

Kohut, Joseph, and Walker, John. "Allocating the Book Budget: Equity and Economic Efficiency." *College and Research Libraries* 36 (1975): 403-410.

Lancaster, F.W. *Toward Paperless Information Systems.* New York: Academic Press, 1978.

Leggate, Peter; Rossiter, B.N.; and Rowland, J.F.B. "Evaluation of an SDI Service Based on the Index Chemicus Registry System." *Journal of Chemical Documentation* 13 (August 1973): 192-203.

Library Journal 105 (February 15, 1980): 2370.

Machlup, Fritz; Leeson, Kenneth W.; and Associates. *Information through the Printed Word.* vol. 1-4. New York: Praeger Publishers, 1978-1980.

McClure, Charles R. "The Planning Process: Strategies for Action." *College and Research Libraries* 39 (November 1978): 456-466.

McGeehan, Thomas. *Decision Analysis Technique for Program Evaluation* (Goal Programming). Alexandria, VA: Defense Documentation Center, April 1977, ADO 38800.

McGrath, William. "An Allocation Formula Derived from a Factor Analysis of Academic Departments." *College and Research Libraries* 30 (January 1969a): 51-62.

_____. "Classifying Courses in the University Catalog." *College and Research Libraries* 30 (November 1969b): 533-539.

_____. "A Pragmatic Book Allocation Formula for Academic and Public Libraries with a Test for Its Effectiveness." *Library Resources and Technical Services* 19 (Fall 1975): 356-369.

Meadows, Jack, et al. "What is the Future for New Research Journals in the 1980's? A Discussion." *Journal of Research Communications Studies* 2 (November 1980): 137-147.

Miller, Edward. "User-Oriented Planning." *Special Libraries* 64 (November 1973): 479-482.

Miller, Laurence. "Liaison Work in the Academic Library." *RQ* 16 (1977): 213-215.

Morrow, Carolyn Clark. "A Conservation Policy Statement for Research Libraries." University of Illinois, Graduate School of Library and Information Science *Occasional Papers Series,* no. 139 (July 1979).

_____. *Conservation Treatment Procedures: A Manual of Step-by-Step Procedures for the Maintenance and Repair of Library Materials.* Littleton, CO: Libraries Unlimited, Inc., 1982.

Musselman, K., and Talavage, J. "A Managerial Tool for Evaluating Information." (Working Paper). Lafayette, IN: Purdue University (August 1978).

National Fire Protection Association. *Recommended Practice for the Protection of Libraries and Library Collections.* Boston, MA: National Fire Protection Association, 1980 (NFPA, no. 910-1980).

Newell, Allen, and Simon, Herbert A. *Human Problem Solving.* Englewood Cliffs, NJ: Prentice-Hall Inc., 1972.

Oboler, Eli. "Public Relations and Intellectual Freedom." *Pacific Northwest Library Association Quarterly* 38 (1974): 17-21.

Orr, Richard H. "Measuring the Goodness of Library Services: A General Framework for Considering Quantitative Measures." *Journal of Documentation* 29 (September 1973): 315-332.

Patterson, Robert H. "Organizing for Conservation: A Model Charge to a Conservation Committee." *Library Journal* 104 (May 15, 1979): 1116-1119 (LJ Series on Preservation, no. 2).

"Prepare: The Library Public Relations Recipe Book." Preconference publication of the Public Relations Section, Library Administration Division, American Library Association, 1978. Mimeographed.

Raburn, Josephine. "Public Relations for a 'Special' Public." *Special Libraries* (December 1969): 650.

Raffel, Jeffrey. "From Economic to Political Analysis of Library Decision Making." *College and Research Libraries* 35 (November 1974): 412-423.

Roderer, Nancy K., and Schell, Colleen G. *Statistical Indicators of Scientific and Technical Communication Worldwide.* Rockville, MD: King Research, Inc., 1977.

Rosenberg, Kenyon C. "Evaluation of an Industrial Library: A Simple-minded Technique." *Special Libraries* 60, no. 9 (November 1969): 635-638.

Rosenberg, Victor. *Studies in the Man-System Interface in Libraries, Report No. 2: The Application of Psychometric Techniques to Determine the Attitudes of Individuals Toward Information Seeking.* Bethlehem, PA: Lehigh University, Center for the Information Sciences, July 1966b.

Rouse, William B. "Optimal Resources Allocation in Library Systems." *Journal of the American Society for Information Science* 26 (May-June 1975): 157-165.

Rubenstein, Albert, and Birr, David. *Designs for Field Experiments on Accessibility, Quality and Use of Sources of Scientific and Technical Information.* A report submitted to NSF. Evanston, IL: The Technological Institute, Northwestern University, 1976.

Scholarly Communication: the Report of the National Enquiry. Baltimore, MD: Johns Hopkins University Press, 1979.

Sellers, David Y. "Basic Planning and Budgeting Concepts for Special Libraries." *Special Libraries* 64, no. 2 (February 1973): 70-75.

Strable, Edward G., ed. *Special Libraries: A Guide to Management.* New York: Special Libraries Association, 1975.

Summers, F. William. "The Use of Formulae in Resource Allocation." *Library Trends* 23 (April 1975): 631-642.

Swift, D.F.; Winn, V.A.; Bramer, D.A.; and Mills, C.T.R. *A Case Study in Indexing and Clarification in the Sociology of Education: Development of Ideas Concerning the Organization of Materials for Literature Searching.* Milton Keynes, England: Open University, Faculty of Educational Studies, June 1973, 2V (OSTI Report 5171).

The Technical, Scientific and Medical Publishing Market, 1981-82. White Plains, NY: Knowledge Industry Publications, Inc., 1982.

Ulrich's International Periodicals Directory, 20th ed. New York: R.R. Bowker Co., 1981.

Urquhart, Donald. "The National Role in Resource Allocation." *Library Trends* 23 (1975): 595-601.

Van Deerlin, Cf. Lionel. "Information Overload: What the Congress and Information Professionals Can Do About It." *Special Libraries* 72 (January 1981): 107.

Walch, Timothy. *Archives and Manuscripts: Security.* Chicago, IL: Society of American Archivists, 1977.

Webster, Duane. "Strategies for Improving the Performance of Academic Libraries." *Journal of Academic Librarianship* 1 (May 1975): 13-18.

Weinberg, Charles B. "The University Library: Analysis and Proposals." *Management Science* 21 (October 1974): 130-140.

White, Herbert S. "Cost-Effectiveness and Cost-Benefit Determinations in Special Libraries." *Special Libraries* 70, no. 4 (April 1, 1979b): 163-169.

_____. "Publishers, Libraries, and Costs of Journal Subscriptions in Times of Funding Retrenchment." *Library Quarterly* 46 (October 1976): 350-377.

Wills, Gordon, and Oldman, Christine. *A Longitudinal Study of the Costs and Benefits of Selected Library Services: Initial Exploration and Framework.* Cranfield, Bedfordshire: Cranfield School of Management, 1974.

Wooster, Harold. "Books and Libraries in the Scientific Age." *Library Journal* 92 (July 1967): 2511-2515.

Zipf, G.K. *Human Behavior and the Principle of Least Effort.* Cambridge, MA: Addison-Wesley, 1949.

ABOUT THE AUTHORS

Michael R.W. Bommer is associate professor of management at The School of Management, Clarkson College. He was project director of a National Science Foundation grant to develop a management information system for academic libraries. Co-author of *Library Planning and Decision-Making Systems* (1974), Professor Bommer has been a contributor to several other books and has published articles in numerous professional journals.

Ronald W. Chorba is associate professor at Clarkson's School of Management. He was co-principal investigator of the National Science Foundation study on developing a management information system for academic libraries. Professor Chorba was previously associate professor and associate dean of business at the University of Calgary, Canada. His articles have appeared in *Management Science, Health Services Research, Decision Sciences* and the *Journal of the American Society for Information Science.*

Audrey N. Grosch is director of the Library Services Division, Library Systems Department, at the University of Minnesota. She has been a consultant in information systems and facilities in numerous institutions including the Pahlavi National Library of Iran, the Library of Congress, Division of the Blind and Physically Handicapped, and the Hawaii State Library. She was author of *Minicomputers in Libraries, 1979-80,* and has written over 30 articles for various professional journals.

Richard W. Boss is Senior Management Consultant, Information Systems Consultants Inc., Bethesda, MD, and Boston, MA. He has served as a consultant to more than 100 libraries and library consortia on the selection and procurement of automated library systems. Mr. Boss was formerly University Librarian at Princeton and Director of Libraries at the University of Tennessee at Knoxville. He is the author of *The Library Manager's Guide to Automation* and many other publications.

David C. Taylor is undergraduate librarian, University of North Carolina, Chapel Hill. Previous positions were as serials librarian, Michigan State University; interlibrary loan and reference librarian, University of Rhode Island; and circulation librarian, Union Theological Seminary. Mr. Taylor was editor and publisher of *Title Varies,* a newsletter on serials issues, from 1973 to 1980.

Carolyn Clark Morrow is conservation librarian/assistant professor at the Morris Library, Southern Illinois University at Carbondale. She is also project director of the Illinois Cooperative Conservation Program (ICCP). Previous positions include conservator, Department of Rare Books and Special Collections, Washington University Libraries, and head, bindery section at the Morris Library. She is the author of *Conservation Treatment Procedures: A Manual of Step-by-Step Procedures for the Maintenance and Repair of Library Materials* and coauthor of *A Conservation Bibliography for Librarians, Archivists and Administrators.*

Benedict A. Leerburger is president of the Board of Trustees, Scarsdale (NY) Public Library and member of the Board of Directors of the Westchester (County) Library System. He is the author of *Josiah Willard Gibb, American Theoretical Physicist* and editor of *Cowles Encyclopedia of Science, Industry & Technology.* A freelance writer and editor, Mr. Leerburger previously held numerous editorial positions, including editor in chief of McGraw-Hill Book Co.'s Webster/McGraw-Hill Division, editorial director of KTO Press and managing editor of the Book Division of *Look* magazine.